KU-714-946

Max Hastings was educated at Charterhouse and University College, Oxford, which he abandoned after a year to join the *Evening Standard*. He spent most of his early career reporting for newspapers and BBC TV from far-flung places, including eleven war zones, of which the most notable were Vietnam and the 1982 Falklands conflict. In 1986 he became editor of the *Daily Telegraph*, then after almost a decade moved to edit the *Evening Standard* until 2002. He is the author of more than twenty books, of which the most recent are *Armageddon, Nemesis* and *Finest Years*. He has won many awards both as a reporter and historian, including the 2009 Edgar Wallace Trophy of the London Press Club, and the RUSI's Westminster Medal for his lifelong contribution to military literature. He has two grown-up children, and lives with his wife Penny in west Berkshire, where they garden enthusiastically but – he says – much less expertly than his mother.

From the reviews of *Did You Really Shoot the Television*:

'Hastings' portrait of his absurd and loveable father is extraordinarily touching; that of the failure of his relationship with his mother scarcely less so . . . extremely funny in places, extremely poignant in others and extremely well-written throughout – in fact, I haven't enjoyed anything so much in ages' Tom Fort, *Sunday Telegraph*

'Deeply moving . . . one of the legends of our time, Sir Max Hastings gives us an intimate portrait' *Private Eye*

'A brilliantly entertaining book, full of funny, well-told stories about [Hastings'] talented, eccentric, sometimes rackety predecessors' David Sexton, *Evening Standard*

'Funny and moving . . . Few family histories are written with as much skill and sensitivity as this one. Moving without being mawkish, Hasting's book is a trove of marvellous stories' Dominic Sandbrook, *Sunday Times*

'[Hastings] reveals himself as never before . . . This memoir is regretful, wise and forthright. It deals with unnecessary cruelties and self-delusions and ends with a sense of completion and understanding' Andrew Marr, *Financial Times*

By the same author

MAX HASTINGS

Did You Really Shoot the Television?

A Family Fable

Harper
Press

Harper Press
An imprint of HarperCollins*Publishers*
77–85 Fulham Palace Road
Hammersmith
London W6 8JB

Visit our authors' blog at www.fifthestate.co.uk

This Harper Press paperback edition published 2011
1

First published in Great Britain by HarperPress in 2010

Copyright © Max Hastings 2010

Max Hastings asserts the moral right to be identified as the author of this work

A catalogue record for this book is available from the British Library

ISBN 978-0-00-727172-6

Set in Minion by Palimpsest Book Production Limited,
Falkirk, Stirlingshire

Printed and bound in Great Britain by Clays Ltd, St Ives plc

Mixed Sources
Product group from well-managed
forests and other controlled sources
www.fsc.org   Cert no. SW-COC-001806
© 1996 Forest Stewardship Council

FSC is a non-profit international organisation established to promote the
responsible management of the world's forests. Products carrying the FSC
label are independently certified to assure consumers that they come
from forests that are managed to meet the social, economic and
ecological needs of present and future generations.

Find out more about HarperCollins and the environment at
www.harpercollins.co.uk/green

All rights reserved. No part of this publication may be
reproduced, stored in a retrieval system, or transmitted,
in any form or by any means, electronic, mechanical,
photocopying, recording or otherwise, without the
prior permission of the publishers.

This book is sold subject to the condition that it shall not,
by way of trade or otherwise, be lent, re-sold, hired out or otherwise
circulated without the publisher's prior consent in any form of binding or
cover other than that in which it is published and without a similar condition
including this condition being imposed on the subsequent purchaser.

For Charlotte, Harry and Calypso:
the next generation

CONTENTS

ILLUSTRATIONS

Great-grandfather Edward Hastings
Great-grandmother Lizzie Hastings.
Grandfather Basil Hastings.
Great-uncle Lewis, with rifle and hunting party in South Africa in 1910.
Lewis as a gunner officer in World War I.
Lewis sketched in old age by Tom Purvis.
Grandfather Rolfe Scott-James.
Grandmother Violet Scott-James.
Menu for a Savage Club 'Country Members' Night' chaired by Basil in 1925.
Menu for a matching occasion at which Mac presided in 1953.
Anne as a member of the 1930 St Paul's tennis team.
Mac with bride Eleanor Asprey at his first wedding in 1936.
Anne photographed by Cecil Beaton in 1937, when she was working for *Vogue*.
Mac taking delivery of a new pair of 12-bores in 1939.
Mac delivering one of his wartime 'London Letters' to America.
Mac attending debriefing after a bomber raid on Germany.
Mac exploring the finer points of a Bren gun.
Mac peering towards the German front line in Holland in October 1944.
Major Stephen Hastings with his partisan escort in northern Italy on a 1945 SOE operation.
Stephen with an Italian friend.
Anne as women's editor of *Picture Post*.
Anne pulling a cracker with an American flier.

Anne as an apprentice bus conductor in Coventry.

Anne showing off the virtues of borrowed men's clothes to readers of *Picture Post* in 1941. *(© Getty Images)*

Anne carries the author to his 1946 christening, flanked by Nanny.

Anne with the author and sister Clare.

The exterior of Rose Cottage in about 1946.

Rose Cottage interior.

Mac in idyllic rural setting.

The author serving as an extra in a fashion shoot for *Harper's Bazaar*.

The author fails to enter into the party spirit.

The author and Clare at a Butlin's holiday camp in 1956.

Circus performer Hal Denver throws the knives, while Eagle Special Investigator acts as target.

Mac as a Bedouin in the Jordanian desert.

Mac learning to fly a Tiger Moth.

Mac as a cowboy in Alberta.

Mac practising the snake charmer's art in southern India.

Mac's 1956 adventure in the Kalahari Desert, where he sought out some of the last wild bushmen.

The author escaping from boarding school for the holidays.

Mac purporting to take an interest in the author's steam engine.

Anne on assignment for the *Daily Mail* among Masai in Kenya, 1960.

The Hastings men at Brown's Farm in 1964.

Mac's arrival on Ressource.

Mac feeding Friday.

Mac near to despair, with pitifully little in the pot.

Mac signalling for rescue, just before he collapsed.

Mac with Cliff Michelmore and Donald Baverstock in the BBC *Tonight* studio.

Mac filming a makeover of Rose Cottage's garden.

Weekend party at Rose Cottage in 1968.

Osbert Lancaster's perception of Maudie Littlehampton and Anne in cocktail party conversation.

Anne at Rose Cottage in the 1970s.

Anne with Osbert.

Mac at Brown's Farm in his final decade.

Anne at ninety.

The author aged twenty-one, steeplejacking on a South London chimney for the *Evening Standard*.

Introduction

I am the least significant character in the story which follows. But it was an enquiry about the fate of the TV set in the London family flat of my childhood which prompted me to embark upon it. Throughout the long life of my mother, the journalist and gardening writer Anne Scott-James, I wrote little about our tumultuous family experiences. In 1986, featured as the castaway on the BBC's *Desert Island Discs*, I dodged tricky questions about parental relations. I incline to my mother's view, that 'All families are dysfunctional.' However, when she enjoyed the same experience on *DID* in 2003 – and of course, most of us find it pleasing to talk about ourselves in such a context – at the age of ninety, she was much less inhibited. To the audience's delight and my toe-curling embarrassment, she regaled Sue Lawley with tales of our old squabbles, and of my admittedly pretty frightful childhood behaviour. For weeks afterwards, people came up to me in filling stations and other unlikely places, demanding: ''Ere – did you really shoot the television?' We shall address that question in due course, but I want to make plain immediately that it was not a big set.

The latter part of the book evokes personal memories of my parents and childhood, partial and fragmentary as all such yarns are. Until we reach the 1950s, however, I have sought to sketch some of the doings of the Hastingses and Scott-Jameses who came before me. Their experiences, journalistic and adventurous, fed my own aspirations. The tale is not founded upon delusions that our family has been important. The bylines of Macdonald Hastings and Anne

Scott-James, which were modestly celebrated in the mid-twentieth-century media, are quite unknown to a younger generation, as is the way of the world. Most of us have been 'nearly' people. Some of the clan, indeed, barely kept their heads above water. We have spasmodically proved capable of making a little money, but never of hanging on to it. Though our collective experiences all over the world in the past century of war and peace have been varied and picaresque, other English middle-class families can boast similar excitements. What is unusual, I think, is that our lot wrote it down. Even the least materially successful were highly literate. They committed to paper what happened to them at school and at home, in fashion studios and newspaper offices, on battlefields, in the African bush, and even on a desert island.

The story is based upon published and unpublished autobiographical material assembled by its principal characters. Beyond the miscellany of family papers which I possess back to the 1850s, my grandfather Basil wrote a book entitled *Memoirs of a Child*; his brother, great-uncle Lewis, published an anecdotal autobiography, *Dragons are Extra*; Lewis's son, cousin Stephen, likewise wrote *The Drums of Memory*. My father, Macdonald Hastings, published *Jesuit Child* and *Gamebook*, together with accounts of his most memorable journalistic exploits – *The Search for the Little Yellow Men* and *After You, Robinson Crusoe*. My mother wrote *Sketches from a Life* and *In the Mink*, which professed to be a novel, but was an almost undisguised memoir of her time in the fashion business. Her father, Rolfe Scott-James, published mostly literary criticism, but left a manuscript account of his relationships with some literary idols of his day. My stepfather, Osbert Lancaster, wrote a memoir of his childhood, *All Done from Memory*.

In addition, they produced millions of words of journalism, more than a few about themselves. Wherever possible here, I have allowed them to tell the tale in their own words. Such an approach is not a formula for objectivity. Leslie Stephen, creator of the *Dictionary of National Biography*, observed that 'No good story is ever quite true.' But this is a book designed to divert and entertain, rather than to enrich the annals of the times.

A very ordinary family's doings attain interest when its domestic details are preserved from a century ago. There are lots of gaps – things which I have been unable to discover. For knowledge of feuds and scandals, for instance, I am dependent upon anecdotage rather than documentary evidence. Tolstoy famously observed that all happy families are alike, while every unhappy family is unhappy in its own way. That line prompts me to recall a sally of my mother's, one day as we were lunching together, when she was a mere adolescent of eighty. 'You still haven't forgiven me for your childhood, have you?' she said, with her customary abruptness. I replied that she was quite wrong about that. One should judge things by how they turn out. Most of my life has been uncommonly fulfilled. I probably inherited from her whatever talents I possess. I added, however: 'If you try a different question – did I enjoy my childhood? – the answer is "no". When I was three or four, I doubt that you and I would have recognised each other in an identity parade.' Mumsy paused for a moment, brooding. Then she said: 'Whoever did you hear of who did anything with their lives who had' – the next bit in tones of withering scorn – '*a happy childhood?*' She claimed that Frank Muir, her fellow panellist on the 1960s and 'seventies BBC radio quiz game *My Word*, was the only clever man she ever met whose domestic life appeared satisfactory from the cradle to the grave.

There may be something in what she said, though I doubt that its moral would deserve a place in a manual on child-rearing. On my side, there seems merit in writing a book like this at sixty-three, rather than at thirty-three or forty-three. Whatever follies Mummy and Daddy committed, I have had time to learn, as we all do, that the only privilege of children is to make different mistakes from those of our forebears. I have so often failed as parent, husband and everything else that I now understand, as few of us do before middle age, how hard it is to get things right.

Some details: in the text below, I refer to each family member by name rather than relationship. Thus, my parents are 'Mac' and 'Anne', rather than 'Father' and 'Mother', except when I write explicitly about our dealings with each other. I have mentioned money a good deal, because when I read books about other people's lives I like to be told how they did, or did not, make ends meet. Trollope shocked his contemporaries by itemising in print the earnings from each of his novels, but posterity is grateful. I have said less about my sister Clare than her part in the family experience deserves, because it would be wrong to associate her with my perspective and judgements. Six years younger than me, a big gap in childhood, she saw things in her own way, invariably more temperate and less jaundiced than my own. Mac, Anne and I alike owed her more apologies than ever got expressed, for many and various injustices which we inflicted upon her. Likewise my half-sister Harriet Hastings, born in 1964, near the conclusion of the story told in these pages, has plenty to forgive us all for. I am happy here to make my own act of contrition to both siblings.

I have not written much about my own schooldays, which were disagreeable in the usual banal way. This is the story of a family, not about the miseries of English boarding education for boys who are no good at games. I have described in earlier memoirs – *Going to the Wars* and *Editor* – my experiences first as a foreign correspondent, later running the *Daily Telegraph* for a decade. *Did You Really Shoot the Television?* is a prequel. I have written it in fits and starts, and held back from publication until my mother, last of her generation of Hastingses and Scott-Jameses, was dead. My admiration for her will become plain, but she never appreciated my jokes.

I grew up with an exaggerated pride in my family's journalistic and literary heritage. I only realised in adulthood how modest this is by the standards of serious writers. At the outset, I was obsessed with sustaining it. At seventeen, I had read almost all the forty-odd books which the previous two generations of Hastingses and Scott-Jameses had then published. Like most children, I passed through a phase of awe towards my parents, into one of scepticism which persisted for several decades. Today, I can enjoy the memory of my own mistakes alongside theirs, and draw pleasure from the fact we alike experienced adventure, editorship and authorship. A condescending critic might say that we scrambled on the lower slopes of literary endeavour. I prefer to think of us all as reporters, sharing many of the same thrills and spills – three generations in turn discovering that you are as good as your last story, until finally, as Tourneur observes, 'That which would seem treason in our lives is laughter when we are dead.'

Max Hastings
Hungerford, Berkshire

ONE

The Tribe

Lots of families possess delusions of grandeur about their ancestry, and ours is no exception. Tess Durbeyfield's feckless peasant father liked to indulge a fantasy about his descent from the grand Dorset family of d'Urberville. Some modern Hastingses of our branch of the name cherished a notion that they should be earls. Both my father and his cousin Stephen were at pains to assure me that if there was any justice in the world, the Huntingdon peerage would rest in our hands, rather than in those of the upstart Hastingses who possess it. They wasted several hundred pounds, significant money fifty years ago, on a joint attempt to prove as much, with the aid of professional genealogists. Steve, a veteran Tory MP and Master of Foxhounds, married *en secondes noces* into the grand Fitzwilliam family. In old age, he became rather cross when I suggested that in truth – and as the evidence shows – our paternal ancestors were a pretty humble lot. Though some important people in British history have been called Hastings, it is impossible to trace connections between them and us. Walter Pater, asked if he was related to the French painter of the same surname, answered: 'I hope so; I believe so; I always say so.' This is charming, but silly.

I have no idea what our family did with itself before the nineteenth century, when we emerged as small-town Northern Irish Catholics, in an era from which few records of such people survive. Since Hastings is not an Irish name, I would surmise that some ancestor crossed from England in the sixteenth or seventeenth century, perhaps as a soldier. The first of my forebears of whom I know anything is James, who lived at Brookeborough, Co. Fermanagh, in the early 1800s. The most notable characteristic of the Brookeborough Hastingses was that they were not merely Papists, in that fiercely Protestant society, but devout ones. God played a dominant part in their lives throughout the ensuing century. In the bitter years before Catholic Emancipation, when the 1798 uprising was a recent memory, several of them emigrated to the United States, where two became Jesuits.

My own great-great grandfather, Hugh, born in 1810, briefly attended Queen's University in Belfast, moved to England in 1827, married a Wiltshire girl named Ann Sweatman, and taught mathematics and classics at various schools. He worked for a time in the 1850s as a jobbing writer at Knight's Agency in Fleet Street, producing essays and articles on any subject required, including the geography of Fermanagh and the topography of London. This was the family's first association with the Grub Street world which would loom large in our lives in the following century. In 1857 Hugh emigrated to America, where he taught at a school in Harper's Ferry, Virginia. He was living there with his five children, among them my great-grandfather Edward, born in 1850, when John Brown staged his famous raid, which helped to precipitate the US Civil War. I still possess my great-great aunt's narrative of the drama.

Conflict brought only grief to the Hastingses. Hugh was too old to fight, even had he wished to. His enthusiasm for the Southern cause prompted him to invest his tiny savings in Confederate bonds, an early instance of the family's hereditary improvidence. When he decided to return to England, he was obliged to borrow the passage money from a friend. Late in 1862, broke and disappointed, Hugh Hastings reached London once more with his family. He spent the last years of his life teaching at University College School.

Somehow, despite their modest income, there was just enough cash to send Edward to Stonyhurst, the grim Jesuit public school in Lancashire 'for the education of English Catholic gentlemen's sons'. In 1867, the boy had just completed five Spartan years when his father suffered a stroke and died. Family hopes that Edward might study science at London University were dashed. He had to make a living. He was articled to a solicitor at a salary of thirteen guineas a quarter, and remained a solicitor's clerk, albeit later a valued and well-paid one, for the rest of his life. Fortunately, a family friend provided him with an allowance of £75 a year to supplement his earnings.

In 1877, Edward married Elizabeth Macdonald, a Scottish teacher working in Carlisle – heaven knows where they met. The couple produced eleven children. The family's income never much exceeded £400, yet on this they managed to occupy a relatively large and comfortable London house south of the river – 29 Trinity Square, Borough – and to send all the boys to Stonyhurst. Edward and his family inhabited the genteel lower-middle-class world familiar to us through *The Diary of a Nobody*. His writings and experiences echo those of Mr Pooter. Yet the family correspondence also reveals Edward, like his father, as a literate and devout Pooter, fluent in Latin and Greek. His religion was the core of his life.

Basil Macdonald Hastings, Edward's second son and my grandfather, was to become the first of the family who made a living from the pen. His boyhood in that big Victorian family – 'the Tribe', as they called themselves – is minutely recorded, because many years later he published a charming account of it, *Memoirs of a Child*. He said nothing of his father's spiritual torments and worldly disappointments. Basil merely rejoiced in an early life full of incident, in which a modest income somehow sufficed to provide fun as well as education. I first read his narrative when I was twelve, and it inspired me with a sense of heredity which is usually the privilege of grander dynasties.

Probably because Edward's financial circumstances made close budgeting essential, as well as because he possessed a meticulous temperament, he commissioned custom-printed account books. In these, he recorded every detail of expenditure on behalf of each member of the ever-expanding Tribe. Ethel, his first child, arrived in 1879; Lewis, the eldest son – named for Leyson Lewis, the family benefactor who provided Edward with his vital allowance – in the following year; my grandfather Basil in 1881. Thereafter babies, all born at home, followed in a profusion that must have gladdened the

Home for the holidays. One of the illustrations from my grandfather's 1926 book *Memoirs of a Child*

heart of the family priest. Like Dickens's much-put-upon clerk, 'the Cherub' Reginald Wilfer of *Our Mutual Friend*, Edward had a 'limited income and an unlimited family'. The account books eventually contained separate pages for:

Hastings Mrs E
Hastings Ethelreda Agatha Gordon
Hastings Lewis Macdonald
Hastings Basil Macdonald
Hastings Gladys Mary Fraser
Hastings Beryl Angela Macdonald
Hastings Claude Hugh
Hastings Aubrey Joseph
Hastings Everard Ignatius
Hastings Eulalia Emily Macdonald
Hastings Muriel Magdalen
Hastings Rene Francis

In 1890 the family's annual income was £416, of which household costs consumed £200, rent a further £70, an annual holiday £17.11s.3d. Edward recorded expenditure upon himself of £6.2s.0d on clothes; 2s on hair cutting; £11.0s.6d on lunches; £3.12s.0d on travel. In 1901, the last year for which the account books survive, his salary was just £312.10s.6d, the family's expenditure £319.17s.5d. This included seventeen tons of coal at £22.10s.6d; lunches at £6.2s.6d; £10 on a holiday; £6.2s.0d for clothing; one penny for a diary; half a crown for postage; £20 for Elizabeth; £3 or £4 apiece on the children, including 3s.5d for dress-lining for Beryl, and 2s.4d for Claude's sand shoes. There were also assorted halfpennies for orphanages and the destitute; a few pennies apiece to the church choir, school treats and various Catholic charities. Edward bought one suit a year, collarless to save on the expense of ties. He paid £10 in income tax.

He was obsessed with keeping records, a habit honed by thirty years in a solicitors' office, and he made his children follow suit. From their earliest years, transgressions were minuted. They were required to make formal confessions or promises of future good behaviour, like this one signed by Lewis:

I Lewis Macdonald Hastings do hereby pledge myself to my father
as under
1. not to buy on credit
2. not to apply again to my father for a loan
3. to repay present loan of £2.5.0 by weekly instalments of 5/-
4. I represent to my father that I want the present loan to repay R.
   Gray for a liability they have incurred on my behalf for a suit of
   clothes
5. to buy myself a nightshirt.

Basil suffered similar embarrassments, which he was also obliged to confess. Edward debated his own dilemmas in writing, as in this memorandum to himself, dated 2 May 1901: 'Question: whether having power either to send Claude and Aubrey to Stonyhurst or to Wimbledon we ought to exercise that power in favour of Stony-hurst when the consequences will be that Muriel cannot be sent to school till she is 16.' Stonyhurst's fees were £14.18s.5d a year, plus £2.8s.6d clothing allowance. Edward considered, and rejected, a notion that if he borrowed money, Muriel might be sent away to school at fifteen. Instead, he made minute calculations about the cost of journeys to Lancashire. He concluded that a few pence could be saved by ensuring that the boys always took the college trap from the nearby station at Whalley. It was decided that Claude and Aubrey should indeed be sent to Stonyhurst, 'using portmanteaux bought for Basil and Lewis'.

Edward's children lived in awe of their father, perceiving his profound commitment to conducting life as religion taught. Basil wrote later of his father's 'nobility', his behaviour as 'an example of light and guidance'. Edward kept a secret journal in Greek characters, in which he described strivings with his own conscience which became more pronounced and indeed tortured as he grew older. He scarcely ever lost his temper. Once, after displaying anger to their maid, in the midst of the following Sunday lunch he summoned the girl and apologised in front of his children. Basil described him: 'Silent, always apart, he passed through the world shunning company, afraid that he might become too attached to temporal things.'

A priest who was a family friend described him as 'the ideal Catholic layman'. Basil said: 'You cannot write down how people are good. You just know it and cannot get away from it. I don't think any of us remember his ever doing anything or buying anything for himself. He just worked and worked and prayed and prayed. Sometimes, the mater would buy him a packet of cigarettes and he would smoke one each evening. I think he was a little ashamed of that luxury.' Each night, Edward blessed each of his children before they went to bed. In May there was always an altar to Our Lady on the staircase, before which the family gathered for prayers. Even by the standards of the Victorian era, the severity of the regime which Edward imposed upon himself seems flagellatory.

Yet nobody could exercise effective control over eleven children once their father disappeared to his office. Basil wrote: 'Our garden was enormous, actually hedges and a mulberry tree. The hedges were absolutely right for ambuscades and sitting behind to eat all your sweets if you didn't want to give any away. Once the garden was all dug up into trenches in the most perfect manner (in connection with the drains) and the kids played at the Boer War, which was on at the time . . . They must have done it pretty well because we had a genuine Spion Kop where all the garden refuse had been piled up.'

When it rained, the back garden became swamped. Two French boys named Louis and Albert were then summoned from next door to re-enact the battle of Trafalgar. Lewis played Nelson, of course, though Basil as Hardy refused to kiss him. The Tribe were bemused by Louis and Albert's ready acquiescence in defeat, but in those days the French seemed resigned from birth to English superiority. On other days the children enacted the battle of Lake Regillus, or put planks across the garden inundation and played Horatius holding the bridge across the Tiber. The Pater made them learn reams of Macaulay by heart, and they put the knowledge to good use. Lewis acted Horatius. Small members of the Tribe served as Tarquins, who fell in the swamp after being stabbed, 'so that we were usually dragged in to tea and dripping instead of butter'.

Their father, ever the legal pedant, conducted 'trials' to mete out justice for his children's outrages against each other, at which evidence was solemnly taken, witnesses cross-examined. Edward then pronounced a verdict, typically: 'No jury could convict on such conflicting evidence. Case dismissed. Parties to kiss each other.' Basil wrote: 'That was the sort of trick the pater usually played on us. When we were all dead tired he'd stop the case and make us kiss when we'd much rather have been thrashed. It's bad enough to have to kiss your sister, or any girl, but a brother – pah!'

The girls and boys fought each other relentlessly. Whenever it was the Mater's day to go to the Stores, and Edward was safely absent at his office, there was a war. This might be started by Lewis snatching a book from Ethel, or Ethel making a sneering reference to the colour of Basil's hair. Once hostilities had been joined, the girls flew to entrench themselves in their room, usually accompanied by a hostage, perhaps baby Everard.

In the ensuing siege, pepper might be squeezed through the keyhole, smelly chemicals pushed under the sill, the lock smashed with a hammer and pincers. When the door was breached, the girls flew for protection to the servants – even in that modest household, there were three. Gladys might then avenge the girls by sneaking into the boys' room and tearing a page out of a favourite book Basil had been given for Christmas. Basil wrote: 'The funny thing about all of us was that none were particular chums. We all liked each other and fought each other constantly. No one was particularly popular and no one was unpopular.' He speculated that one reason for this was that they were rigorously segregated from other local children, who were deemed socially unacceptable: 'This probably had the effect of making us think that we belonged to quite a superior order of beings.' Little Eulalia, once rebuked for speaking to strange children, replied serenely: 'God made them,' then, as an afterthought, 'and made them like hens.'

Lewis was inevitably chief. All the children grew tall, the boys over six feet, except Basil who stopped at five feet seven. They developed a ruse for raising cash. Sometimes the older children were allowed to take the younger ones for a short walk without Nurse. They would station themselves outside a sweetshop then, at the sight of a benign-looking old gentleman or lady, overturn the pram containing baby Muriel Magdalen. The ensuing shrieks usually prompted the passer-by to still the clamour by proffering a penny, immediately appropriated by the baby's siblings to buy sweets.

In times of penury, they sometimes purloined their father's books, 'mostly trash about science and philosophy and so on, that he could hardly miss', and sold them at a curiosity shop not far from the house. They christened the old dealer 'Tuppence-the-Most', because that was the largest sum he offered for anything. By degrees, most of the contents of the Hastings attic ended up in the shop of 'Tuppence-the-Most'. The boys always wondered what the neighbours thought of the sight of them crawling round the roof leads, laden with goods. Nobody ever said anything, however. When in funds, they hired a bicycle from the old dealer for sixpence an hour. Six of them would take it in turns to try to master it, taking ten minutes apiece. Most of the boys' money, however, went to the turnstiles at The Oval, a few minutes' walk away. Passionate cricket fans all, devoted to the fortunes of Surrey, day after day they watched play from first ball to last.

Tuppence-the-Most

When his offspring were small, Edward Hastings subjected them to an hour's lessons each day before he left for the office – Latin, Greek, Roman history and maths. Homework was set for the rest of the day, while Lizzie Hastings taught handwriting, history and geography. As the children grew older, tutors visited twice a week, including a bearded Frenchman who smelt of snuff, instructed them in his language, and prompted disgust by kissing them. Edward was too gentle a man to thrash his children, but Lizzie, in this as in most things a dour Scots biddy, applied the birch vigorously.

Their father liked to reward members of the Tribe for good behaviour or feats of prowess by inviting them to write down what presents they wanted, come their next birthdays. When Lewis was seven, on 8 March he wanted a whip; on 10 March, a box of tools and an alarm clock; on 7 June, implausibly, a bowl of flowers; on 13 June, a little pump; on 19 July, boxing gloves. When Ethel was eight, on 8 June she asked for handkerchiefs; four days later for a little pump. When

15

Basil was five, on 13 June he bespoke a little pump; on the twenty-sixth a camp stool; on 19 July boxing gloves. The shared mania for 'a little pump' was prompted by a fascination with one which their father used for filling his bath, in the absence of taps. The children loved to work it, though when they grew up they puzzled in vain to remember why. 'Needless to say,' recalled Basil ruefully, 'we never got any of the presents we asked for. All we got was money, which had to be put into the Savings Bank at once and dragged out afterwards to pay for broken windows.'

Yet another mystery of the family's financial affairs is how Edward Hastings, on an annual income which rarely exceeded £400, contrived each autumn to take his enormous clan to the seaside for six weeks. The children adored the holidays, but dreaded the journeys. Edward, obsessive as ever, wrote down lists of every item of baggage, and insisted that each was ticked off as it was carried out to the railway omnibus, while the children stood in line, at attention in the hall. Besides the pram, camp stools and suchlike, a large table from Trinity Square was thought indispensable, because it was the only one at which Edward felt himself able to write in comfort. Each child was likewise ticked off the list, as the Tribe filed out of the house. In a characteristically quirky letter dispatched to Lewis, by then missing from the family party because he was at Hodder, Stonyhurst's prep school, Edward rehearsed one such journey, in a fashion which suggested that he was a court reporter *manqué*:

Herm, 1.10.92

At 8.20am on Friday 23 Sept 1892 a (Victoria) omnibus with pair horses pulled up at 29 Trinity Square. In the hall there were seventeen pieces of luggage as under. (1) cutter stand. (2) cutter (3) office bag (4) Elizabeth's box (5) my wraps (6) CSSH grub box (7) mamma's wraps (8) cradle (9) children's box A (10) children's Box B (11) hatbox (12) hamper (13) portmanteau C (14) portmanteau D (15) mamma's tin box (16) children's hat box (17) Margaret's box.

The following persons were in the square looking on while the driver loaded the luggage: The Jacobs – the Smiths – the inhabitants of the Brockham Street corner house. Caroline Attwood the sister of Margaret Attwood came to see us and travelled with us to Waterloo. Mr Jarvis's old woman was left in charge. I gave her a matchbox. Before the driver started Gladys and Beryl went on top of the omnibus. They saw the driver take a bottle. We were too quick for him.

Edward concluded with a brief inquisition, also characteristic:

(1) Have you been allowed to have your notebooks?
(2) What is the name of the archbishop who visited Hodder on 20 Sept? If you don't know, find out.
(3) Furnish list of school books, stating a) name of book b) author c) edition d) date e) publisher
(4) Ask Father Graham the name of the Jesuit who drowned.

Herm, in the Channel Islands, was the family's favourite destination. For several successive years, Edward rented a house on the island, the whole of which was the private property of a Prussian nobleman, Prince Blücher. Their holiday routine was as precisely regimented as everything else in their lives: 7 a.m., rise; 8 a.m., breakfast; 9 a.m., compile journals; 10 a.m., free time; 11.30 a.m., bathe; 1 p.m., lunch; 2.30 p.m., family walk; 5 p.m., tea; 5.30 p.m., evening prayers; 5.45 p.m., free time; 6.30 p.m., all children under seven go to bed; 8 p.m., supper; 8.30 p.m., retire to rest. The only part of each day which the children found intolerable was the requirement to compose a journal of its predecessor. Here is a typical entry of Lewis's:

> Bathed in the morning. Pater swam out five or six miles, perhaps, and a man said, 'What is that man doing that for?' It was Aubrey's birthday. He got a pile of prayer-books from the pater and mater and somebody else gave him 2s 6d and a watch and chain, which broke while we were all winding it. Borrowed sixpence from Aubrey and went rowing with Basil. Dinner roast pork, beans, potatoes, stewed plums and rice pudding. Sardines for supper. Buns for tea. Yesterday the sky was an Italian blue. There was no wind. The sea was studied [sic] with boats of all kinds. There are some books in this house. Some of their names are *God's Glorious Creation*, *The Plant World*, *On Foot in Spain*, *John Halifax*, *Cresswell's Maxima And Minima* and *Map And Plan Drawing*, all rotten.

The children's favourite companion on Herm was a fat, grizzled old sailor named Tom Duffy, who served as engineer of Prince Blücher's private steam yacht. A man of infinite good nature, who had travelled the world as a seaman, Tom told them tales of Africa, the West Indies, Constantinople, Iceland. 'It was so very much better than the stories in *The Boy's Own Paper*,' wrote Basil. The old salt took the children fishing for whiting and mackerel, and rigged their model boat. They spent hours standing at the door of his curious little cottage, in which he kept everything hung on the walls – even his prayer-book, attached to a piece of string. He said that it saved an old man the bother of reaching down. Tom, to the Pater's gratification, was a good Catholic. When they saw him chewing tobacco, the boys tried it themselves. They were horribly sick, and were later soundly thrashed by the Mater. The aged sailor laughed heartily next day when he heard the story. He resumed his usual duty, answering the children's incessant questions.

Tom Duffy

'Ever been to Jersey, Tom?'

'Rather.'

'What's it like?'

'Jersey? Jersey's a place for five-pound swells. A five-pound swell? That's one of those young fellers cutting a dash on five pounds because that's all he's got.'

'But you can do anything with five pounds, Tom.'

'No you can't, missie. It sounds a lot to you, but if you have to pay for your own lodgings and your own fares and your own food and your own amusements, it don't last more than a fortnight. And then you've got nothing to show for it.'

Herm was full of fascinations for children. There were snakes, which the boys caught and sometimes tried to take home. They once caused consternation in the Customs shed at Southampton when the reptiles staged a mass escape. For some reason, Herm's princely owner had elected to keep kangaroos, which roamed wild, and seemed untroubled by having stones thrown at them. No ordinary visitors were allowed on the island, so that it was a paradise for digging caves in the sands, playing pirates, hunting for treasure. 'We were so happy that we couldn't quarrel very much,' wrote Basil. They also dreaded the prospect that a row might result in one of the Pater's show trials, which would waste precious holiday time.

Each Sunday, the family boarded the proprietor's glittering steam yacht to attend Mass on Guernsey. At sea, the boys watched Tom Duffy working the engine. If Prince Blücher himself was aboard, he passed the trip shooting seagulls. The children marvelled at their father's almost inextinguishable holiday good temper. Edward seemed happier on Herm than at home, delighting in his children, perhaps because the Tribe was easier to manage amid the wide-open spaces. To Basil, each one of those September days in the Channel Isles was an idyll.

Back in London, during Victorian winters when there were annual freezes, the Pater taught his brood to skate on the Ladies' Pond in Battersea Park. They never minded skating days, because lessons at home were cancelled. Indoors, most of the boys' games involved model soldiers and bangs. In those days, gunpowder could be bought loose across the counter, like tea or sugar. It was regarded, even by Edward, as a perfectly normal playroom accessory. One day Lewis and Basil made a bomb by wrapping sixpence worth of black powder in an oily rag, placing it inside a tin and wooden fort, then laying a powder trail to the door of the nursery.

The Pater was summoned to join the children and witness the climactic moment. Blinds were drawn to make the room dark, then the fuse was lit. They watched enthralled as the flame raced across a desert made of silver sand and entered the fort, defended by broken lead soldiers, their uniforms glinting in the firelight. When the trail caught the oily rag, for an instant the fort became brilliantly lit. Then there was a thunderous crash as it blew apart. The watchers coughed and spluttered in a nursery full of smoke. The Mater ran upstairs and threw a fit when she observed a deep burn on the floorboards. She scolded Edward for allowing it all, as well she might. He, however, chuckled and chuckled, and was still laughing as he went downstairs. In his own life he had allowed himself so small a quotient of fun, of recklessness, of self-indulgence. A moment such as that one released all manner of unexpected emotions. At heart, the poor man may have yearned to unleash a wilder spirit than ever he allowed. In any event, the explosion provoked no recriminations for Lewis and Basil. Heredity must count for something, because an enthusiasm for bangs has been a persistent attribute of the Hastings family ever since.

The Tribe reserved its utmost scorn for visitors, who were received with almost unfailing discourtesy. A woman before whom they were paraded in the drawing room said to Lewis: 'Well, you are a big boy! Do you know that I nursed you when you were a tiny baby in arms? You must give me a kiss.' Lewis glared blankly back and demanded: 'Are you going to give us any money?' This caused her to become very red in the face and leave quickly. The children categorised visitors who offered no tips as 'the paupers'. Young Claude cannot have been best pleased when old grandmother Mary Hastings died in 1885, and bequeathed him only her red rosary blessed by the Pope.

Children often recoil from the banality of grown-ups' remarks. My grandfather winced when a woman visitor gushed: 'And is this really Basil?' The Mater, who had thrashed her offspring that very morning, assented with an indulgent smile, which increased her son's disgust.

'He is a very big boy – and he looks so healthy.'

'Oh yes, but just a little bit troublesome at times, aren't you, Basil?' said the Mater, beaming.

'Oh no, I'm sure not!' said the visitor, lifting her veil as well as her glass of sherry, the better to inspect the youthful prodigy.

'I am afraid so. He had to have a little whipping this morning.'

'Well, there now, but he's going to be a good boy always now, isn't he?'

If these performances were repugnant enough, the children's worst ordeals took place when parties were held at Trinity Square. Never much liking outsiders anyway, their resentment intensified when they were ordered to confine themselves to bread and butter, so that visitors could scoff the cakes and éclairs. After tea, the Tribe was required to sing for the assembled company, to their mother's piano accompaniment. The worst of the ditties they performed was entitled 'O Tea, O Tea, O Fragrant Tea'. Once, old General Hastings, Edward's uncle who had spent most of his life in the US Army, arrived on a visit. He was very old and very deaf, supposedly in consequence of cannon-fire, and his wife shouted at him through a speaking trumpet. The children quite liked his stories of the Mexican expedition and the US Civil War, 'but he was horribly ignorant about real history like Horatius and Castor & Pollux'. Their best visitor ever was a girl cousin, whose father gave her a sovereign with which to amuse herself and the Tribe. They were able to go to the Zoo and back in cabs, as well as gorge themselves on ten shillings' worth of ices, mince pies, Banbury cakes, ginger beer, meringues, angel cake, chocolates and tangerines. Basil said: 'It was the best feed we ever had.'

But that huge family was always happiest in its own company. Both Lewis and Basil became accomplished story-tellers, regaling the younger ones with tales of slave ships, pirates, treasure, ghosts. There were more than enough of them to perform plays and tableaux in the big kitchen, which had lots of doors. The nurse was conscripted to print a programme on Edward's typewriter. 'I don't think the pater liked anything so much on earth as these plays,' wrote Basil. 'He was always frightfully solemn at the solemn parts, and roared like mad if there was anything comic. At the end he clapped and clapped till he was tired. If you wanted to cheer him up you only had to tell him that there was to be a play the next Saturday.'

Edward carried to extremes a refusal to display signs of alarm, less still panic. Once, two of the younger boys hired a steam engine from Tuppence-the-Most. After it had been running for some time, delighting the Tribe, their parents went to bed. Lewis and Basil set about discovering how fast the engine could be driven. They poured fuel into its furnace, even breaking up their siblings' toy theatre to feed the flames. There was a thunderous explosion, smoke filled the house. The nurse woke, and hammered in terror at the Pater's door. 'Come out sir, come out!' she cried. 'The house is on fire!' The Pater's response caused the children to howl with laughter: 'All in good time, Nurse, all in good time. Wait till I find the coat I usually wear on these occasions.' When Edward emerged, however, he went out into the street and rang the fire alarm, causing the brigade to appear, its horse-drawn engines galloping up the street. The children were ecstatic, the Mater furious. She pointed out that the fire could have been extinguished with a few buckets of water. She was neither the first nor the last Hastings wife invited to endure much at the hands of her husband and offspring.

At ten, Lewis and Basil were sent to Hodder, Stonyhurst's prep school. They proved successful schoolboys, both in the classrooms and on the sports field, winning prizes, Basil wrote later, without extravagant effort. Edward's letters to his sons display the same relentlessly didactic spirit as do those of his own father Hugh to himself, a generation earlier. Because the boys had never known any other kind of father, and lived in an age and a family powerfully influenced by religion, they seem to have been untroubled by screeds which were, more often than not, exam papers.

'My darling son Basil,' Edward wrote from Herm on 10 October 1892,

I have your letter of 6 October. I notice you by mistake left the
name of the archbishop blank. Please (1) supply the blank.
Mamma has received the manual of Prayers for Youth, and I have
got the list of books, for which I thank you. (2) please send the
timetable. Please (3) answer question 34 more fully. I have told
Gladys you thank her for her letter. (4) find out the derivation of
the word 'blandyke'. (5) what does 'Night Studies' in the Stonyhurst
Calendar mean? (6) have you got Ethel's umbrella? (7) have they
any rules at Hodder, and can you send me a copy of them.

There followed an extract from Gladys's journal of their Channel
Islands holiday, then further bullet points, culminating with:

(17) I regret to hear of the drowning of the Jesuit you mention
. . . By the bye – don't call us your parents, but 'my dear pater and
mater'. It is a point of the utmost significance that when you leave
Stonyhurst you should enter the world well apprised of its dangers
and infinitely on your guard against bad company and the love of
vanities and pleasures. You cannot fortify yourself too much
against these evils. You must bring along with you all your religion.
I wish you to pray to God to know your vocation.

The barrage of questions was punctuated with fragments of whimsy:
'Have you asked for Lumley's *Select Plays Of Shakespeare*? – which
you lost. *Responde mihi*. Have you found Smith's Latin Grammar?,
respondez s'il vous plaît. I thank you for the programme of the concert
of the 1st of November 1892 which was not, as you allege, a Sunday,
but a Tuesday – Please apologise.'

Soon after Basil was promoted from Hodder to the main school
at Stonyhurst, on 15 February 1893, his father demanded:

Did you cry when you left Hodder?
Do you suck your thumb still?
Do you feel at home at Stonyhurst?
Do you like any of the boys?

Do the boys kick or ill-treat you?
Please answer all questions.

And a week later:

We were sorry to hear that you were spending your holidays in the
Infirmary. Did you offer up the sickness to God 'all for thee, Oh
my God – To do thy will, o God'. If you did not – you missed a
grand opportunity of earning merit in the sight of God, for this
sickness was a great disappointment to you – entailing as it did the
loss of 15 days skating. Did you get any skating at all before you
were taken ill? The 3rd term's Report has come. You have attained
only 13 marks in Religious Doctrine as against a possible 75 of
marks attainable!!!

Edward's obsession with recording trivia amuses his descendants,
but suggests eccentricity of heroic proportions. In great-grandfather,
pedantry tipped over into dottiness.

Basil's Stonyhurst diary was as banal as most schoolboy records,
as shown by this entry in 1894: '84 more days . . . Retreat began
today. Association. I played right-wing and got two goals, 17 marks
for my Greek theme. I have saved 9d. Xmas presents: Lewis got 2
pocket knives, a top hat, a purse; I got a pack of Snap cards, 2 coloured
tops; sweets; a steerable balloon; parlour cricket; an artificial nose.'
More interesting was his catalogue of books read. First, there were
those from the Spiritual Library: *St Paul of the Cross*, *St Elizabeth of
Hungary*, *The Little Flowers of St Francis*. Then came works that he
read for pleasure. He listed seventy-six titles, and many were exactly
those tales of adventure which his own son, and later I, his grandson,
in due course learned to love. G.A. Henty and Walter Scott figured
prominently among favourite authors. Basil mentioned with special
enthusiasm *Bonnie Prince Charlie*, *Tales of Daring and Peril*, *The
Talisman*, *St George for England*, *In the Dashing Days of Old*, *A Cornet
of Horse*, *Stirring Stories by Land and Sea*, *Cutlass & Cudgel*. A passion
for books, and for historical romance, has persisted in the family. To

give Edward his due, he did not allow his preoccupation with religion to deny the children fun.

More and more of his father's letters to Basil included lines of congratulation on prizes won, runs and goals scored. But Edward could never abandon the habit of admonition, as in April 1894: 'Your poem on Stonyhurst is disfigured by things attractive to the senses being given more prominence than things in which the mind plays a part.' Nine months later, in January 1895, Edward was quoting Samuel Butler: 'Nothing is more dangerous and nice and more difficult than for a man to speak much of himself without discovering a complacency in himself . . . and without discovering symptoms of secret self-love and pride.' On 22 March, he advised Basil: 'In your essay on the capture of Gibraltar you might bring in these saints as follows: "Not only did the capture of Gibraltar lead to the establishment of the Moorish dominion in Spain, but indirectly it may be said to have led to numberless martyrs sealing their fidelity with their blood. Had not Gibraltar been captured by the Moors it may be doubted whether saints like ss Nunilo and Alodia would have had the opportunity of winning their crowns."'

As Lewis and Basil grew older, money matters intruded with increasing frequency into their father's postal injunctions to them, as in this succinct note of 12 October 1896: 'Dear Basil, please return enclosed bills with your observations. Don't have any more neckties. *Pater tuus* S. Edward Hastings.' Immense pains were taken to economise on their journeys to and from school. As an end of term approached, Edward dispatched a banknote to Basil with these lines: '3rd class railway ticket Whalley to S. Pancras 17-6; margin for contingencies 2-6. £1 supplied. Please give me a written account of how you spend it, and hand back to me the balance. Lewis omitted to write and acknowledge receipt of the £1.10s. This was a solecism on his part.'

Shillings mattered to the Hastingses.

TWO

Lewis and Basil

In 1898 Edward's eldest son Lewis, my great-uncle, was in his last year at Stonyhurst when a seismic shock fell upon him and the family. He was accused by the Jesuits of a homosexual relationship, and sacked. Lewis – big, bold, passionate Lewis – emphatically denied wrongdoing. His father, however, insisted that the Jesuits could not be mistaken. Edward took the part of the school against his eldest son, prompting a breach between them that was never healed. Here was the most unsympathetic aspect of the Pater's religious fervour – a belief that Mother Church was incapable of error.

Lewis responded in a manner worthy of one of G.A. Henty's wronged young men, of whom he had read so many tales. Always attracted by the notion of wild places, he had devoured the writings of the great African hunters, Selous and Gordon-Cumming. Now, shaking the dust of England from his feet, he ran away to South Africa, working his passage before the mast on a sailing ship, with all his worldly possessions crammed into an orange box. On landing at Cape Town in the midst of the Boer War, he joined a group of young professional hunters who eked a living supplying meat to the mining community. Later, still conforming to a storyline stolen from fiction, he served for a couple of years in the Cape Mounted Police. In its ranks he found himself perfectly at home among other runaways, adventurers and remittance men. He fell in love with Africa, and spent the happiest years of his life there.

There is no record of the row about Lewis, but it must have inflicted a deep trauma on such a family as the Hastingses. Basil's last years at Stonyhurst were clouded by the memory of his elder brother's disgrace, whatever his own academic successes. After leaving the school he briefly enrolled at King's College, London, but quit almost certainly because there was insufficient money to fund him. For the third time in three generations, the education of a young Hastings was cut short. In 1902 he became a clerk in the War Office at a salary of £75 a year. There he remained for the next eight years, though his energies and ambitions became increasingly focused upon free-lance journalism.

Only a few months after Basil started work, the family suffered a new blow. Edward's health was never good. In April 1896 he had visited a specialist, Sir Dyce Duckworth, to discuss his persistent cough. He recorded afterwards that Sir Dyce 'noticed certain blood vessels below the breast and said I was a hot-tempered man but the temper was soon over. Advised me to discontinue shaving – go for my holiday to a district without trees like Tunbridge Wells or Malvern; eat fat bacon – avoid catching cold; open window of bedroom at night – said I would live 90 years more.' This diagnosis emphasises the quackery which prevailed a century ago, among even supposedly distinguished medical men.

In September 1903, at the age of fifty-three, Edward suffered a heart attack, collapsed and died while bathing at Shanklin, Isle of Wight. Only a few weeks later his eldest child Ethel, just twenty-four, died of consumption – tuberculosis, then still an incurable blight upon mankind. Lying in a Bournemouth nursing home with her mother at her bedside, she said feebly, 'I am very sorry for you, Mamma . . . Oh, Mamma, I'm dying.' Lizzie Hastings said, 'Never mind, darling, dear Jesus will take care of you.' The girl said, 'Oh yes, I will be with Jesus tonight.' Her mother asked Ethel to give her love to Edward, then the girl was gone. Lizzie wrote to Lewis in Natal: 'It would be selfish to wish her back, God's will be done. I'm sure she will pray for us all very much in her Heavenly Home. Father Luck said he was sure she had gone straight to Heaven. She had a lovely hearse and two mourning coaches.' Lewis arranged his own Mass for his sister at Kimberley's Catholic church.

I have no idea how the family coped financially after Edward died. There was probably some life insurance, because people such as the Pater took pains over such things. Somehow, the younger children's education was completed. Fortunately or otherwise, when the First World War came four of Edward's sons proved eligible for commissions, in an age when to become an officer it was necessary to 'pass for a gentleman'. One of the younger boys later attracted public attention of the most unwelcome kind, being tried at Winchester assizes, convicted and imprisoned on charges of homosexual behaviour. But that scandal lay in the future. In the Edwardian years, Edward's children had neither fame nor notoriety.

Their circumstances remained very modest. Almost all set up London homes south of the river. They remained inhabitants of the world of Mr Pooter, albeit a literate corner of it. A typical entry in the *Catholic Herald* for May 1904 reports: 'A successful concert was given on Thursday evening in the aid of the mission, at Peckham Public Hall, under the direction of Claude H. Hastings. The vocal talent was represented by the Rev. W. Alton, Miss Beryl Hastings, Miss Muriel Hastings and Mr A.J. Hastings. The following gentlemen acted as stewards: Messrs. J.D., W.D., and J.A. Newton, Master E.J. Hastings.' The Church still loomed large in the family's existence – their aunt Emily, Edward's sister, presided as Mother Superior at a convent in Roehampton until her death in 1920. Basil, who lived in Denmark Hill, became a pillar of local Catholic charities, notably the St Vincent de Paul Society, for which he organised and acted in local theatricals and concerts. The *South London Press* reported in March 1906: 'Few Catholic laymen are better known in South London than Mr B. Macdonald Hastings . . . because of the work which he has done for the Church in Southwark, for the poor and destitute. Year after year he has organised an entertainment for the benefit of the poor at St George's Cathedral mission.'

A jovial, enthusiastic, eagerly sociable man, Basil contributed with increasing regularity to newspapers and magazines. He published light verse, much of it about cricket, together with snippets of wit in gossip columns such as: ' "Kiss and never tell" is a poor adage for the billiard table. It is just the kissing that does tell' . . . 'The consistent borrower has the immense satisfaction of knowing that when he dies he will have finished ahead of the world' . . . 'A clean straw hat in May is an infallible sign of solvency.' This sort of thing may not make a modern audience roll in the aisles, but a century ago it played well with readers of the *Bystander, London Opinion*, the *Star* and suchlike. Basil yearned to escape from his servitude at the War Office. As the first decade of the century advanced, he acquired a modest journalistic reputation.

In 1907 he started to 'go steady' with the girl who became his wife, the love of his life. Billie – her full name was Wilhelmina Creusen White – was pretty, gentle, and Catholic. She lived with her parents in Peckham. Later, when some members of the family developed social pretensions, they treated Billie with condescension, complaining that she was dull, unlettered and 'common'. This was unjust. A woman full of kindness and good nature who had much to suffer, she proved a devoted wife in good times and bad. And the Hastingses of Trinity Square, Borough, were scarcely pillars of *Debrett's*.

Basil began a correspondence with Billie on 19 January 1907, dispatching the first of many passionate letters which, *inter alia*, reveal a fascination with her underclothes: 'Dear Little Wilhelmina with the very long name . . . I am going to bed to dream of your tantalising little feet, your brown stockings, your blue garters, your pink knees and lovely foaming petticoats and things. I send you heaps of kisses for all of them.'

On 6 August 1908, he wrote her his last letter as a bachelor, on War Office crested paper, anticipating the joys of married bliss the following week: 'I am going to kiss you in an entirely different way next Monday night, and somewhere you never dreamt of . . .'

In less fanciful vein, the day after their marriage in Peckham, Billie's mother wrote to her daughter, describing what happened at the wedding party after the bride and groom went away. Mrs White's letter conveys a nice sense of the genteel society in which they lived, and of its simple pleasures:

The Pines, Lyndhurst Road, Peckham S.E.

My dear Mina, you asked me to tell you everything what happened after you went. First they made a beastly mess with the confetti, & I think I am developing a new complaint. The symptoms are putting my finger in my mouth & making a dab at some coloured pieces of paper on the floor, well to return to the beginning again as soon as you left Willy and Harold had to see about getting home because Willy had to get to Windsor. So while Harold was racing around Peckham to try and find a taxi, I made tea which was very much liked by the ladies and also the strawberries and cream. Mr Smith had arrived by then and joined us. Mrs Mont was obliged to go by tram, then Mr Eastern waltzed *The Merry Widow* with Mrs Gordon, their tall hats stuck at a most ridiculous angle. Then the girls waltzed a little to Beryl playing. She was very jollie [sic] and nice, she kept us alive. After a while Father Alton had to go and Mr Eastern also. I think myself that he is rather afraid of his brother George. He made two or three trys [sic] to go, and at last ran down the road like mad. Then Mrs Hastings and the girls went, leaving us alone with pere Leo *il y avait encore quelque chose dans le bouteille n'est ce pas.*

This narrative continues for many pages, before concluding: 'There is no need to send you my hopes & wishes for you both because you know them, but may God and the blessed Virgin shower you both with blessings and may you and your *husband* be Pals to the end, is the one wish of your loving *mother*.'

Liz Hastings, Edward's widow, also wrote to her new daughter-in-law the day after the wedding: 'Does Basil know he had a column in the *Morning Leader* on Saturday? I forget the title . . . You must have had dreadful trouble with confetti. Well, dearest Mina, I must draw this scribble to a close with much love and the hope that you will always be very happy in *this* world and the *next*. Very affectionately your mother L. Hastings.'

Basil indeed found happiness with his Billie. They had two children: a son, my father Douglas Macdonald Hastings, born in October

1909; and a daughter, Beryl Ursula, who arrived two years later. The Basil Hastingses gradually drifted apart from the rest of the Tribe. Only Lewis featured much in their later lives. None of the other brothers or sisters made much mark on the world. Gladys, indeed, chose to leave it, following her great-aunt Emily into a convent and taking the veil. Among the others, though all remained churchgoers, religion no longer played the dominant, indeed oppressive, role which it had done in the lives of Hugh and Edward Hastings. Basil addressed worldly concerns with more ambition and greater success than either his unlucky father or grandfather.

Lewis, meanwhile, was cutting an exuberant swathe across South Africa. He adopted a lifestyle so remote from those of his forebears as to defy any notion of inherited values. It was as if he set out to compensate for generations of stiff-collared family respectability and piety by cramming a century's misdeeds and extravagances into a single lifetime. He was also writing verse. Here is a fragment of doggerel, inevitably Kipling pastiche, published in a South African newspaper in 1903, while he was serving with the Mounted Police.

When I was out in Africa amaking of my pile,
I met a sort of auxiliary bloke got up in reg'lar style;
He was sitting over a Kaffir pot concocting a sort of stew,
'And so,' says I, 'excuse me please, but who the deuce are you?'
Says he, 'I'm His Majesty's half-and-half, policeman and soldier too.'

They can handle a sword or carbine, a lance or a billiard cue,
And what they learned of botany was never learned at Kew.
They can follow the spoor of a cattle thief from the bleating of a ewe,
Though they're only blooming hermaphrodites, policemen and
    soldiers, too.

Since then I've met them everywhere, a-sleeping under the skies,
Hard as a packet of tenpenny nails, the sort as never dies.
They ain't quite strict teetotallers, they like their Mountain Dew,

And like it, of course, just half-and-half, whisky and soda too.
With some dop and a government blanket, they lie in the air so clear,
On the wide veldt in the moonlight with their troop-horse hobbled
    near.

Lewis wrote much later, at the end of a life rich in incident:

> In De Quincy's words, I have taken happiness in its solid and its liquid form, both boiled and unboiled. The world is so full of beasts, birds, fishes. The swoop of pratincoles on a Kalahari locust swarm. Rosy circles of flamingos above a salt marsh. Crocodiles on Zambesi sandbanks, and the great shapes of hippo walking by night past the camp-fire. Salmon leaping the fall in a Highland river. And sounds – the thunder of hooves of a great herd of wildebeest. The high, singing note of a ship's rigging in a full breeze (the crew of that ship lived in a filthy rat-haunted fo'c'sle, but they had a new Bible apiece given to them by the kind shipping company). Smells – the damp smell of Africa around the Primasole Bridge in the Sicily campaign. The linked odours of horse and leather in night marches of the older war. The smell of a beech wood in autumn, and the sweet scent of a flue-cured tobacco barn.
>
> Then there are people – bushmen with their bows and arrows in Ovamboland. The stripped divers at Monkey Island. Early Brown-shirts waving their antennae at the Brandenburger Tor. The black and the white and the brown, the hairy-heeled and the sophisticated, the hard-boiled and half-baked.

Lewis made a career as an adventurer, or, if you like, as a sensationalist, in the sense of one who pursued sensations, preferably in wild places. He took the title of his published fragment of autobiography from an early experience at a circus in Delagoa Bay. Having paid his half-crown for admission, he was dismayed to discover that he was expected to put a hand in his pocket again, to view one special attraction. Challenged, its cockney keeper responded impenitently: 'What do you expect, gents? Dragons are extra!' In Lewis's life, not much else was. His experiences would have adorned the pages of a Rider Haggard novel. He became well known in bar rooms and around campfires across southern Africa; uncomfortable without a rifle in his hand, or at least in his saddle bucket; welcoming a 'rough-house'; heedless of where next week's grubstake would come from. In the second decade of the century he became briefly prominent in South African Unionist politics. When the First World War ended in 1918 Lewis, who had acquired a reputation as a public speaker, was dispatched around France to address disgruntled soldiers about their demobilisation. At one such gathering, a man called out accusingly from the crowd: 'Aren't you the same Lewis Hastings who murdered a man in Eloff Street during the Johannesburg diamond riots of 1913?' Lewis, quite unabashed, called back: 'I didn't murder him. I broke my rifle stock over his head.'

Lewis argued that the disease-carrying insects of Africa fulfilled an admirable function by preserving the virginity of the vast tracts of bush he loved so much. He was irked when, in later life, he received a cool reception from the British Empire Society for his proposal, advanced not entirely in jest, to form a committee to protect the tsetse fly. In his early days as a professional hunter in Natal, he worked with two young Boers killing springbok, which in Kimberley fetched as much as a sovereign apiece for a ninety-pound carcass. He and his companions rode out to spend three days at a time pursuing the vast herds, shooting scores to be carried to market on a groaning wagon drawn by sixteen oxen. 'To be nineteen years old,' wrote Lewis, 'to wake before sunrise with Halley's Comet overhead, a rifle by one's side, and a whole perfect day before one on the plains, that was surely very near the crown of life. It was so cold at early morning that the frost crackled beneath our feet and the rifle barrel seemed to burn one's fingers.'

Having stalked a herd, often hundreds upon hundreds of springbok dancing across the veldt in great irregular columns, Lewis and his companions aimed to fire three, four, five shots apiece as fast as they could push bullets into the breeches of their old falling-block rifles, dropping as many beasts. Then they snatched the bridles of their ponies and set off in pursuit, racing to overtake the herd, bent low over their saddles: 'The nearest waiting horseman goes for all he is worth, not towards the buck but across their line. Hardly checking from the gallop, he flings the reins over his horse's neck, throws himself off, and firing from the knee, picks off one flying buck after another as the frantic multitude run, spring, and jink at close quarters . . . The excitement is packed into a few vivid minutes. Then it is over. The herd swings out of the danger zone.' The hunters then retraced their trail, gathering and cleaning carcasses for the wagon.

Lewis lived long enough to see the civilised world recoil from the slaughter of African game. What men such as he did in the early years of the century came to be regarded with revulsion. The breech-loading rifle and improvements in transport enabled hunters to kill and market animals on an industrial scale, accomplishing in the first thirty years of the twentieth century an unprecedented depletion of the conti-nent's wildlife. In fairness to Lewis and his generation, over the ensuing eighty years habitat loss – the consequence of exploding human popu-lations – has proved an even more fatal foe of Africa's game than were the massacres committed by the old white hunters. But Lewis, looking back later, confessed that he regretted the wholesale killings of elephant and buffalo in which he participated so eagerly – by which, indeed, he made his living – in the years before 1914.

Around 1911, he became fired with the new craze for aviation. He formed a friendship with a man named John Weston, who brought the first aeroplane to South Africa – the usual double-kite contrap-tion of the period, laced with piano wire and christened the 'Weston-Farman biplane'. Lewis adored his flights with Weston: 'The pilot occupied a flimsy sort of box open on all sides, and his passenger a kind of Madeira chair, just behind and above him. The sensation for anyone conveyed in this way, when the unwieldy machine drooped its nose earthwards, was terrific. No modern passenger can have any conception of the ecstasies of horror and rapture induced by a trip in a thing like the Weston-Farman.' Weston the pioneer was so obsessed by the beauty of mechanical science that when a daughter was born to him, he insisted that she should be dressed in dungarees, and play only with nuts and bolts, in the hope that she might grow up into an aviatrix. In this he was disappointed, but unlike most of the early airmen, he survived to die in bed.

Weston's plane and his own beloved Greener .303 falling-block rifle were the only examples of modern technology which Lewis enthusiastically embraced. Despite his use of firearms for hunting, he applauded the fact that the many quarrels in the Kimberley diamond diggings were settled with bare knuckles. He himself was a keen boxer, with or without gloves. In South African mining towns, he said, 'the flourishing of guns was a mortal offence. I remember one case where a gentleman newly arrived from Western America, in the course of an argument in one of the canteens, drew a six-shooter. That was the end of him. A dozen willing hands cast him and his weapon into the muddy Vaal River. The diggings never saw him again. And yet, oddly enough, years afterwards in the Kalahari Desert during Botha's campaign, I recognised this same American filibuster in the ranks of one of our mounted regiments. So his heart must have been in the right place, after all.'

Lewis became intimately acquainted with a host of buccaneers and freebooters such as Leander Starr Jameson of Jameson Raid notoriety, and the bandit-smuggler Scotty Smith. Far from harbouring any dislike for the Boers – the English war with them, remember, was not long finished – Lewis admired the hardy Dutch farmers. Courage and uncomplaining fortitude were the first qualities which he sought in a man, and most Afrikaners possessed them. He also warmed to black Africans, especially Khama, paramount chief of Bechuanaland – modern Botswana. Lewis was once hunting, with the chief's permission, in remote bush five days' march from Khama's capital. A native runner appeared, bearing in a cleft stick a message written at the chief's dictation by his European-trained secretary: 'Please to take great care now on the Shoshong, for it is this month the breeding season of the black mamba.' Lewis was enchanted by the solicitude of the old chief, who had sent a messenger a hundred miles across country with his kindly warning.

Lewis's first body-servant and gun-bearer was a Zulu named

Shakespeare, who stayed with him for years, and often entertained him with tales of his tribe's 1879 war with the British, only a quarter of a century earlier. Shakespeare claimed that his own father had been among the party which cut down the Prince Imperial, son of the exiled French Emperor Napoleon III. Perceiving that the dead man was a chief of some importance, Shakespeare asserted that, in accordance with tribal custom, his killers extracted and shared a mouthful apiece of the Prince's raw heart. Lewis believed this story to be true. It left him puzzled about what might therefore repose in the casket supposedly containing the boy's heart which had been returned by Lord Chelmsford with much ceremony to his grieving mother, Empress Eugénie, in Surrey.

Lewis loved the legends of the African tribes, of which he often included samples in his own anecdotage. But in his attitude to the continent's indigenous peoples, he was a man of his time. 'A lot of nonsense is talked about the yearning for freedom of this and freedom of that,' he observed characteristically. 'The only freedom Africans want is freedom from trousers.' That line appeared for years in a dictionary of quotations, until a squeamish modern editor deleted it. Lewis loved to meet Africans in what he perceived as their natural setting – villages amid the vast expanse of the bush. He was moved to pity when he saw them in the towns of South Africa and Rhodesia, where they seemed to him to shrink and become lost souls.

In the last years before the First World War, Lewis devoted increasing energy to journalism and politics, to which he was intro-duced by the ex-Jameson raider turned financial magnate Sir George Farrar. Farrar persuaded Lewis to help organise the Unionist Party in the Transvaal. He worked closely with two former members of the 'Milner Kindergarten', Patrick Duncan and Richard Feetham. In July 1913, in their company Lewis played a dramatic part in suppressing the huge, violent miners' strikes which convulsed South Africa. Thousands of rioters, many of them armed, converged on Johannesburg. Lewis, though the youngest man in the Rand Club that day, found himself called upon to command a local 'Civic Guard'. This was the occasion when he broke a Mauser rifle over the head of a man whom he saw raising a gun to fire at his company. Lewis cheerfully admitted afterwards that he held no special opinion one way or another about the merits of the authorities' case, or that of the strikers. He merely took his usual view that if there was a fight, he wanted to be in it. Botha and Smuts suppressed the rioters by promising generous concessions, none of which were fulfilled. A few months later, Lewis found himself with a real war to fight, on a scale which satisfied even his own gluttony for trouble.

I was brought up to idolise Lewis, as my father did. Even in old age, he retained his magical speaking voice. He presented a magnificent tawny figure, about whom no legend could be doubted. He was entirely of his time and place. A sceptic would have said that his life was selfish and reckless. Most of his virtues were those of the Clubland Heroes of fiction, founded upon courage, physical prowess, a boundless appetite for excitement and fellowship. His views and prejudices lacked any shading: somebody was a white man, or a rotter; a cause was worthless, or to die for. Yet Lewis possessed real literary gifts, not least a talent for verse. When he exercised his brain and pen, the results were sometimes remarkable. His accomplishments were much slighter than they might have been, because he always chose to please himself, to forswear discipline, to pursue whatever overhead star momentarily seized his imagination.

To my father and later myself, when we read of the Hastingses of the nineteenth century, they seemed respectable, hard-working, decent Christian people. But glamour and romance were lacking from their lives. Lewis, by contrast, towered over every room he entered. Even in old age, in any company he looked willing as well as able to knock down any man who deserved it. Like so many black, or at least grey, sheep he was much more fun than the chaps who got made head of house at school or lived blameless lives in – well, Trinity Square, Borough, where the Tribe grew up. And by 1914, the fun in Lewis's life had hardly started.

THREE

Stagestruck

My father disliked the name with which he was christened, Douglas, almost as much as his own father Basil resented being Basil. Grandfather sought to assuage the pain by signing himself in print Basil Macdonald Hastings. Once Douglas Macdonald Hastings escaped from infancy, he became universally known as 'Mac'. At the time of his birth in 1909, his father was a struggling freelance journalist. A year later, Basil became assistant editor of the *Bystander* magazine, then in its heyday. In this role, he once sought to persuade Max Beerbohm to contribute an article about his schooldays at Charterhouse. 'Dear Hastings,' Beerbohm wrote back, 'I fear that I must decline, for if I accepted I know that the poison would creep into my pen.' How well I recognised this sensation as I read the letter seventy years later! By then I had myself experienced the miseries of the same school.

Basil prospered at the *Bystander*, and spread his wings. In 1911 he wrote a comic play entitled *The New Sin*, and sent it to the Vendome-Eady theatrical management. They accepted it at once, gave him a princely £10 on account of royalties, and a contract promising him 5 per cent of weekly receipts, rising to 10 per cent on anything over £1,000 a week. After the play's first night at the Criterion, there were fears. A pessimistic producer muttered about 'complete failure' – then was confounded. *The New Sin* became the hit of the season and ran for two years. It was translated all over Europe and performed on Broadway with an all-star cast. Basil travelled to New York on the *Lusitania* for its opening. Six thousand copies of the play were sold in bookshops. There were negotiations

Basil (seated on the left, beaming benevolently through his spectacles) as assistant editor of the *Bystander* in 1911, in a view of its office sketched by one of the magazine's illustrators. The exquisite figure draped on the sofa is editor Comyns Beaumont.

for the cinematograph rights. Basil wrote: 'Heaven send me a few more such "complete failures".'

The plotline of *The New Sin*, a comedy, concerns a man who needs to stay alive, because if he dies ten feckless siblings stand to collect large inheritances. Originality derived from the fact that its characters were all male. Pasted into the flyleaf of our family copy of Saki's *Beasts and Superbeasts* is a note from the Cocoa Tree Club in St James's Street: '12.2.12 Dear Mr Hastings, congratulations on your brilliant play, sincerely yours, H.H. Munro.' A host of other literary stars, including J.M. Barrie, paid tribute. Great things were predicted for Basil. By the time young Mac became conscious of the world, his father was a recognised figure in the London theatre.

Basil's subsequent plays, though cast with such starry names as H.B. Irving (elder son of Henry) and Cyril Maude, were notably less successful. *Love – and What Then?* flopped. 'Though witty and amusing,' said *The Times*, 'it has a weak and unconvincing story.' *The Tide* in 1914 did no business. When *The Advertisement* opened at the Kingsway Theatre in April 1915, *The Times* was again unenthusiastic: 'There are in it excellent passages, interesting ideas and some dramatic situations, but on the whole it resembles the chief character in being good only in parts.' A 1915 collaborative effort with Stephen Leacock, *Q*, was likewise a box-office failure.

Basil was much more successful, however, as a writer of revues, which enjoyed immense popularity throughout the First World War, especially with men back from the trenches. At one moment in 1915 he had three productions running simultaneously in the West End, of which *Razzle-Dazzle* at Drury Lane, starring Harry Tate, was the biggest hit, running for over four hundred performances. Basil collaborated with the famous trench cartoonist Bruce Bairnsfather, creator of Old Bill, to write *The Johnson 'Ole*. He continued to contribute light pieces to newspapers, and was for a time a regular columnist for the *Evening Standard*. In 1916 he earned £1,100, a good income for the time. His own health was poor, rendering him ineligible for active service, but three of his brothers were fighting in France, and often wrote to Basil seeking tickets for his shows for fellow officers coming home on leave.

Today, it is taken for granted that the First World War was an unspeakable experience for all those who participated. Yet, as in all conflicts, there was a small minority of eager warriors, who welcomed the opportunities and challenges which the battlefield offered. Among these, inevitably, was Basil's elder brother. In South Africa in August 1914, at General Smuts's request Lewis managed a recruiting campaign for the Imperial Light Horse, to fight in German South-West Africa – modern Namibia. Lewis, by then thirty-four, possessed notable gifts as an orator. He used these to effect in a barnstorming tour, addressing meetings up and down South Africa. When the recruiting drive was over, he was invited by the Transvaal government to accept some token of its thanks. In those days, volunteers for the ILH were expected to supply their own kit. Lewis asked for a horse and saddlery, to outfit himself for the campaign. A dinner was thrown by the Transvaal Unionist Party at the Noord Street concert hall in Johannesburg. A pretty girl rode Lewis's charger, a big chestnut named Ensign, up the steps and into the hall for presentation. During the speeches, Ensign disgraced himself by lifting his tail, to riotous applause. Then Lewis rode the horse down the steps into the city street, and off to war.

'D' Squadron of the Imperial Light Horse was composed of the sort of men whom Bulldog Drummond would have applauded – Currie Cup rugby players (who included Lewis himself), boxers, athletes, horsemen all, well accustomed to firearms. Together with the troopers of other units such as the Natal Carabiniers and Rand Rifles, they celebrated riotously at their camp outside Cape Town before boarding the ships which carried them to South-West Africa in September 1914. Once in the Kalahari Desert, Lewis and the other Light Horsemen were deployed as scouts and intelligence-gatherers for the main British column. The South Africans found themselves skirmishing with Uhlans of the German regular cavalry, quite unversed in bush life. 'The squadron bag in the first three days consisted of about a dozen Huns, three camels and an adolescent seal,' wrote Lewis. The latter poor creature, miles from the sea, had been the mascot of a German unit, and was now adopted by the Light Horse. Lewis was delighted to meet the seal again a few months later, 'pleased and glossy in Pretoria Zoo'.

Trooper Hastings enjoyed himself shamelessly, despite the atrocious conditions prevailing on the battlefield. 'All desert campaigns have much in common, and we suffered the usual pests of sandstorms, veldt sores, heat, dirt and flies. The supply system was scandalous. It wasn't only that we were on starvation rations and that a diet of dry biscuit and bully caused rampant desert sores, but the equipment supplied by rapacious profiteers in the Union was rotten. Nearly all the water-bottles developed leaks in the first twenty-four hours.' In one skirmish, Lewis was hit on the shin by a spent bullet, and dismounted to have the wound dressed. His hard-living general, old Sir Duncan McKenzie, chanced to gallop by at that moment. He blazed at Lewis: 'What the hell are you doing here? You can ride, can't you? Then why the hell aren't you with your troop?' Lewis hastily remounted, though when the action was over he was obliged to retire to hospital for a fortnight.

He loved his time in the South-West, mostly serving under a tough old Boer named Jacobus van Deventer, who when war came in 1914 had mustered his Commando, then cabled General Botha: 'All my burghers armed, mounted and ready. Whom do we fight – the British or the Germans?' On one march in April, the South African horsemen covered two hundred miles in eleven days, despite being obliged to haul forward in trucks every gallon of water for horse and man. German resistance was feeble: in the entire campaign only 113 South Africans were killed by enemy action, as against 153 who died from disease or accidents. Hardship rather than peril was the hallmark of the experience, as Lewis readily acknowledged.

By early 1915, the South Africans deployed 43,000 men in South-West Africa. The Germans, heavily outnumbered and lacking a commander to match the genius of von Lettow-Vorbeck in Tanganyika, surrendered in July. When Lewis's unit returned to Cape Town, he was among many men who hastened onwards to England, to join a vastly more serious war. Commissioned into the Royal Field Artillery, he spent the rest of the war in France, entirely happy commanding a battery of eighteen-pounders, finishing as a major with the Military Cross. He saw the terrible first day of the Somme from an observation post in the front line, and never forgot 'the orderly rows of British dead in front of the German wire'. He wrote to Basil on 29 April 1917: 'Recently I've seen dozens of air fights, which are the cream of spectacles when you get anything like a near view. The Bosch is now getting it in the neck up above, thank goodness. For the present, we're more or less in trenches again – but a moving order may come at any moment. I'm writing this in an OP in the outpost line on a comparatively peaceful and sunny morning. Love to Billie and the youngsters, yours ever, Lewis.'

For the rest of his life, though Lewis readily acknowledged the scale of 1914–18's horrors, he was exasperated by those who professed that the experience was worse in kind than any other conflict. In 1963, when I was working as a researcher on what became a legendary

BBC TV series, *The Great War*, he wrote me a letter about his own memories. He said that he had just finished reading a new book on the Waterloo campaign. 'You know,' he said,

> those three days in 1815 were as full of mud and blood and horror and blunders as the long Somme agony was. A review of Henry Williamson's book on the Somme by some hysterical nitwit claimed that all the good and brave and the potential leaders were annihilated, and apparently on the first day! Frightful as it was, one must remember that it was followed by the large-scale battles of '17 and the bloody squalor of Passchendaele. British fortitude and capacity for sacrifice were not written off in November 1916. Moreover, though I know beyond peradventure that our chaps in 1918, especially after the great German attacks in March and April, were on the whole below the heroic standards of the British armies of 1916, they were still capable of inflicting upon the German Army in August, September and October 1918 the greatest defeats in German history, and of capturing *more men, more guns, and more territory* in that final victorious onslaught than all our bloody allies put together – French, Belgians, Americans etc. This is always forgotten. Wish I could tell you some more – about horses! About mules! Yes, the poor bloody mules!

Basil's other brothers found the experience of war vastly less rewarding than did Lewis. Aubrey, twenty-eight years old, was commissioned into the 7th East Surreys, a unit of Kitchener's New Army, in the spring of 1915. His battalion was sent to France that summer. Thereafter, Aubrey wrote frequently to Basil, in a vein much more familiar to modern students of the First World War than Lewis's exuberant scribbles. He described, with mounting dismay, the usual murderous manifestations of trench warfare – shelling, bombing, sniping, losses, flies, relentless tension. By August he had become desperate to escape, and wrote to Basil asking whether his brother could exercise any 'pull' to secure him a transfer to the Royal Flying Corps: 'I've got a certain amount of mechanical knowledge and I think my CO would recommend a transfer, on the ground of being married.' Actuarially, had the poor man but known it, his prospects of survival as a pilot would have been more precarious than as a junior infantry officer. But in that place in those days, any posting seemed preferable to serving in the line with an infantry battalion. Aubrey wrote to Basil on 17 August 1915:

Thanks very much for enquiring about the Royal Flying Corps. I do hope it comes to something. My appearance in the casualty list for 13 August refers to the second time I've been hit – only slightly, Thank God! The Hun put over some shrapnel – registering shells, I think. Willie Martin and I were in command of Support trench with 3 platoons (Willie is our second captain – a ripping fellow – regular officer) we got the men in dugouts and were returning to the telephone dugout . . . We heard the usual whizz, it went off bang and I felt a sting in my right shoulder. As soon as it was over we emerged and I took my coat off and found I'd been hit with two splinters. They only made a small patch of blood on my shirt. It's not the fact of being hit, Basil, it's the frightening effect of shells etc that make you so nervy. I'm much more nervy today than when I first came out.

PS I don't say anything to the women about the fighting, of course.

On 21 September, Aubrey wrote:

My company commander Capt. H.J. Dresser is going on leave today. Could you give him two seats for the play? He is going to stay at the Jermyn Court Hotel, Jermyn Street. I expect to go to a rest camp, in a day or two. Had two nasty heart attacks in the trenches. The first time it occurred was the day we were being relieved. I had been fooling about and joking etc, delighted at the thought of getting into billets, when suddenly at teatime I collapsed. The 2nd time the Germans were sending over rifle grenades. Suddenly they started bombing us with trench mortars as well. One went off quite close to me, and my heart started again. I've seen the MO and he says I've got a large heart, and must take a fortnight's rest. He is

45

seeing the colonel also. He has stopped me smoking cigarettes &
alas! struck me off beer! I think it is only excessive excitement that
brought it on. I've not told Mother.

Then on 29 September: 'We are in a bust-up tomorrow, so I thought
I'd let you know. The artillery starts today. I only told the colonel
the other day I was married and he said it was a pity I had not told
him before, for in case anything happened to me, it would be difficult for Elly to get a pension. I just mention this in case of events,
as I know you would help to straighten it out. Give my love to dearest
Mother.' On 5 October, at Loos, the 7th Surreys' war diary recorded
laconically: 'A [trench mortar] battery in D Coy's trench got a severe
shelling about 8am resulting in several casualties. Lt. Hastings was
killed also two men and 9 others wounded.' Aubrey was among four
officers and sixty-eight men from the battalion who became fatal
casualties that month. His letters reveal no lust for glory, only a deep
dismay at the predicament in which he found himself. Since he was
the family's only fatal loss of the war, among three brothers who
served in France, the Hastingses came off lightly. But it cannot have
seemed so to Aubrey's hapless widow.

Even as casualties rose, Basil continued to be rejected for active duty
– the medical examiners categorised him B2. Mac described his father
as 'Pickwickian'. Part of this persona was that Basil, short and stout,
was ill-constructed for physical exertion. Nonetheless, so desperate
was the demand for men that in 1917, at the age of thirty-seven, he
donned the uniform of a corporal in the King's Royal Rifle Corps.
It seemed absurd even to the staid spirits of the War Office that a
talented writer approaching middle age should waste his time
guarding some remote encampment. Thus he was transferred to the
Royal Flying Corps, and spent the last year of the war producing a
weekly newspaper for flight trainees, entitled *Roosters and Fledglings*.
Many of its columns were taken up with recording the grisly roster
of training accidents, which killed more embryo British pilots in
World War I than did the Germans. Basil finished with the rank of

lieutenant in the new Royal Air Force, though his commissioning letter emphasised: 'He is clearly to understand that he is appointed for ground duties only, and in no circumstances will he be permitted to go into the air, except in connection with the actual duties of his appointment.'

Throughout the war, Basil continued to work on further plays, though West End audiences craved light entertainment. He embarked on a collaboration with the novelist and playwright Eden Phillpotts, who wrote from Torquay in January 1917:

Dear Hastings, Now I hear [H.B.] Irving has changed his mind again and may use [the stage adaptation of Phillpotts's novel] 'The Farmer's Wife'. But there is something so volatile and contradictory about the actor's mental make-up that one rather despairs. It is because the game is worth the candle – one real success worth working for – that we put time into play-writing. It's a pure gamble of time. Drinkwater suspects that there will be a tremendous demand for plays after the war; but not khaki plays. I like your construction, but feel it won't be worth putting the time into until we both feel we've got a likely proposition for [the actor-manager Gerald] du Maurier, or somebody of that sort. I'm holding 'A Happy Finding' and will send it in at once, when you let me know. With [Sir Charles] Hawtrey it would be bound to do well, for it is very funny, and a shrewd hit at our disgusting divorce laws. Try and get Hawtrey interested again. Yours always EP.

Mac was seven when, in 1917, he followed the usual family path to Stonyhurst's preparatory school, Hodder. A two-horse brake carried him from Whalley station to his new abode, full of fears which were soon fulfilled. Unlike his father and grandfather, Mac possessed no piety. He found his new residence mindlessly cruel, was himself 'unutterably miserable', and was bullied from the moment of his arrival. When his tormentors suspended him from a ladder in the gym, the prefect who released him – at Stonyhurst masters rather than senior boys were called 'prefects' – slapped his face to check his tears. 'Physical violence, so it seemed, was a way of life . . . I make no excuse for the bitterness of my pen,' he wrote long afterwards. At seven especially, but likewise afterwards, he found incomprehensible the religious tracts which he was obliged to read. At confession, he was driven to invent imaginary sins. 'The round of daily mass and prayers was hateful to me . . . I parroted the words, I fingered the rosary. But deep down inside, I was wondering what it was about.'

Mac achieved a brief spasm of happiness with his introduction to school theatricals, playing Morgiana the slave girl in *Ali Baba and the Forty Thieves*. But he found the brutality of the Stonyhurst system unforgivable. In that last year of the war, boys with richer parents were permitted to pay for extra food such as bacon and eggs, which Mac did not receive. Because the Jesuits censored the boys' letters home before dispatch, it was impossible for him even to reveal his miseries. Bullying was institutionalised. Not long after his arrival, in that cold, dank, draughty, cavernous place, Mac contracted pneumonia. Their matron, 'the hag', shrugged her shoulders and wrote him off. A Jesuit gave him the last rites with an insouciance the memory of which disgusted the boy when he defied probability by surviving. He never forgot the readiness of his keepers to deliver him to his Maker.

At Stonyhurst, he wrote later, the Jesuits 'devoted an unconscionable time getting us ready for the next world before we were even ready for this one'. His 'beaks', like most pedagogues, were poor pickers of people. Boys who achieve office in their schooldays often sink without trace thereafter, ending up as secretaries of suburban golf clubs. The qualities which commend prefects and games-players to teachers are seldom those which will prove of much value thereafter. Willingness to conform is perceived as the highest good in schoolboys, but it ill fits them for any subsequent attempt to reach the stars. Schoolmasters are also the only people on earth who claim a right to place money on horses after races have been run. Decades on, they seek to embrace former pupils who have prospered in life, however abominably they treated them in childhood. This was Mac's experience.

While recuperating after his bout of pneumonia he was granted a respite, staying with his family at St Leonards-on-Sea for the duration of one glorious missed school term. Then he was returned to Lancashire, his father assuring him, with timeless fatuity, that modern Stonyhurst was much less harsh than it had been in his own and Lewis's day.

Mac learned to live with the place, if never to love it. When he advanced from Hodder to the main school, and began to achieve some academic success, his life brightened. From an early stage he displayed a gift for public speaking, and always applauded the fact that the school taught Elocution as a specific skill: 'I am best in the class at Latin, English, History by heart and all oral work,' he wrote exuberantly in November 1918. He urged his parents to come and see him perform in the Shrovetide play, but said he realised that the expense of the journey to Lancashire would probably be prohibitive, as indeed it proved. 'We have had two holidays because the armistice has been signed. I have learned two pieces of poetry for you when I come home, *The Jackdaw of Rheims* and the other *King John and the Abbot of Canterbury Cathedral*. I wish you would tell Daddy to send me some of his articles now, especially out of the *Sunday Herald*. He has made a name for himself here. I'd love to tell you more but *Tempus Fugit*.' A Stonyhurst report for 1919 suggested that Douglas 'showed distinct talent as an actor'.

Mac shared the enthusiasm of almost every Hastings schoolboy through the generations for tales of war and adventure – Conan Doyle's *Sir Nigel* and *The White Company* – 'the fights are simply ripping' – together with all of Kipling, especially the *Just So Stories*. He loved the school cadet corps, and relished any opportunity to use firearms – there were no guns at home. His toys were those of his time: Meccano, model soldiers, cigarette cards. The arrival of a new Gamages' catalogue was a big event. He was increasingly fascinated by the countryside. Roaming the fields and woods around Stony-hurst, he developed a knowledge of birds and plants remarkable in the child of a family which was anything but rustic.

His language reflected not only the period, but also a natural exuberance which persisted for most of his life. He was always 'working like blazes', his latest acquisition was 'topping', 'ripping', or 'hairy'. He developed a mild interest in racing, and was extravagantly impressed by a schoolfriend whose father owned two horses. To the end, he tolerated Stonyhurst rather than loved it. Thank Heaven, he never considered sending me, his own son, there. Its oppressive devotion left him almost entirely irreligious. The Catholic Church's spell upon our family was broken. But Mac retained a grudging gratitude for the education he received, for the classical and literary enthusiasms Stonyhurst awakened, and for the eloquence and powers of self-expression the school promoted.

At home, he grew up in a mildly bohemian literary world, focused upon family homes with such coy addresses as Wella Willa, Pickwick Road, Dulwich; then later in rented country cottages, of which the longest-tenanted lay near Winchester. He sat at the feet of such friends of his father as Hilaire Belloc, whom he asked breathlessly whether he had indeed, as he recounted in print, walked from London to Paris with only sixpence in his pocket. 'Young man,' responded Belloc magisterially, 'I am a journalist.' Mac remarked later that this exchange provided him with an early hint about the merits, when composing contributions for newspapers, of tempering a strict regard for truth with some savouring of romance.

G.K. Chesterton, another Catholic author, likewise favoured him with advice: 'As I went out into the world,' the old sage said, 'I would meet two sorts of great men: there were the *little* great men who made all those around them feel little; and the *great* great men, who made all those around them feel great.' Mac shook the hand of Kipling, and was much in awe of his father's familiarity with such literary stars as J.M. Barrie and James Agate, as well as of his constant appearances in newspapers and on theatre bills. Yet Basil's efforts to repeat the success of *The New Sin* yielded continuing disappointments.

His first post-war play, *A Certain Liveliness*, opened at the St Martin's in February 1919, then swiftly closed. A month later, his dramatisation of Joseph Conrad's novel *Victory* received its first performance at the Globe. This was a project which had been almost three years in the making. In July 1916 the actor-manager H.B. Irving had written to Conrad, then fifty-eight, urging him to agree that Basil, 'a dramatist of some standing', should adapt *Victory* for the stage. Here was implausible casting. The novel is a dark work which ends in wholesale death and tragedy, while Basil was at his best composing light pieces. But Irving persuaded both playwright and novelist that a collaboration was feasible. A month later the three met at the Garrick Club for discussions.

Basil wrote a vivid account of his first encounter with Conrad, whom he found surprising. 'Unlike my books?' demanded the novelist with a smile. Basil replied: 'On the contrary – just like your books, and not in the least like a retired captain of sailing-ships.' Conrad put his head on one side,

> a birdlike gesture that was common with him. When he talked to me he showed enthusiasm only when I said anything challenging. His eyes would light up, and he would argue eagerly, at the same time giving the impression that he was trying to satisfy himself that I was right. Never was there a more flattering talker. He raised all those with whom he came in contact. It was as if one had been blessed. I do not suppose he bared his soul to anyone save in his books. He charmed you into telling your thoughts. Never was there a more courteous man, and I think he was conscious of this quality and proud of it.

Basil wanted to create the play in active collaboration with Conrad. At the outset, the novelist insisted that the theatrical adaptation should be the dramatist's work alone. But over the next two years Conrad wrote Basil many letters, advising on passages of dialogue, details of clothing and sets. He explained, for instance, that the character Jones is 'at bottom crazy . . . a psychic lunatic'; that the façade of Schomberg's Hotel on Java, the principal setting, had three arches, with wooden tables beneath them. 'A play must be written to *seen* situations,' he observed. Sometimes Conrad was moved to write to the dramatist explaining the profound emotions which stirred him in passages of his own novel: 'I give you my word, Dear Hastings, I wouldn't have let out a whisper of it if your letter had not prodded me to the quick . . . *Victory*, don't forget, has come out of my innermost self.' They met often, usually at Conrad's urging, when some special problem was identified. Basil sustained deep respect for the passion and intellect of the novel's originator. Yet he became increasingly doubtful about the commercial prospects of the play. He was eager to ensure that both he and Conrad received the cheques for their parts in the production well before its opening. Basil felt that the novelist's 'mental attitude . . . did not allow him to appreciate what was theatrically significant'. As he urged Conrad that the plot must be modified to take account of the requirements of the stage, Conrad replied that he did not wish to see the stuff of his novel become too diluted: 'Not too much water! My dear Hastings, not too much water!'

Basil's first draft was finished in the spring of 1917, but Irving then changed his mind about which character he himself wished to play. This meant substantial script changes. By autumn, Irving had lost confidence in the whole project, and decided to abandon it. But Conrad had become enthusiastic about Basil's work, so much so that he contributed an article to *Roosters and Fledglings* under the title 'Never Any More', about his own sole experience of taking to the air. The two men obviously liked each other. Conrad suggested that once *Victory* had reached the stage, Basil might dramatise his novel *Under Western Eyes*. In place of Irving, the actress Marie Lohr, who was co-lessee of the Globe Theatre, agreed to stage the play and herself play a leading part. The script was heavily rewritten – yet again – after a brief and unsuccessful American production of an early draft. After Conrad attended the first rehearsal, he declared that he 'carried away an intense impression of hopefulness and belief in the play'. It opened on 26 March 1919, received some warm notices, and ran for eighty-three performances. Basil made useful money. But literary and dramatic critics never thought much of his dramatisation, and it has rarely been revived. This reflected two realities. The first was that *Victory* was ill-suited to the stage. Basil, who himself became conscious of this difficulty early in the drafting process, wrote after the event: 'It was really a crime to turn that wonderful novel into a play.' Second, though Basil was a successful entertainer, he was out of his depth realising themes of the intellectual profundity addressed by Conrad.

There is an exchange in *The New Sin* where one character says to another, who is a playwright: 'Bah! Your plays are just prostitution.' The playwright answers: 'I'm not proud of them, but I'm proud of the fact that I can sell them.' Basil was a professional, wholly unembarrassed that he wrote for money. At his first meeting with Conrad to discuss collaboration, he said frankly: 'There are not two forms for a work of art. This thing is only worth doing for the money there may be in it. If you are rich, it would be absurd for you to agree.' In truth, Conrad was anything but rich – at that time, his income was smaller than Basil's. But the playwright minded about the money much more than did the novelist. Having experienced middle-class poverty after his father Edward's death, Basil was determined to cling to the place he had won for himself, significantly higher up the economic and social scale than that of his nineteenth-century forebears.

Hanky-Panky John, a farce of his creation, achieved a modest success in 1921, but by that date he was earning much of his income as a dramatic critic and journalist, mostly for the *Daily* and *Sunday Express*. The tenor of his essays is well captured in a sample from the index to one of his published collections, *Ladies Half-Way*: 'Actresses, insulted; Americans, affectionate; Bennett, A., prostrate; Carnations, eating; Conrad, letter from; Crocodiles, kinder to; Eggs, awkward with'. Basil was a humorous columnist whose pieces about – for instance – the merits of cocktails and changing women's hairstyles would fit as readily into the feature pages of a modern newspaper as they did into those of the 1920s. At that time also, he published a bad novel entitled *The Faithful Philanderer*, but we should not hold that against him.

I am a shade doubtful about the quality of Basil's judgement. He opposed the mooted creation of a National Theatre, on the grounds that such an institution would encourage endless productions of Shakespeare, an author whom he thought better read than performed: 'All the world's worst actors, the offspring of what is known as Shakespearean experience, would flock to the stage door.' When he was theatre reviewer of the *Daily Express*, he incurred the wrath of Arnold Bennett, a director of the Lyric Theatre, Hammersmith. Basil dismissed a Chekhov production at the Lyric as 'fatuous drivel', and described its author as 'a great writer of stories, but a paltry dramatist'. In similar vein, Basil listened to some 1926 radio broadcasts by Winston Churchill, then commented: 'I hope political hopefuls do not listen in when Mr Churchill broadcasts. He speaks clearly and powerfully, and every word, I am sure, could be heard in Tattersall's in the five minutes before the start of a big race, but his pauses between sentences – and even between words – suggest an Olympian contempt for the value of time. How often must listeners have shouted out the word he was groping for!'

Yet Basil's verdicts were perhaps no worse advised than those of many newspaper pundits of the past century, including others named Hastings. He understood that a good columnist must be a professional controversialist, seeking to tease and provoke. At home as well as in print, though essentially benign, he liked to play the part of the irascible grumbler. At Christmas, he hung a sign in the hall of the family house in Holland Road, West London, proclaiming 'Peace and goodwill to all men, with the following exceptions:'. He appended a pencil, with which visitors were invited to make their own additions to his list.

In that clubbable age, he loved the Savage, whose members were almost all writers, painters, actors, musical hall stars. He was a regular performer, sometimes producer, at the club's smoking concerts. Poems were recited, songs sung, turns rehearsed by some of the great comics of the day, including George Robey and Wee Georgie Wood – who lived long enough for me to be introduced to him at the Savage. Though Basil was a Londoner by upbringing and instincts, he professed a devotion for rural life, which caused him to rent a country cottage, tend his vegetable garden, and enthuse about the superiority of Sussex pubs to London ones. He organised a regular Savage 'Country Members' Night', at which his friends dressed in yokels' smocks and sang jolly rustic songs. Keenly gregarious, Basil was never happier than when chattering in the club bar with a cluster of theatrical friends

He never made a fortune, but achieved a comfortable living by

the standards of the day. His account books, meticulously kept by
his wife Billie, who also typed his manuscripts, show him earning
£1,333 in 1912; £870 in 1914; £815 in 1915; £1,100 in 1916. In 1922,
his most successful year, largely because of back royalties, he received
£2,550. It is interesting to notice the scale of payments for journalism
at the period. In 1905, Basil received a guinea apiece for occasional
contributions to newspapers; by 1915 this had risen to seven guineas
a time from the *Evening Standard* and four guineas from *Punch*. His
books earned tiny sums, and theatrical royalties were never large,
but he was well paid for *Victory*.

His 1923 adaptation of A.S.M. Hutchinson's novel *If Winter Comes*
failed in London, but Basil cherished high hopes for its New York
production. For its opening, he crossed the Atlantic on the *Aquitania*,
which he adored, as he did the play's star, Cyril Maude. From the
ship, he wrote to his wife full of hopes:

26 March 1923
Adorable Bill,

No, I'm not a bit worried about the London failure. They are
cowardly and incompetent and one can only pity them. The play is
a great success in Australia. Sir George Tallis cables: 'Winter opened
splendidly. Excellent performances. Prospects good. Think
undoubted success.'

We shall succeed here, don't you worry. How I will fondle you
when I come home. I almost reel when I think of pressing your hair
to my face. Billie, I love you, I love you. If you don't spend *at least
£10 on yourself, I shall be angry*. Everything you have on when I
come home must be new to me . . . There is a certain amount of
dancing every night, but the ship rolls too much for it to be enjoy-
able. Maude is splendid company. I have had the entire story of his
past life, as I fancied I would, not to mention complete details
about all his family . . . Cyril is very perturbed as to whether to be a
bad man for the rest of his life or very religious. I have persuaded
him to be very religious. We lunch today with Lord Chichester in
the Ritz Carlton restaurant. His name is 'Eggy Eric'.

There is a priest on board, and there will be mass tomorrow in the card room. I was amused to find that the water is rough in the swimming bath.

From the St Regis in New York a fortnight later, he wrote:

About a million damned Irishmen have just marched down Fifth Avenue because of St Patrick's Day. I longed for a machine-gun. Did all the shows. David Belasco rang me up this morning and offered me seats for *The Comedian* on Thursday, and *Kiki* on Friday. *Kiki* has been running for years and is said to be wonderful. Here's a letter I've had from Mac. I think I'll write to him now – and Beryl. I'll buy them both wrist-watches – and for you a handbag, silk stockings, & (I hope) some undies. [On dress rehearsal night] over 1000 dollars advance booking yesterday! Laurette Taylor has asked me to dinner and is going to show me the film of *Peg o' My Heart* at her house. She's a darling, but I can't fall in love with any more girls just now. Rather rotten for you about the drains – keep Weston up to the scratch. No, I'm not dancing, but I have a good time apart from aching for you.

We open at the Gaiety (perfect theatre) on Easter Monday. Cast splendid. It will be a vastly better show than London. Peggy is a divine Effie . . . Everyone predicts gigantic success – but, oh dear, how often have I heard that word! Gave a dinner party and bought a bottle of whisky for *two guineas*. Saw *Nazmura* last night – worst play I've ever seen . . . Your eternal lover, BASIL.

Mac wrote to his father from Stonyhurst: 'Thanks awfully for your letters, you seem to be staying at a ripping hotel. I hear you are having filthy weather in New York. I should like if you please a present of a wrist watch from America, a little one. So with heaps of love and good luck to the success of the play . . .'

However, to Basil's bitter dismay, the New York venture failed. The play closed within a month. He returned to London, still the man who wrote *The New Sin*, a pillar of the Savage Club, friend of George

Robey and Edgar Wallace, favoured literary protégé of Lord Beaver-brook. He was painted by the fashionable portraitist James Gunn, but though he was still in his early forties, Basil's features already suggest a disappointed man, rather than a rising one. His income declined steadily. He had saved nothing in the good times. From 1925 onwards, his health declined rapidly. Late in 1926 he was diagnosed with bowel cancer, which had killed his mother Lizzie only six years before. The last months of his life were a torment of pain and financial fears. Like all the family, Basil had lived for the day, spent freely, taken no heed for the morrow. Royalty income from his plays had dried up. He was soon almost incapable of writing. The family lived in a rented house, and owned no property. Mac, in his last year at Stonyhurst, was abruptly brought home. School fees could no longer be paid.

Basil was driven to increasingly desperate measures, begging loans. He wrote to a friend in March 1927, appealing for £50: 'If I die before I have paid, I shall tell Billie that the £50 has first call on my estate . . . Feel good today – I have done a comic article about my broad-casting experience for 2 LO.' 2 LO was the forerunner of the BBC. Basil's first radio broadcast, a reading from his own essays, was almost his last professional engagement. Most of his friends, struggling writers like himself, felt unable to respond to his pleas for loans. The Royal Literary Fund sent him a modest cheque, which sufficed only to keep the family fed. In the opiate-drowsy months which followed, Basil scribbled desperate, almost incoherent instructions to Billie: 'Big ledger must be shown to no one, not even solicitors.' He urged her to seek financial help from Lord Beaverbrook and other former mentors, and to dispose carefully of his books, especially those signed by famous names. There was £2,000 in life assurance money, he said. He died in agony early in 1928, aged forty-seven. It was a dreadful end to a life and career which had seemed full of promise barely fifteen years earlier, yet lapsed into disappointment, indeed misery. Having striven so hard to achieve a prosperity and celebrity which eluded his father, Basil quit the stage knowing that he left his wife and children almost penniless.

FOUR

Mac

Basil's wife Billie suffered a nervous breakdown following his death. His last years had been overwhelmed by financial troubles overlaid upon the horrors of a disease whose symptoms contemporary medical science could do little to ameliorate. She was left struggling in a morass of debts. Theatrical friends organised a West End benefit matinee which raised a little money. Lord Beaverbrook and Edgar Wallace made a generous offer, which Billie accepted, to pay for her daughter Beryl to go to finishing school in Paris. Those two rich benefactors also offered to fund Mac through Oxford. With a delicate sense of honour, which he afterwards regretted, the young man refused. He said that he thought it his duty to go out and make a living, to support his mother. For the rest of his life, Mac was nagged by self-consciousness about his lack of a university education, and displayed an exaggerated deference towards those who possessed it. Though in old age he talked volubly about most of his experiences, he said nothing about this period, which left enduring scars. For a few miserable months, he devilled as a clerk at Scotland Yard. Then his fortunes improved. He found a job in the publicity department of J. Lyons, located at 61 Fleet Street, where he hugely enjoyed himself for the next nine years.

Lyons dominated Britain's catering industry. The company processed and retailed all manner of foods, owned teashops in almost every town in Britain, together with prestige hotels and restaurants in London, of which the Trocadero in Piccadilly Circus was the most famous, Lyons' Corner House in Coventry Street the most popular.

58

Mac, in those days eagerly gregarious, discovered that he was good at writing advertising copy, and that Lyons offered unparalleled opportunities to enjoy what a somewhat credulous young man perceived as the high life. Almost every night, dressed in white tie and tails, he disported himself at one or other of the company's restaurants or show palaces. He learned to call C.B. Cochrane's Young Ladies by their first names – and more important, as he observed gleefully, they learned to know him by his. He practised the 'Buchanan roll' with the famous performer Jack Buchanan, and was dispatched on a notably unsuccessful ballroom dancing course at Lyons' expense. Less happily, offered unlimited access to free drinks, he acquired a taste for alcohol in extravagant quantities.

Mac had charm, enthusiasm and talent, and made the most of all three. He was a true believer in almost everything except God. He possessed that gift more useful than any other in public relations, of espousing passionately any cause to which he was professionally committed. He did not pretend to love Lyons, he really did so. He became a protégé of Montague Gluckstein, the company's boss, who indulged him. 'Major Monty', as the staff called him in accordance with common practice so soon after war service, often sent for Mac in the morning while he was being shaved in the barber's shop of the Royal Palace Hotel. The young publicist was expected to pass on gossip from the shop floor, and also to make Major Monty laugh. Once, Mac was summoned to account for an outrageous expenses claim following a press dinner he had given on Lyons' chit, opening with cocktails and champagne, ending with Château d'Yquem, old port and cigars. After an inquest, the great man put down the frightful bill and said: 'When you leave this firm, Hastings, I sincerely hope that you will remain one of our customers. God knows, you are the sort we need.' Mac continued to party not merely night after night, but year after year. In his twenties, he could take it.

He prospered in the job, for he was good at stunts. When Lyons were building the Cumberland Hotel by Marble Arch, he arranged for them to complete a room on the top floor first, then gave a big media lunch, for which guests had to ascend ladders through the building's skeleton. This might not win the approval of modern Health & Safety gauleiters, but it played big with the press in 1934. On another occasion, Lyons showcased the great novelty of frozen foods. Journalists were invited to throw steaks at the wall, then sit down and eat them.

When his sister Beryl had completed finishing school and a secretarial course, through Mac's intercession she became personal assistant to 'Major Monty'. After a few years at Lyons, she used the expertise she had acquired to start her own restaurant in the City of London. She ran successive places with her mother Billie, and eventually her husband Leslie, for forty years. Though mid-market catering never made them rich, it provided them with a decent living. Beryl, devoid of the social pretensions which have been the undoing of so many Hastingses, was a tough, cheerful professional who worked hard all her life, neither demanding nor receiving a break from anybody. The harsh experiences of her youth rendered her prudent and cynical. She admired her brother's gifts and later success, but despaired of his excesses, alcoholic and financial.

Mac's trouble was that he never knew when to stop. It was tremendous fun to party with chorus girls, but in 1936 he went a disastrous step further, and married one. He was twenty-six, she was a thirty-two-year-old divorcee named Eleanor Daisy Asprey. The alliance lasted only a few months, but he was obliged to pay his ex-wife maintenance almost until the day he died. With misplaced chivalry and a dislike of rows, even when a well-wisher informed him thirty years later that his ex-wife was cohabiting with a man whom he, Mac, had been effectively supporting for years, he refused to go back to court. He admired women, and they were often attracted to him. But he lacked the slightest notion about how to treat them as human beings, or else was too selfish to learn, a vice which some claim can be hereditary.

It took time for Mac to achieve his ambition of becoming a journalist. While working at Lyons, he offered occasional contributions to newspapers and magazines, then in the late 1930s began to do some broadcasting. He performed first for the commercial station Radio Normandy, graduating to becoming a contributor for the BBC. His early 'talks' were whimsical, rather in the style of Basil's essays. Mac was deeply, indeed exaggeratedly, conscious of his father's reputation, which flickered on for some years. He often asserted that one of the best days of his life came when a stranger said, 'I really enjoyed that piece of yours.' Mac said, as he had grown accustomed to saying, 'I think you mean of my father's.' The stranger replied, 'No, no – it really was yours.' In due course, I would experience the same sensation myself.

Mac was prompted to make a clean break with Lyons by an experience one night as he stood waiting for a girl in the foyer of a restaurant, clad in carnation, white tie and tails. Tapping a patent leather shoe impatiently, he was reflecting upon what a fine figure he cut when a stranger approached, demanding: 'Have you got a table for two?' To Mac's horror, he perceived that instead of looking the perfect man-about-town, as he supposed, he had acquired the proprietorial demeanour of a head waiter. He resigned from Lyons amid expressions of mutual regret – sufficiently sincere that years later, Monty Gluckstein sought to woo him back on generous terms – and set about making his living as a freelance writer and broadcaster.

Mac's surrogate father in the 1930s was his uncle Lewis. Indeed, Lewis became a far more potent role-model for him, and later for me, than was his father Basil. Although Mac remembered Basil with love and respect, his memories were tarnished by the horrors of the last years, and of financial ruin. Basil was also a domesticated body, a man of the pavements. Mac's imagination had become fixed on the wide-open spaces. He wanted adventure, and his uncle was its embodiment. Lewis stood six foot two, and was broad to match, a leonine figure with flowing hair and military moustache, in all respects larger than life. He was forever bursting with ideas and enthusiasms. Having relished the war, he set about securing a livelihood. In 1920 he married a Scottish heiress named Marigold Edmondstone, whom he met while recuperating in a military hospital from the after-effects of a bad trench gassing. Marigold was divorced, an unusual condition in grand families of the time. C.S. Forester's General Sir Herbert Curzon, meeting his future wife for the first time, was struck by a sudden thought that her features resembled those of Bingo, 'the best polo pony he ever had'. This seemed to me true of Marigold when I met her in later years, but I doubt whether Lewis bothered to look much at her face. Her fortune kept him in some style for the rest of his life, and her earlier mis-hit at marriage was a matter of indifference to him.

Uncharacteristically bitchy family gossip, broadcast by grandmother Billie and my aunt Beryl, held that Lewis never bothered to divorce his first wife, Clare – acquired and discarded in South Africa with equal insouciance around 1911–12, and recalled by his sister-in-law in shameless period vernacular as having 'a touch of the tarbrush' – before marrying Marigold. Such a solecism would certainly have accorded with his ruthless, reckless character. The notion of Lewis as a bigamist caused some later family amusement. Both Marigold and her son Stephen – who became Sir Stephen Hastings, MP – were keenly conscious of pedigree. Marigold recoiled from the vulgarity of Basil and family, especially his wife Billie. Class, class, class reared its head in the Hastings family as often as it does everywhere in British life. Billie was a woman of exceptional good nature, who endured her tribulations without bitterness. But she extracted from Mac a promise that he would never be nice to Marigold, because this queen of the hunting field was so damnably condescending to her. I always wonder why Lewis gave no financial help to Basil in the desperate circumstances of his brother's last months. Either the two were no longer close, or Marigold held the purse strings too tightly. In any event, the gulf between the financial circumstances of Basil's widow in her little West London flat and those of Lewis's family in a succession of manor houses obviously exacerbated tensions between them.

Having secured Marigold's hand and fortune, and thereafter produced two children with her, Lewis resumed his old roaming habits. He acquired a tobacco farm in Southern Rhodesia, and spent many of the interwar years there, leaving his offspring and often his wife to amuse themselves as they saw fit. He published a slim volume of poetry, became first president of the Tobacco-Growers' Association, a member of the Rhodesian parliament and eventually of its cabinet, and indulged a lifestyle that would have commanded the respect of Kenya's Happy Valley set. The novelist Doris Lessing, who grew up in Rhodesia, encountered Lewis when she was a gawky teenage girl. In her memoirs she left a pen-portrait of him, as MP for Lomagundi in the 1930s, which has always delighted me.

He was famous for his oratory. He was famous for his love affairs, possibly because he wrote poems not unlike Rupert Brooke's, and a good many were love poems. Very handsome he was, like a lion. He was a dandy, with a suggestion of military swagger, but this was used for dramatic effect. He would stand at ease on his box platform and entertain the farmers and their wives and their children with speeches . . . garnished with Latin and Greek. The crowd stood about in the red dust, the men in their khaki, the women in their best dresses, the children behind him on the verandah, while the ox wagons went groaning past on their way to the railway tracks, and Major Hastings said – he was talking about Native Policy, but don't imagine that he disapproved, '*Volenti non fit injuria* – which means, as of course you all know, "No harm is done to him who consents."' And everyone laughed . . . Major Hastings loved his audiences too much to despise them . . . [He] did it all with just a touch of parody, his smile inviting us all to share with him his style, his bravura. How could wives not fall in love with him? Not to mention daughters. There are men who – with not so much as one second's impropriety, with no more than a look – perhaps without even intending it, promise a half-grown girl that one day she, too, will be a member of the freemasonry of love.

Lewis blew into London at irregular intervals, towering over the bar of the Savage Club as he captivated Mac with his tales of shooting elephant and lion, of camps in the bush under the stars. A passionate nationalist, pillar of the Empire Society, he foresaw a splendid future for East and Southern Africa, producing food for Britain – this, though his own agricultural ventures in Rhodesia were wholly unprofitable. Lewis's personal behaviour, not least towards the wife whom he exploited without scruple, may not deserve admiration. The violence of his enthusiasms and enmities could alarm more temperate folk. But he was no line-shooter. He lived as he talked – physically fearless and bent upon draining every cup to the dregs. His son Stephen, who found it hard to relate to him, wrote: 'He strode in and out of our lives like a whirlwind. As well as weaver birds' nests he brought exhilaration, suspense and uncertainty. His was a life of stirring and haphazard adventure.' In Rhodesia in 1973, I met an old Afrikaner who had farmed next door to Lewis forty years earlier. '*Ach*, I never forget Major Hastings,' he said, in the inimitable accents of the veldt. 'I used to see him go out to hunt in the morning with his rifle, wearing only a cartridge belt and tennis shoes. He said he felt closer to nature that way.'

By courtesy of Marigold's money, in England Lewis was able to hunt, fish salmon, shoot pheasants and inhabit country houses appropriate to his acquired status as a country gentleman. His writings and later broadcasting made him modestly well known, but I doubt whether his earnings would have paid his cook's salary. Lewis didn't care. He believed that life was for living. Mac spent time with him whenever he could. In 1933 they drove to Germany together, to take a first-hand look at Nazism. Irked by hearing constant renditions of 'The Horst Wessel Song', at the famous Femina nightclub in Berlin Lewis insisted upon leading a rousing chorus first of the Cape Mounted Police song, then of 'The Red Flag', to the stunned horror of Brownshirts in the audience.

I still possess his heavily annotated copy of the English edition of Hitler's *Mein Kampf*. Lewis did not doubt for a moment that it would soon be necessary to fight Hitler. Although approaching sixty in the 1930s, he looked forward eagerly to a second round with the Hun. Meanwhile, Africa remained his happy hunting ground, its peoples his favourite companions. He wrote: 'When I think of the African it is not as a kind of raw material for sociological experiment, but instead as clear-cut individuals, like Chidota my devoted and ruthless camp boss; Mafuta the dandy; Chiunda the tracker, and my old fighting Swazi and superb ox-driver Hendrik. I remember their separate ways and tricks and quite unquenchable laughter.'

In Rhodesia he kept a cheetah about the house: 'Zunzu was often a bit of a trial to human visitors. To have a great animal suddenly leap in through the bathroom window was a test of character.' One overnight guest objected strongly to discovering on awakening what he described as 'a tiger sitting in my suitcase'. Lewis read a great deal, especially poetry. But he believed that excessive attention to intellectual pursuits dulled the physical senses, which grew more intense if denied books and newspapers. 'You hear more – you see more things, you see more of them and you see further. That heightened sensibility to external impressions which shepherds have, and gamekeepers and gardeners and hunters – that's one of the chief rewards. Awareness of movement and growth and seasonable signs, of footprints in the dust, of wind and the stars – these are the things that are blunted by books.'

Although nominally farming in Rhodesia, Lewis contrived to spend many weeks hunting in Mozambique and the Okavango Delta in Bechuanaland, as well as shooting lion and leopard closer to home. For years he was accompanied by his camp boss, Mafuta, a wartime veteran of the King's African Rifles, 'who could throw as pretty a salute as any Grenadier. If I hadn't gone out with my gun-bearer at first light, Mafuta would materialise somehow out of the bush, stand rigidly at attention and deliver himself in his official voice somewhat as follows: "Good morning, *n'kosi*. Klass has cleaned the shotgun and gone out to get some guinea fowl. The elephants went over the river into the reed-bed last night. The *n'tombi* has come from the village with some eggs. A hyena has come in the night and taken a buffalo hide. The sugar is finished." So there you were – all the real news in headlines. But Mafuta always put the good news first and the bad last, which is a much better idea than the one current in Fleet Street.'

One day when Lewis was out on a long trek, at evening he went out alone with a shotgun, in search of an antelope for the pot. After walking for some time, there was a sudden eruption in the bush in front of him. A bushbuck sprang out, he took a long-range snap shot, and was delighted to see the beast drop, apparently stone dead. Leaning his gun against a tree, Lewis walked forward to collect the carcass.

> The moment I bent down to handle him, he came to life. I threw myself down, and grabbed him by the throat. The next second his razor-sharp hooves cut clean through my belt, just missing the skin. Many and many a time I had handled calves for branding, but this thing was like a bundle of steel springs. I twisted my legs round him and bore down as hard as I could. My weight at that time was 190 pounds, the bushbuck's no more than ninety, but it took everything I had to hang on and prevent his hooves ripping me in pieces. At last I managed to shift my grip from the throat to his horns, and with that additional leverage I wriggled him round underneath me until I could reach my knife, and open it with my teeth. All this time the buck was blowing foam in my face, his tongue was lolling out of the corner of his mouth, and he was making the fiercest kind of ram noises. But I got him where I wanted him in the end, drove the knife in and cut his windpipe. For quite some little time I sat down after this struggle covered with blood, mostly the buck's. Then I tore my tattered shirt into strips, and fastened the antelope's legs together. I draped the heavy body over my shoulders and started back for the camp. The buck seemed a great deal more than ninety pounds by the time I got there.

At their best, Lewis's descriptions of his life in the bush achieved a lyricism not unworthy of being compared with those of Karen Blixen or Robert Ruark: 'The dawn breaks on the wide plain of tawny grass and the scattered clumps of tall ivory palm. It is the air and light and visible world of the First Day, virginal and unblemished . . . Far ahead of you there are some glittering motes of light that suddenly resolve themselves into a group of impala, most beautiful of all antelope. At long range they dance like snowflakes and are almost as effervescent.' Mac was intensely impressionable, and Lewis conveyed to his nephew a sense of the romance of Africa which never faded.

Less usefully, he also imbued him with some of his own contempt for the practical issues of life, solvency among them. Lewis's values were those of Buchan and Sapper, which were starting to seem dated even in the 1930s. He never made the most of his considerable talents, because chronic restlessness caused him to go walkabout before finishing anything he started.

The most notable influence on Mac's life, in the last phase before war came, was a woman. He struck up a friendship with a successful gentleman dentist named Bertie Pallant, who continued to practise despite having a country estate and considerable fortune. Bertie eventually squandered his money in a series of increasingly fanciful investments, but in those days plenty of cash remained. His rural acres lay in Sussex, south of Haslemere, and he was a keen shooter and fisher. Mac yearned to adopt these pursuits, but lacked experience, opportunities and cash. Now he began to edge into the rural world, and to explore a path to its pleasures. In 1938, for £50 he rented a cottage and rough shooting rights in Vernley Wood, a few miles from the Pallants' place, and acquired an uncontrollable black spaniel which he christened Ruins, because the puppy was born in the old castle at Cowdray. A keeper looked after the dog while Mac was off earning a living.

Bertie Pallant had a smart, stunningly beautiful wife named Ruth, possessed of infinite Irish charm and considerable Irish recklessness. She and Mac embarked upon an affair which persisted for some years. Bertie was apparently acquiescent, for the three often went shooting and fishing together. Ruth sized up Mac, and decided that his years working at Lyons had given him some sorely mistaken ideas about what constituted the high life. She set about purging his vulgarities, and transforming him into a gentleman. With the aid of Savile Row and Ruth's generosity, his wardrobe dramatically improved. He acquired his first made-to-measure shotgun, along with an impressive array of sporting impedimenta. He discovered that the Trocadero did not, as he had supposed, represent the summit of sophistication. Years later Ruth, who became my godmother, told me without embarrassment that she regarded herself as the architect of the new-model

Macdonald Hastings. The phrase 'make-over' had not then been invented, but that is what she imposed upon Mac. It had only one unfortunate consequence. Forever afterwards, he sustained a style of living without much attempt to reconcile this with his income. Ruth turned Mac into a dashing country-gentleman-about-town, lacking acres and cash to support his enthusiasms. This would lead to many tears before bedtime, mostly shed by Mac's wives.

Yet his career was taking off. In December 1938, a few months before the outbreak of war, he achieved the highest ambition of many of his generation of journalists: at the age of twenty-nine, he was given a job on the new weekly magazine sensation, *Picture Post*. Created and edited by the Hungarian Jewish refugee Stefan Lorant, it burst upon Britain with a force only matched, a decade later, by the coming of television. Indeed, with its bold use of live-action photographs, its elevation of the 35mm Leica camera to an instrument of magic arts, it represented the last old-media print revolution before moving images seized the ascendant. *Picture Post* became the most thrilling workplace in British journalism, and Father one of its stars.

Mac had a fine visual sense, as well as natural skill as a word-smith. Far from being uncomfortable about working in close partnership with a photographer, he adapted readily to the discipline. At the outset, he specialised in country topics. Then as now, journalists were an overwhelmingly urban breed, knowing little about rural life. This offered notable opportunities to a writer stricken with a romantic enthusiasm for the English countryside, such as Mac. There were more people who wanted to read about rural life than there were journalists capable of satisfying the demand. Political correctness being unheard of, Mac contributed big pieces to early issues of *Picture Post* on pheasant-shooting, badger-digging and otter-hunting, as well as British farming, the life of a tramp, the work of vets. When King George VI paid a state visit to Canada, Mac was given a wonderfully glamorous transatlantic assignment. With a photographer he travelled to New York on the *Queen Mary*, recording the passage, then wrote two features on the city before travelling north into Canada. The King and Queen had just crossed the continent on the Canadian Pacific Railway. Mac was sent to trace the same journey, and describe what the King saw.

Afterwards, he travelled to the far north to write about life in the Yukon, visited a logging camp in British Columbia and the wheat prairies of Alberta, before catching the boat back to England. Back home, he persuaded the magazine to let him do a feature about buying a pair of handmade shotguns from Robert Churchill – though I doubt whether the £240 which he paid for them was chargeable to expenses. By the autumn of 1939, still just short of thirty, he had established himself as one of the young stars of *Picture Post*. The fears and sorrows of his teens were behind him. Journalism is more generous than any other career to successful young practitioners, offering not only a living, but almost unlimited opportunities for fun and adventure. Avidly, Mac set about exploring them.

FIVE

Anne

My mother disliked her own family considerably. No photographs
of them were visible in any house in which we later lived. She spoke
dismissively of their professional doings, and recalled with distaste
the oppressive atmosphere in their home. Born in 1913, she was
'frightened of my parents, and grew up too soon for Dr Spock. I
caught the tail-end of the Victorian philosophy that parents were
perfect, and children always in the wrong, a righteous target for
round-the-clock criticism. This made me very shy in company.' Her
paternal grandfather was a Congregationalist minister, a heavy,
bearded Victorian, named Rev. John Scott-James, who presided over
a church in Stratford-on-Avon and somehow contrived to educate
eight children with the aid of scholarships. One such enabled my
own grandfather, Rolfe, born in 1880, to attend Mill Hill school and
then read classics at Brasenose, Oxford. Most of his sisters spent their
later lives as spinster teachers in far-flung corners of the world. One,
like her Hastings contemporary, became a nun.

On leaving Oxford, Rolfe spent some time living and working
in the London East End missions at Canning Town and Toynbee
Hall – he remained committed to liberal social causes all his life.
He then embarked on a career devoted to literary journalism. After
joining the staff of the *Daily News* in 1902, he was its literary editor
between 1906 and 1912, when he became editor of the *New Weekly*.
As a member of a prominent literary club of the day, the Square,
he forged acquaintance, which in several cases ripened into friendship, with Galsworthy, Yeats, Walter de la Mare, Ford Madox Ford

and suchlike literary giants of the day, who seem to have thought well of him.

Ford whimsically addressed him as 'James' when feeling formal, and 'Scottie' at moments of affection. Rolfe noted Ford as appearing to have pink eyes – in truth they were light blue – sandy hair, 'and looking rather like a guinea-pig'. One evening as they emerged from a dinner and walked together along Gerrard Street, Ford murmured wryly: 'Oh, who would go into dark Soho/to chatter with dank-haired critics?' He then turned laughing to his companion and said that he forgave him for being himself one of that breed, for Rolfe was always so kind to his books. For a time the young man was a lodger in Ford's rooms in Holland Park, where he listened for hours to the novelist extolling the virtues of his literary heroes, Flaubert and Henry James – 'the great panjandrum', as he called him. Rolfe was unconvinced when Ford asserted that he had taught Joseph Conrad how to write. But his relationship with the novelist became one of the most important in his life.

Rolfe was a regular attender at Edward Garnett's Wednesday-evening soirées. He dined with Galsworthy in Addison Road, to discuss how best to further the novelist's enthusiasm for a National Theatre, and later stayed with him at his house in Devon. Hardy, whom Rolfe encountered several times, once took him for a walk around Dorchester, pointing out to the enthralled young man places which had inspired passages in the Wessex novels. He showed him the house in which he had imagined Henchard, the Mayor of Caster-bridge, to live; the grey Palladian mansion which he appointed to Lucetta Templeman; the church and other landmarks woven into his fiction. As they passed one cottage, Hardy said that it held deeply sinister associations in his mind: 'When I was a boy, the hangman lived there. When very young I would hurry past it in fear. But later I watched it, still a little frightened, but fascinated. When the hangman himself put his head out of the upper window, I have never forgotten the dreadful impression which it made on me. I gazed at it for a moment with fear and wonder, then scampered off.' At a later meeting, when Rolfe sought to quiz Hardy about his novels, he was dismissive: 'If I am to be remembered at all,' he said, 'I should like it to be for my poetry.'

Rolfe wrote an account of dinner with Algernon Charles Swinburne at his home, The Pines on Putney Hill, richly adorned with paintings by Rossetti and other members of the Pre-Raphaelite Brotherhood, in 1908, the year before the poet's death. When the young man arrived with a friend, Swinburne's longstanding companion Theodore Watts-Dunton announced that they would sit down without their frail host.

> When soup was over, he made a sign to us. We waited, listening, expectant. Then a slow tap-tap on the stairs in the hall. Swinburne was coming down, one step at a time – a solemn, prolonged tap . . . tap . . . tap . . . as one foot followed the other. He opened the door himself: small, slight – he seemed to be all head and eyes, wisps of hair on his face and scarcely any on his scalp. But although his voice was a little shrill, it was vigorous; he greeted us heartily, ate heartily, and talked robustly. His deafness made it necessary to repeat every sentence. When Swinburne got the point a glint of understanding lit up his eyes, and he began at length to answer and expound the point. Asked about a rival poet, William Watson, who like himself was an unsuccessful contender for the Poet Laureateship, Swinburne said contemptuously: 'He made an assault on a Princess's horse in order to qualify for the laureateship.'
>
> He spoke of Meredith, saying: 'I cannot read Meredith. I can't stand the *literary flowers* which disfigure his style on every page. How affected he is, and what a snob. There is too much gentility in Meredith for a novelist or for any man.' He asserted that he himself was a Jacobite: 'All my ancestors were Jacobites. I pride myself that they were in all the rebellions. I have carried on the torch, yes, and I have made converts.'

Rolfe was a highly disciplined and prolific journalist who imposed strict regulation on his three children – Marie was seven years older than Anne, John two years younger. He was a self-consciously intellectual figure, which helps to explain his weighty, indeed often leaden, prose style. Yet his work won contemporary respect. His first book, *Modernism and Romance*, was published in 1908, when he was twenty-eight, and was widely and generously reviewed. Two years later, he produced a plodding account of a summer canoe trip, entitled *An Englishman in Ireland.* 'The chill mist and the distressing rain-clouds which had covered England for half the summer were gone,' he wrote in a characteristic passage. 'There was a transparency in the air by which every visible object gained a fine edge, and a kind of vast decorativeness in the deli-cately-tinted scene as if Nature had bathed and come forth glittering.'

How Rolfe persuaded Dent to publish this atrocity (for the narra-tive gets worse) seems mysterious to a modern reader, but the book attracted surprising enthusiasm from critics at the time. The young author became friendly with Norman Douglas, greatest travel writer of his generation. In 1912 Rolfe visited America, contributing accounts to the *Morning Leader* of Theodore Roosevelt's unsuccessful presidential re-election campaign. Most of the trip, however, was devoted to studying US newspapers for his book published the following year, *The Influence of the Press*. This was ponderous in tone, often absurd in substance. Almost all poor Rolfe's judgements reflected a monumental naïveté. He convinced himself, for instance, that Britain's newspaper proprietors had suddenly discovered God, and seen the error of their past ways:

> The controllers of the popular Press have learnt the market-value of decency. They have discovered that accurate information pays; that an irresponsibly sensational manner no longer makes a sensation; that news must be news; that the largest newspaper audience in the world is not devoid of common-sense. This is the amazing discovery which has recently been dawning upon the world; and it has emanated, not from 'respectable' England, but from the Press which had once been called the 'Yellow' Press . . . Assuredly I hold no brief for the *Daily Mail*, but it seems to me a fact of extraordinary significance that the most popular organ in England should be adopting a policy of decency.

In the First World War, Rolfe won a Military Cross as a captain in the Royal Artillery, and published several articles about the work of the heavy guns. Norman Douglas wrote to him from his sanctuary on Capri, appropriately named Casa Solitaria, in July 1916: 'Hope you are all right? It is very pleasant here – a great calm. Dim rumours of war going on somewhere far away. No foreigners.' Rolfe himself, by contrast, spent almost two years on the Western Front. One of his daughter Anne's earliest memories was of being awakened in the small hours at the family's holiday lodgings in the little village of Burghfield Common, near Reading, by her father's return on leave from France. Many rural communities did their best to ignore that war, and cared astonishingly little for those who were fighting it. The countryside and its people, in those days, were rather nastier than modern nostalgia acknowledges, pervaded by a parochialism often manifested in hostility to outsiders of any kind or purpose. When Rolfe, having walked seven miles through the darkness from Reading station, knocked up the landlady of a pub to ask directions, she slammed the door in his face.

Rolfe's post-war books on English literature displayed wide reading, both ancient and modern, but Anne always urged me not to bother with them, because they are written in the style of a pedant's pedant. 'Literature, as regarded by a Schlegel or a Taine,' he wrote in 1928 in a characteristic passage of *The Making of Literature*, 'is a social product. It is circulated, or stored, for the use of all who desire to help themselves from the sum-total of finished thought-work available in men's writing. All the parts of it are food for the mind, and collectively constitute world culture. When Coleridge said that "No man was ever yet a great poet, without being at the same time a profound philosopher," he was not confusing two different faculties of the mind; but he was affirming the importance of the one to the other.'

I see what Mummy meant when she urged me to skip reading her father's works. Much of what he said is sound enough, but he expressed it in the tones P.G. Wodehouse adopted when parodying intellectual bores of the kind who terrified Bertie Wooster. Rolfe never used one word where three would do. A reviewer in the

Westminster Gazette observed of one of his books in 1928: 'When we finished Mr Scott-James's work, we had a comfortable feeling that he had said the right things and said them adequately, but precisely what he had said we find it difficult to remember.' Arnold Bennett said abruptly to Rolfe one night: 'Scott-James, why haven't you written a novel? You should write a novel.' Yet when Grandfather later acted on Bennett's advice the outcome, entitled *Knights and Knaves*, remained unpublished, as judging from the typescript it deserved to.

After the First World War, Rolfe spent a decade as a leader writer on the *Daily Chronicle*, then two years as assistant editor of *The Spectator*. In 1935 he followed J.C. Squire as editor of the *London Mercury*, the literary monthly which Squire had created, and presided until its extinction in 1939. There is no record of Rolfe ever having made a joke, either in person or in print, though he was once the recipient of a passable one. As editor of the *London Mercury*, he wrote to A.E. Housman, inviting a contribution. Housman replied: 'I am obliged by your letter, but my career, and it is to be hoped my life, are so near their close that it is to be hoped they will concern neither of us much longer.' The poet duly expired nine days later.

Between the wars, Rolfe bolstered his income by moonlighting as London correspondent of the American *Christian Science Monitor*, which paid him three or four guineas a time for his contributions. He reviewed books for several newspapers, and for a time wrote the Atticus column of the *Sunday Times*, eschewing any hint of frivolity. He was a dogged labourer in the literary vineyard, immensely prolific, and eventually received an OBE for his work for the British Council. A staunch lifelong Liberal and pillar of the Reform Club, his hero was Lloyd George. This represented perversity on Grandfather's part. The austere Scott-James esteemed truthfulness above all other virtues, while Lloyd George's dearest friends would have hesitated to claim it among his. Rolfe, a diligent researcher into educational and social conditions among the working classes, contributed to Lloyd George's 1924 Liberal Party inquiry into the coal industry. He had a dry commitment to virtue which would have commended itself to Edward Hastings, but did not do so to his daughter Anne.

Rolfe's wife Violet, an almost uneducated but nonetheless highly cultured woman, seems also to have found her husband unexciting, for she indulged herself with affairs on the fringes of literary London. Her origins were somewhat smarter than those of her husband. She came from a West Country family which had squandered its money on hunting and high living. Her father, Captain Arthur Brooks, was a veteran of the 13th Foot, the Somerset Light Infantry (I have always mistrusted ex-officers who cling to junior rank after retirement from the army). The captain lived in some style until his money ran out. Heaven knows what brought his daughter Violet together with Rolfe Scott-James – they married in 1905, when he was twenty-six and she twenty.

After the war, for some years she contributed a witty 'London Letter' to the *Yorkshire Post*, for which she served as its first women's editor, and later as dramatic critic, writing above the coy byline 'V.S-J'. Family folklore fails to determine whether her long liaison with the paper's celebrated editor Arthur Mann inspired him to hire her, or whether the connection evolved the other way around. A highly strung, intense woman who suffered constant ill-health, her restlessness rendered contentment elusive for Violet. She faced the further burden that her son John was epileptic, at a period when no effective treatment existed. Responsibility for caring for him fell heavily upon Anne, who loved John dearly. She was troubled all her life by the tragedy of her brother's plight.

In London, the family occupied a terraced house in Bayswater. During school holidays in the 1920s the three children were sent to lodge without their parents at the cottage of a retired nanny in Sulhampstead, Berkshire. Anne adored those experiences, and forged a passion for wildflowers and woodlands which she retained all her life. She loved the white roads, unmetalled ribbons of stone and dust, 'as poignant a memory of my childhood as cowslips, kingfishers, scarecrows, collecting pinecones in a go-cart, stirring pigwash in a tub, finding heartsease and corncockle in the cornfields, or filling jamjars with tiny frogs in a stream'.

The children walked everywhere: 'It is only by walking that one gets to know a district and its inhabitants intimately. I knew every cottage, every bird's nest, within our little territory. For me, the country was never a slow cabbagey sort of place, but was rich in incident. And, though I didn't understand it at the time, I realise now that many of the country people we knew were absolutely cracked.' A woman just up the road killed herself by drinking a bottle of disinfectant. A nearby farmer, faced by financial ruin, shot himself. The local vicar, 'burdened with many children and a defeated wife', lived in threadbare poverty and played tennis in his socks. The local gamekeeper commanded a special interest, because despite his gun and appearance of robust self-sufficiency, he was rumoured to be beaten by his spouse. As late as the 1920s, in southern England barely forty miles from London, Anne remarked that rural life was conducted in a manner far more closely resembling that of the mid-nineteenth century than that of the twentieth.

The Scott-Jameses possessed one mildly upmarket connection. Violet's elderly aunt Eleanor Craven, Captain Brooks's sister, a childless widow, maintained considerable state in a large flat in Westminster. Rolfe's three children were dispatched to lunch with her on alternate Sundays. On these occasions, they were torn between delight in the delicious food and trepidation provoked by Aunt Eleanor's stern formality: 'She wore long black or grey dresses over petticoats, high wired Edwardian collars, a diamond brooch, doeskin gloves and highly polished buckled shoes over black open-work stockings, and her hair was piled into an elaborate coiffure which I later learned was a toupee.' Any child who resorted to slang at her table – 'top hole', 'ripping', 'She's a beast' – was sternly rebuked. Although Mrs Craven was deeply religious, with a horror of Roman Catholics, it was not faith which dominated her conversation, but etiquette: 'A lady never makes personal remarks'; 'A lady never mentions the food at luncheon'; 'A lady always wears gloves.' Bedspreads must be of real linen, writing paper die-stamped. Anne once arrived at the flat clutching *Tiger Tim's Weekly*, her favoured leisure reading at the time. This was removed in the hall, and returned in stony silence on her departure.

During the winter, Aunt Eleanor decamped for three months with her maid, a parrot in a cage and ten pieces of heavy leather luggage to rooms at Bath or Ventnor on the Isle of Wight. Anne and Marie were occasionally dispatched to spend a week with her, and found these experiences tedious. Their best features were substantial tips – Aunt Eleanor was generous to all her family offshoots, especially in their financial crises. In her company, however, 'there was much kindness in the air, but not much laughter'.

At the Scott-Jameses' home in Bayswater, strict economy prevailed, on the lines practised a generation earlier by Edward Hastings. To avoid running up electricity bills, they fed a slot meter with shillings. One night before a dinner party, Rolfe forgot to top it up. The house was plunged into darkness as soup was served. This was an embarrassment, for the guests included the visiting American editors of the *Christian Science Monitor*. The family never ate in restaurants, and took taxis only in cases of sickness or when burdened with luggage. Many of the girls' clothes were second-hand. They never resented this, however, because Violet, Marie and Anne often received the cast-offs of a rich and fashionable godmother. They spent hours darning stockings and altering dresses. They shopped at Barker's rather than Harrods. Save for Rolfe's whisky nightcaps, alcohol was served only at dinner parties, but they found this no hardship: 'We were a non-alcoholic family from preference, not principle.' Their one notable luxury was the theatre, which they indulged enthusiastically, queuing night after night for seats in the pit. They also enjoyed annual seaside holidays in the wildernesses of Wales and Cornwall. The latter, especially, became one of the most beloved places in Anne's life.

She was sent to school first at Norland Place in Holland Park, then to St Paul's, where she became a star. She was one of those unusual people who adored her schooldays, which she found far more rewarding than home life. A precocious child in classes two years older than herself, she flourished academically, socially, athletically. She even enjoyed regular visits to a settlement in Stepney which St Paul's helped to support, in a manner common to most public schools of the day. She played tennis for the school team and in 1931 won a classical scholarship to Somerville, Oxford. Her only subsequent regrets about her education were that she learned nothing of science, which remained a lifelong mystery to her, and that she was denied the smallest opportunity to form acquaintances with boys. 'We complained bitterly to each other about the shortage of young men as dancing partners and had callow longings for a romantic friendship, Hollywood-style, with some charming hero who would kiss one lightly on the cheek, send one bouquets of flowers, and take one on platonic trips to Paris. So total was our innocence that I thought of marriage as a specially pleasant form of social life. As for homosexuality, I had never heard of it.'

Anne's university life, however, proved much less happy. Oxford cast no more of a spell upon her than it did upon me, thirty-three years later. Having attended London day schools, she bitterly resented the confinement, under mediaeval rules designed to preserve chastity, which prevailed in women's colleges in the early 1930s. She wrote later: 'Oxford was a good place for female swots with their minds concentrated on their degrees, and doubtless for lesbians, although I never consciously met any. It was a tolerable place for the few who broke all the rules and led a heady mixed social life. For the others, it could be a lonely world, with every twinge of melancholy aggravated by the rain-washed spires, tolling bells, and miasmas from the river.'

Like so many adolescents, and indeed undergraduates, Anne felt that somewhere in the city, wonderful things were happening, to which she was not invited. She was dismayed to perceive that it was not only acceptable, but fashionable, for the university's young men to cling to each other rather than to women: 'The whole point of Oxford is that there are no girls,' as Compton Mackenzie's priggish hero Michael Fane says in *Sinister Street*. Romance was administratively impeded by the locking of Somerville's gates at 10.30 p.m., which made it necessary for a girl to climb in over the wall, even if she had merely been to the cinema: 'It was all so silly.' In 2007 a book was published entitled *Singled Out*, tracing the fate of the generation of girls who found themselves without men after the slaughter of the First World War. Anne was deeply moved by it. Although a decade younger than the women depicted in the book, she perceived herself, too, as a social victim of the period which it addresses.

In her second year she fell in love with a third-year Balliol undergraduate, with whom she conducted a passionate affair. In 2003, interviewed for *Desert Island Discs*, she was at pains to emphasise that even if there was not much heterosexual sex in the Oxford of 1932–33, she herself was not deprived. She was galled that this titbit was edited out of the broadcast, for she was always oddly eager that the world should know that she had enjoyed an active love life as well as a career. She and her lover drifted apart after he went down. In place of romance, she was obliged to rebuff two proposals of marriage, one from a spotty young historian, the other from a rugby Blue in whose face she laughed 'with a callous contempt which makes me shudder with remorse to remember'. Another young man was sufficiently stricken to offer a charmingly original compliment. Years later, he described Anne to a friend as 'the most orchidiferous girl I met at Oxford'. On her side, she said that the two most striking men she encountered there were Adam von Trott, later executed for his role in the July 1944 bomb plot against Hitler, and George Steer, who became a famous foreign correspondent, notably for his reporting of the Spanish Civil War. Both were, however, too mature, glamorous and remote to reciprocate her interest.

She was strikingly good-looking, though very conscious of her six-foot height, which made her socially uneasy. She forged some close and lasting friendships, but was much less comfortable with casual acquaintances. She sang in the Bach Choir, and developed a passion for Greek which, towards the end of her second year, assisted her to gain a First in Honour Mods. Then, for one unhappy term, she read Greats, and developed an allergy towards Philosophy: 'I am a worldly person, loving people and places and art, but never happy wandering about in a haze of abstract ideas. My father kept telling me that philosophy enlarges the mind, but I chose to keep mine small.' Confronted with the prospect of two more years' study, to the fury of her parents and of Somerville, she dropped out. In June 1933, longing for London and a job, she quit Oxford.

For the first three weeks thereafter, she drove across Europe to Prague with two friends from university, in a car which they clubbed together to buy for £100. In those days, a journey so humdrum by modern standards was intensely exotic. 'Along the road from London to Prague there is a necklace of antiquities, landscapes, local customs, changing languages, varied food.' She was captivated by the Baroque wonders of Germany, shocked by Nazism. In a village in Bavaria, an old man spat at Anne and her friend Sally Graves, calling them painted whores. It was a relief to cross the frontier into Czechoslovakia, following little country roads to visit the churches and castles of southern Bohemia. They slept in farmhouses, once on straw in a barn. The others drank local beer, but Anne never touched alcohol until she was forty, a manifestation of her intensely disciplined character. 'Few journeys have given me more pleasure than that first foreign encounter with no social obligations or business appointments, just unplanned days and companions who were always in good humour. I knew this would be my last carefree outing for a long time, for the serious business of job-hunting awaited me on my return.'

It was the depth of the Depression, a bad time to look for work. Overlaid on national circumstances was the fact that Anne was a woman – worse, an educated one. Few girls entered the professions or the City. A friend of her parents was a director of the biscuit manufacturers Huntley & Palmer. He agreed to see her, but said immediately at the interview: 'We do not employ women, Anne, except at factory level, and we have no present intention of doing so. Women aren't good at business, and it wouldn't be fair on the men.' She asked: was there not the humblest opening in the office? 'No, only in the factory and that leads nowhere. Your mother tells me you went to Oxford. Frankly, that's a disadvantage. There is no room in industry for educated women. The men don't like them.'

She spent some weeks answering correspondence from readers at *Weldon's*, a downmarket women's magazine, and was appalled by the range of troubles which the letters revealed. She felt so sorry for the writers that she set out to answer them individually, and at length.

One girl was going to a dance, and wanted advice on what to do with a short, twenties style evening dress – there was no chance of affording a new one. Anne, already keenly interested in fashion, suggested that her correspondent should make a gathered overskirt of net, short in front and dipping at the back, of which she attached a sketch. Another girl described frightful monthly periods. Anne rang her own doctor, who advised that her correspondent needed medical help, fast. For Anne's services as an agony aunt she was paid twenty-five shillings a week, and soon quit.

She spent a much happier spell as a temporary salesgirl at Harrods' Christmas Toy Fair, though it was debatable whether she possessed the gifts for a hard sell. One of Anne's social handicaps was an irresistible urge to tell the truth, in a fashion worthy of Saki's hostess who told the cook that she drank. At Harrods, she blurted out to one customer: 'This place is much too expensive for Christmas stocking toys – you want Woolworths.' The millionaire publisher Sir Edward Hulton, later an important force in both Anne's and Mac's lives, came searching for a rocking horse for his ward, Jocelyn Stevens, aged two. 'You want the smaller size,' declared Anne firmly, with scant regard for the interests of either her employers or the infant Jocelyn. She loved the store, in those days shamelessly paternalistic. Yet the shadow of poverty hung heavy over most of its staff. In Harrods' staff restaurant, prices were generously subsidised, but as Anne ate crumpets she watched men who confined themselves to tea. They came from homes where every penny counted, and deeply resented the injustice that women like herself should have jobs, while so many men lacked employment.

Only after six months of increasingly desperate job-searching did Anne strike lucky. She answered an advertisement in *The Times* for a personal assistant to the managing director of *Vogue* magazine, Harry Yoxall. She overdressed for the interview, in a bright tartan suit and choker of huge wooden beads. Yoxall, a tall, heavy, dyspeptic-looking figure in his late thirties, asked some penetrating questions and observed – with a bleak glance at the tartan suit – that he doubted whether Anne possessed the chic to work for *Vogue*. But something impressed him. He offered her a month's trial at three pounds a week, rising to £3.15*s* if she was retained thereafter. Part of the deal was that she must double as assistant to Yoxall and the knitting editor. She assured both that she was an accomplished wielder of needles, and on the way home bought a book entitled *First Steps to Stylish Knitting*.

She stayed at *Vogue* for seven years, the first three working on publicity for Yoxall, whom she came to respect deeply. Thereafter she advanced from sub-editor to copywriter, commissioner and then beauty editor. In those days in the media, she observed, there were no teenage columnists, nor indeed were young whizz-kids anywhere apparent. In every walk of life it was deemed necessary to work a passage through the ranks, to serve one's time learning a trade. She was introduced to the vernacular of women's magazine journalism, in which no cliché was left unstoned – 'pencil-slim', 'nostalgic', 'vibrant with colour', 'spiced with white'. Readers were sternly incited to 'Take stock of yourself', 'Re-think your dinner parties', 'Look in the mirror and see what you can take off', invocations as familiar seventy-five years ago as they are today. After the first two years her salary rose to £5, and she earned an extra pound moonlighting as an advertising copywriter. She rented a one-room flat in Meriden Court, a block off the King's Road, for £90 a year, and bought an old Morris Cowley. Off duty she read a lot – Graham Greene, Evelyn Waugh, Hardy, Flaubert, Tolstoy – and became a regular concert-goer, often standing for two or three backbreaking hours in the Queen's Hall to save the price of a seat. Bach was her first enthusiasm, soon supplanted by Mozart, a lifelong passion. Like all her generation, she adored cinema. She holidayed twice in France, learned to love it, and always regretted that she never mastered the language, nor indeed any other beyond restaurant level. Like most of her middle-class generation, she knew nothing of cooking.

Several of her Oxford friends had become academics – Sally Graves ended up as principal of Lady Margaret Hall, Oxford – or joined the Civil Service. Anne felt much more serious about her career than about a love life. She wanted to become a writer, for which *Vogue* offered no scope. She knew that some time she would have to move on. Meanwhile, however, she set about learning the art of glamour, as practised and proselytised by the magazine, which then appeared fortnightly. She learned the basics of layout and typography, and under the tutelage of Harry Yoxall became a meticulous copy editor.

She formed a friendship with one of *Vogue*'s most exotic contributors, Lesley Blanch, later author of *The Wilder Shores of Love*. Lesley displayed a characteristic flourish of imagination when invited to submit an article for a series by well-known hostesses. Earlier published pieces were headlined 'My Cook is a Russian', 'My Cook is Hungarian', and suchlike. Lesley entitled her own contribution 'My Cook is a Catastrophe'. Anne was captivated by her exotic lifestyle, feverish conversation, passionate loves and hates:

> She lived in a whirl of melodrama – something as trivial as a missed bus became a black tragedy. She wore exotic clothes of Russian ballet inspiration and moved in a nimbus of veiling, often topped with a fur shako, to the accompanying music of jangling bracelets. She had the sweetest of smiles, and always seemed penniless. She was devoted to cats, and burst into a storm of tears when informed by a skin doctor that she had a cat allergy. Lesley's favourite country was Russia, and she claimed to have visited its remotest districts with a Russian admirer at some unspecified time in the past. Siberia, Samarkand, the Caucasus were as familiar to her as Piccadilly or Chelsea.

Fashion drawing was then in its heyday – the magazine included Raoul Dufy among its star illustrators. Anne commissioned Rex Whistler to draw family groups of the Royal Family for a 1937 Coronation Gala special issue. He sat in the *Vogue* office with his head in his hands saying, 'I hate it, I hate it, can't I be let off?' and indeed his efforts proved a disappointment. For the same issue, she persuaded Vanessa Bell to paint a royal needlework design. Cecil Beaton photographed five duchesses – Buccleuch, Westminster, Richmond & Gordon, Marlborough and Sutherland – one countess and three viscountesses, with Lady Louis Mountbatten and Lady Diana Cooper thrown in for good measure. This Gallery of Beauties was deemed a great success, save that the New York office expressed incomprehension about the absence of the Duchess of Windsor from the line-up. Anne, however, was underwhelmed. High-society coverage never interested her. She found tiresome this aspect of *Vogue*'s agenda, and likewise the need to address it herself.

Magazine photography, hugely influenced by Hollywood, was a study in artificiality:

> The backgrounds devised by the photographers were of Babylonian luxury . . . Glamour implied not only beauty but wealth, and *Vogue*'s sitters, whether society women or professional models, had to look *rich*. Furred, bejewelled, masked in make-up, set among silks and satins, gilding and flowers, the sitter posed under intense lighting for a photographer who used a plate camera and slow film, so that the pose had to be held for several seconds. Their beauty was much enhanced by heavy retouching of the negatives, every flaw in the complexion painted-out, every bulge in the body tactfully smoothed away. Horst, Andre Durst, Cecil Beaton, Erwin Blumenfeld were pre-eminent among the photographers of this wondrous never-never land, Horst the finest, Beaton a lightweight by comparison.
>
> A recurring element in the fashion photography of the thirties was surrealism, as was not surprising in the heyday of Salvador Dali. Beaton often abandoned his usual tinsel backgrounds and turned to surrealism, with its sinister undertones, photographing the dancer Tilly Losch entrapped in coils of paper, or models standing in empty corridors among broken columns symbolic of decay. I myself worked with Blumenfeld, a brilliant German, to produce a surrealist photograph which was considered a triumph.
>
> I once needed a picture of a beautiful face to illustrate an article on skin care. Blumenfeld had elected to take the model, a fine-boned blonde with an exquisite nose called Cora van Millingen, in profile, smelling a long-stemmed rose. In the studio he changed his mind,

and sent me out to buy a swansdown powder-puff. When I returned, he snapped the rose from the stalk and pinned the powder-puff in its place for Cora to sniff with an expression of ecstasy. It sounds silly, but it was enchanting.

Yet suddenly, studio photography looked dated. Across the Atlantic in 1936 Henry Luce launched *Life*, which hugely impressed *Vogue*'s proprietor, Condé Nast. Two German publications, *Berliner Illustrierte* and *Munchener Illustrierte*, seized the imagination of Europe. London photographers began to shoot fashion pictures outdoors, using models with lighter make-up and flying hair. When the publisher Edward Hulton's *Picture Post* burst upon Britain in 1938, Anne, like Mac, instantly yearned to work for the new magazine: 'It reported news through the eye – the eye of the camera.' The mood of *Post* also appealed to her radicalism, undiminished by the *Vogue* experience: 'It looked into the future as well as the present. It was a young, spirited and provocative magazine, political and reformist, and though it might claim to be non-party, its heart was with the poor, the unemployed, the wretchedly housed.' Yet Anne lacked all reporting experience. She saw no chance of getting a job with *Picture Post*, and for its first three years did not try. Instead, she found herself editing an issue of *House & Garden*, then published as a supplement with *Vogue*. It was a heady experience. She revelled in creative authority. She always knew what she wanted, and by now she had the skills, as well as the natural eye, to get it.

British *Vogue* was a poor relation of its US parent. Beaton was its only contributor whom New York recognised as an international star: 'Otherwise, they patronised us, were friendly but unrelenting critics of our efforts and bombarded us with uncomplimentary cables. At one stage, deploring our old-fashioned typography and lay-out, they sent over an American art editor to buck us up. He was disagreeably surprised at the small resources, being accustomed to an army of assistants to do the donkeywork.' US *Vogue* waxed rich on sales of its paper dress patterns, while its British edition struggled to make a profit.

ABOVE AND RIGHT My paternal great-grandparents Edward and Lizzie Hastings, parents of 'The Tribe'.

BELOW Grandfather Basil strides proudly out of the Criterion Theatre as author of hit play *The New Sin* in 1912.

THIS PAGE AND OPPOSITE Great-uncle Lewis: with rifle and hunting party in South Africa in 1910, spoils draped on a Cape cart; as a gunner officer in World War I; and as I remember him, sketched in old age by Tom Purvis.

My maternal grandparents,
Rolfe and Violet Scott-James.

G. L. STAMPA 1925

The Savage Club, then in Carlton House Terrace, loomed large in the social lives of both Basil and Mac. Above is the menu for a 'Country Members' Night' chaired by Basil in 1925, and right that for a matching occasion at which Mac presided in 1953. The latter was drawn by Mac's friend Tony Wysard, a brilliant caricaturist until marriage into a fortune enabled him to stop drawing for a living.

Country Member's Night
Macdonald Hastings (ME II)
— in the saddle

Savage Club House Dinner
CARLTON HOUSE TERRACE   FEBRUARY 21st 1953

Fried Smelts   Tartar Sauce
Roast Stuffed Hare (from a *sauvage* habitat)
Port Wine Sauce   Red Currant Jelly   Jacket potatoes
Braised Red Cabbage   Brussels Sprouts

Mincemeat Turnovers
Coffee

ABOVE Anne (centre, standing) as a member of the 1930 St Paul's tennis team.

LEFT Mac with bride Eleanor Asprey at his first wedding at Kensington Register Office in 1936. The disastrous alliance lasted only a matter of months.

Anne photographed by Cecil Beaton in a
somewhat self-conscious glamour pose in
1937, when she was working for *Vogue*.

Mac with the toys he loved best: taking delivery of a pair of 12-bores in 1939 from his friend and gunmaker Robert Churchill, heedless of the damage to his overdraft. Churchill's Orange Street shop below Leicester Square, with a pistol range in the basement, became one of Mac's favourite places of pilgrimage.

Mac at war
Delivering one of his wartime
'London Letters' to America
from a microphone in
Broadcasting House.

OPPOSITE TOP Mac attending debriefing by a WAAF intelligence officer among the Canadian crew of a Stirling bomber with whom he had flown to Germany.

OPPOSITE BOTTOM Exploring the finer points of a Bren gun.

BELOW Peering towards the German front line in Holland in October 1944.

Major Stephen Hastings (standing, second left) with his partisan escort in northern Italy on a 1945 SOE operation; and acting the cad with an Italian friend.

Anne's war

LEFT As women's editor of *Picture Post*, a shot which Felix Mann gave her as a wedding present on her 1944 marriage to Mac.

BELOW As an apprentice bus conductor in Coventry.

BOTTOM Pulling a cracker with an American flier at a 1943 party she organised for the magazine.

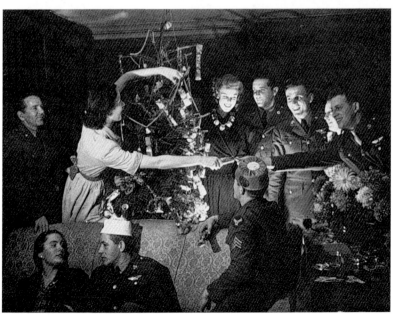

Anne photographed by Bert Hardy with the barman of a London pub, showing off the virtues of borrowed men's clothes to readers of *Picture Post* in 1941. This became one of the most celebrated images of her career.

TOP Mother carries me to my 1946 Aldworth christening, flanked by doughty Nanny, Jessie Strafford. Godmother Ruth Pallant, Mac's former lover, walks behind with handbag.

ABOVE Anne with the author and sister Clare, our family Austin in the background. Mac took the picture.

ABOVE AND RIGHT Rose Cottage in about 1946.

BELOW Mac in the sort of idyllic rural setting he loved.

Most English people in those days were shamelessly condescending to Americans, a habit that would do their nation no favours when war came. Anne, however, had a warm admiration for them. When New York editors visited London she found them twice as energetic as their British counterparts, more imaginative and receptive to new thinking. They were brutally frank, as the London office discovered during a visit from *Vogue*'s fearsome US editor-in-chief, Edna Woolman Chase. 'Who wrote this nonsense?' she demanded, scanning an issue with contempt, and demolished executives before the eyes of their wide-eyed staff. When Chase left for Paris, said Anne, 'We all felt relieved, but stimulated, pleased to be roused from our British lethargy.'

Soon afterwards, she scraped the money for a holiday in New York, outbound – steerage, of course – on the *Bremen*, homeward on the *Queen Mary*. She was awed and enchanted by the city, which she saw at its stylish zenith in 1935: 'I thought I had never seen so many lovely girls, heard such witty conversation, been dazzled by such rich merchandise. I loved the pace, the bright lights, the instant service, the late nights in a city which never went to sleep, and I cried all the way home.' Condé Nast himself offered her a job there, but she did not take it, because when she returned to London she fell in love. She afterwards believed that had she accepted, she would have failed, because she lacked the ruthlessness necessary to prosper in New York. I am not so sure. Though she always perceived herself as a blushing violet, in truth she was never less than formidable, clear-sighted and decisive. All her life she possessed a greater gift for attracting the respect and loyalty of people who worked for her than for social intercourse. What is for sure is that her career benefited from her unabashed enthusiasm for Americans, in an era when so many British people – notably including Mac – disdained their supposed naïveté and philistinism.

In 1937, Violet Scott-James inherited a legacy from her aunt Eleanor, and used some of the money to buy a cottage, The Forge at Upper Basildon in west Berkshire. One weekend a year later, when Anne was staying there with her parents, she and her mother were driving through the local lanes when they chanced upon the hamlet of Aldworth, high on the Downs. Outside a little cottage stood a sign: 'For sale by auction'. Built in 1806, it had recently been lived in by two elderly women who, as often happens, died within weeks of each other. Its two downstairs rooms had only earthen floors. The brick-work crawled with mice and woodlice, and water was drawn from a well outside the front door. Anne fell in love on sight, and borrowed £1,000 from Violet to buy and restore it. For the rest of her life, Rose Cottage remained the only home which she cared a straw for.

In those days when traffic was scarce, the road running downhill past the cottage scarcely mattered. Anne gazed entranced at the view beyond: 'We looked onto a triangular village green, with a group of elm trees in the middle, half-hiding the fourteenth-century church. Just across the green was a pair of thatched cottages inhabited by two ancient men who never exchanged a word except to quarrel over the use of their shared pump. Their front doors would open simul-taneously and they would pop out with buckets and have a row. Behind their cottages was pasture grazed by horses whose dung produced pearly, pink-lined mushrooms in late summer. In the distance was a farmhouse with a mighty barn, and beyond that a copse of wild cherry.'

She designed the cottage interior with inspired simplicity, much influenced by John Fowler, the fashionable decorator of the day. She herself made the red-and-white-striped living-room curtains. She bought a Regency couch for £5, Victorian dining chairs for £10, and a painted dining table from the Colefax & Fowler shop for £15, which together with the builders' bills plunged her into debt. She did not care: 'The cottage looked like a spring morning when I had finished it, and though it has been decorated many times since, I have tried to keep the whiteness and feeling of fresh air.'

She was not alone when she began housekeeping at Rose Cottage. A journalist named Derek Verschoyle, literary editor of *The Spectator*, moved in with her. Verschoyle was a self-consciously raffish char-acter, who kept a .22 rifle at the magazine's office in Gower Street, with which he potted local cats out of the window, or merely conducted target practice addressed at the garden wall, while seated with his feet on his desk. A colleague described him as convivial and hard-drinking. He had some notoriety as a former pupil of Evelyn Waugh at the awful Arnold House prep school in North Wales, being characterised in Waugh's novel *Decline and Fall* as Peter Beste-Chetwynd, the grand, languid, depraved and absurdly precocious boy whose mother Paul Pennyfeather almost marries. Waugh borrowed from real life for the book his attempt to teach Verschoyle to play the organ, while himself absolutely ignorant of the instrument. At the *Spectator*, the now famous novelist became one of his former pupil's favourite reviewers.

Verschoyle's literary enthusiasms, rather than his marksmanship with the .22, presumably recommended him to Anne. But she was drawn to wild spirits, surely in reaction against the rigours of her childhood. In the eighteen months she and Verschoyle were together, they spent every spare hour labouring to make Rose Cottage habitable. On an impulse, in the summer of 1939 she married him. When war came in September, he joined the RAF – Graham Greene took over his role at *The Spectator* – and the following year they were divorced. 'It was as though [the marriage] had never happened,' she wrote later. 'Neither of us seemed to feel anything at all . . . My only excuse [was] that in that summer of 1939 there was a fair amount of false emotion in the air.' Children are the least plausible judges of their own parents' emotional lives. I know nothing of what made Anne love her first husband, or so swiftly become disenchanted with him. Verschoyle continued his exotic career as a post-war spy, then publisher, and enjoyed short-lived relationships with four more wives.

It was not entirely true that he and Anne became painlessly uncoupled. For some reason, Violet Scott-James had made the loan to buy Rose Cottage payable to Verschoyle rather than to her daughter. Always feckless in money matters, he proved, to the Scott-Jameses' exasperation as evidenced by several solicitors' letters, a sticky debtor. This may help to explain why Anne sought to expunge him from her consciousness after their divorce. For years, she never included the Verschoyle marriage in her *Who's Who* entry. When she was ninety, however, he was suddenly inserted. She said that she relented in response to a priggish tease of mine. I suggested that no one who has practised journalism for a living should censor the facts of their own CV.

Again and again during the first fifty years of her life, in her search for love she entered culs-de-sac. Though she yearned for the fulfilment of a partnership, few men met her exacting standards of intelligence and competence. She was intolerant of weakness, save in her brother John, subject to illness and depression all his short life, until he died of lung cancer at the age of forty. She cared for John devotedly, and employed him for some years at Rose Cottage as her gardener, the only work of which the poor soul was capable. She once blurted bitterly to me: 'All my life I have had to take responsibility for people less strong than I am. I think it's about time somebody took care of me.' The price of being so formidable a personality was that, again and again, she found herself in relationships with weaker men, whom she grew to despise. Only in middle age, when she married Osbert Lancaster, did she find a partner for whom she sustained love and respect, yet who also proved capable of relishing her dominance.

SIX

War Work

Mac's war experience made him a successful journalist – not a star, but a reporter respected in his trade, and known to informed people outside it. He was assigned as *Picture Post*'s war correspondent, and adored the role. Between 1939 and 1945 he reported from Channel convoys, destroyers and torpedo boats with the Royal Navy; flew on operations with RAF Bomber and Coastal Commands; described the London Blitz and the home front; then covered the North-West Europe campaign from Normandy to the Elbe. He later recalled gleefully the many occasions when he signed a 'blood chit', absolving the armed forces from responsibility for any mishap that might befall him on operations. He was able to combine his *Picture Post* role with regular broadcasts for the BBC, and indeed often described on the radio experiences which he also reported for the magazine. He was fortunate not to be posted to the Mediterranean or the Far East, where periods of intense action were interspersed with intervals of acute boredom. By staying in Britain, he found plenty to write about even when the war was temporarily quiescent. He contributed profiles of the Cabinet, described the glories of the corn harvest, visited battle schools and tank training camps. Until June 1944, save when he was attached to an operational unit, he was able to sleep in flats and hotels rather than tents and trenches.

Civilians have an exaggerated notion of the perils faced by war correspondents. Though reporters are sometimes under fire, they endure nothing like the continuous risks and discomforts borne by infantrymen, fliers and sailors. Nonetheless, Mac acquired a reputation for courage, indeed recklessness. Photographers who worked with him on the battle-field returned with bloodcurdling tales of his enthusiasm for the fray. But however brave they may be, journalists remain privileged specta-tors. They see far more of their own homes, of hot food and warm beds, not to mention fame, than any fighting man. Mac had a good war, but also a privileged one.

When I first read his dispatches, at the age of sixteen, I put it to him that some seemed too gung-ho. They projected fighting men – especially bomber pilots – as much more enthusiastic about their roles than seemed plausible to me, even as an adolescent. 'For heaven's sake, boy,' he said. 'What I was doing was part of the war effort.' During a struggle for national survival, it was essential for the media to project a positive image of what the armed forces were doing. Especially in the early years of the war, when Britain's continued existence hung by a thread, it was impossible to tell anything like the truth about the inadequacy of the nation's defences, the short-comings of its forces. Mac's wholehearted admiration for the men whose doings he reported contributed mightily to the popularity of his work. But few words written for publication in the midst of such a conflict have enduring merit. Only when the shooting and dying stopped, when peace came, was it possible to start telling the truth about what the war had really been like; about the tribulations, fears and shortcomings of those who fought it.

Anne's passion to join *Picture Post* intensified after September 1939. She found it irksome to be working for a women's glossy magazine while the world dissolved into flame. She tried a bold ploy, writing to *Post*'s editor Stefan Lorant to suggest a feature about *Vogue*. Lorant agreed. A photographer stalked *Vogue*'s offices for some days – almost all *Picture Post* stories were image-led. Anne herself then wrote the words for a four-page article. Soon afterwards, with the Nazis on Britain's doorstep Lorant fled to America, and was replaced by Tom Hopkinson. The new boss invited Anne to come and see him. He had decided, he said, that the magazine needed a women's editor. Would she do the job? She accepted on the spot, moved to *Picture*

Post early in 1941, and stayed for almost four years. Despite her job title, she saw this as her great opportunity to break out of the ghetto of women's journalism. She wrote features on backyard farming, childbirth in the Blitz, clubs for the troops. She spent three days as a bus conductress in Coventry ('Bit tall for the job, isn't she?' said a bewildered passenger). She described service wives, cooking with rations, refurbishing a bombed home, new treatments for war neuroses. Her picture often appeared in her stories, and in those days of *Picture Post*'s awesome market dominance, she became modestly well known. She learned on the job. When sent to interview Dr Shirley Summerskill, the MP had to tell her what questions to ask.

At first, Anne sought to use photographers whom she had known on *Vogue* to illustrate her copy. She soon realised, however, that the fashion magazine's formal, mannered style did not work for *Picture Post*. Instead, she began to work and travel with the tough, buccaneering types on the magazine's staff, notably the famous cockney Bert Hardy, whom both Anne and Mac adored, and who became one of the great news photographers of his generation. 'Travelling with Bert was an education in the art of survival,' she wrote. 'He had a bulbous nose in a purplish face, but his charm moved mountains.' Stuck on a train together, delayed for hours by bombs somewhere on the line, not another passenger could find even a Spam sandwich. Bert, however, returned from a foraging expedition with two steaming cups of tea. 'How on earth did you manage it?' the thankful Anne asked. Bert shrugged: 'I just patted the girl's hand, like, and it turned out she had a spoonful of tea left, so she made it fresh.' Bert, whose links to the black-market fraternity were legendary, once gave Anne a box of chocolates. 'Oh, Bert, I mustn't,' she said. 'You can't have seen yet another overloaded lorry.' 'Anne, I promise you, I ran after that lorry when I saw the crate fall off, but I couldn't catch it up.' After the war, Bert made a fortune in advertising photography and property. But, true to his Elephant & Castle roots, stewed eels remained his favourite dish.

Almost all the Hastingses and Scott-Jameses suffered the kind of Blitz mishaps that were the common lot of Londoners. Mac preserved a hotel-room key, souvenir of a night when he returned from dinner to find the St Regis in Cork Street flattened by a bomb. His sister Beryl went one evening in March 1941 with her boyfriend Leslie to the Café de Paris, dancing to Snakehips Johnson and his West Indian orchestra. The Café was famous for its champagne, of which the manager claimed to have hoarded 25,000 bottles. It was crowded with young officers and their dates awaiting cabaret time – *The Kentucky Derby by Ten Beautiful Girls* – when it received a direct hit from a Luftwaffe raider. Scores of diners were killed, many more injured. 'The macabre scenes which followed were among the most indelibly horrifying of the period,' wrote Angus Calder, one of the historians of the Blitz. 'One woman had her broken leg washed in champagne, while looters plundered rings from the fingers of the dead and wounded.' Beryl and Leslie were dragged from the wreckage uninjured, and stumbled home to fall into a shocked sleep that lasted twenty-four hours. Afterwards, she found the Café's silver menu card still in her handbag. For the rest of her life, she could never look at it without a shudder of horror.

Mac was by chance dining nearby at another restaurant, the Hungaria, when bloodstained and dust-covered survivors began to come in from the Café de Paris. In the men's room, Mac encountered a tank officer scrubbing filth from his face. The man then strode off to find a table, observing in an authentic display of Blitz spirit: 'Well, I'm going to finish my dinner somewhere.' Two girls likewise arrived determined to dance for another couple of hours. They were accompanied by a little fox terrier which found recovery from its trauma at the Café far more difficult. It stood in a corner quivering with terror as the band played through the remainder of the evening.

Anne was asleep at the flat in Westminster she shared with Sally Graves when a near-miss shattered all the windows. Badly shaken as well as slightly burned, she felt obliged to go to the office in the morning after having her injuries treated, because that was what everybody did. She had to move flats, however, and sought refuge at Lesley Blanch's place in Swan Court, Chelsea. Her father, Rolfe Scott-James, suffered more severely. He was blown out of bed by a direct hit on the house next door to his own in Bayswater, suffering shock which imposed lasting effects on his health. The family home had to be demolished, and government compensation was meagre for a mere tenant.

Lewis Hastings adored it all, of course. Aged sixty, he hastened back from Rhodesia in the winter of 1939 to rejoin the army, was passed A1 fit, took a course in anti-aircraft gunnery and assumed command of an ack-ack battery. In the spring of 1941, finding home defence somewhat tedious, he got himself seconded to the BBC as a radio pundit. Lewis asserted that the secret of success as a broadcaster is personal conviction, with which he was bountifully supplied. The posting was initially for three months, but he was then given a title as the BBC's Military Commentator, and filled this role until the end of the war. He made over a thousand radio broadcasts from Britain, the Mediterranean and North-West Europe, and became sufficiently celebrated for Goebbels to mock him on the air from Berlin.

Mac fell in love with Anne almost on the first day he saw her in the office of *Picture Post* in 1941. He told colleagues: 'I'm going to marry that girl,' and set about besieging her with characteristic panache. That summer he invited her to contribute to his weekly broadcast to America. Here is how he made the introduction, in an open love letter across the airwaves, by courtesy of the BBC:

> When I've been blundering about trying to write from time to time on matters of feminine interest, I've often thought that what this column needed was the whisper of the petticoat and imprint of a lipstick. So this week, I've asked one of my most charming colleagues to end this *London Letter*. To introduce her, she looks as if she'd just stepped out of an advertisement. She has got a peaches-and-cream complexion such as men talk about and women envy. She knows more about American men than I do about American girls. She is as high as my heart, or higher, and the nicest girl that ever held a man's hand under such a Bomber's Moon as I've been writing about. Meet Anne Scott-James . . .

Anne's piece which followed was about her garden at Rose Cottage:

> I've been bitten by the gardening bug. At lunch with my girl-
> friends, I discuss not hats, not jobs, not books, not even men
> . . . but cauliflowers, blackfly and the horrible disease called Big
> Bud. At first, the beauties of gardening clothes helped to egg me
> on. I liked myself in dungarees, in corduroys, in linen shorts, and
> striped aprons. I liked the shiny feel of a new trowel and the quiet
> competence of new scissors. But now my motives are purged of
> vanity. I garden for the pure pleasure of digging and sowing and
> planting and pruning and staking and weeding – and picking and
> eating. I glory in a ruler-straight row of peckish young lettuce
> plants. I love my lupins. A pleasant thing, I think, that in the whirl
> of war we've rediscovered the excitement of making things grow.

One night in 1942, Mac flew on an operation over Europe with the
Canadian crew of a Stirling bomber. He wrote his piece for *Picture
Post*, and was busy on another assignment when the base commander
contacted him. The crew with whom he had flown had been killed
on their next 'op'. Since he, Mac, was the last to spend time with
them, would he write to their families? He found those letters among
his hardest tasks of the war, penning plausible words about seven
young men whom he had known for only a few hours, and with
whom his relationship was as careless and transitory as so many
chance wartime brushes. For thirty years afterwards, on the anniversary of their last mission the mother of one of the gunners wrote to
Mac, pleading for any tiny detail of her son's last days. He could offer
nothing, yet felt obliged to pretend.

At Christmas 1942, Anne organised a party for US airmen at a
big Tudor country house which she borrowed, near a Flying Fortress
base in the Midlands. Supported by a bevy of *Picture Post* secretaries
and models, she greeted the airmen with rum punch. They jitter-
bugged till the oak beams creaked, sang and conga-ed frenziedly. Too
frenziedly, Anne thought. She was moved, indeed distressed, by the
emotional extravagance and reckless drunkenness of the airmen,

whose wing had been taking heavy casualties. Many of them were shot down in the weeks that followed.

Lewis made his first parachute jump in company with Mac. The inspecting medical officer at the Ringway parachute school outside Manchester told Major Hastings that he was unable to pass anyone over forty for airborne training. By an odd coincidence, declared Lewis blithely, it was his fortieth birthday the following week. He duly jumped at the age of sixty-two, and was disgusted that the army instructors insisted upon dropping him into a lake, out of deference to his seniority. Later, in Sicily, encountering a rifle company that had lost all its officers, for some days Lewis contrived to take command. He accompanied the advancing Allied armies across North-West Europe, developing a warm regard for Montgomery, whom he often interviewed.

Lewis and his son Stephen never got on. In large part, I think, this derived from Lewis's almost permanent absence during Steve's childhood. Mac had a much warmer relationship with Lewis, and indeed was jealous of Steve's closer blood tie. Whatever the reasons, Steve went through Eton and Sandhurst, and in 1940 became a regular officer of the Scots Guards ('the regiment', as it was known in his mother's family, on the assumption that there was no other), with little contact with his father. It was a surprise to both when they met by chance during the Blitz, at the ack-ack battery Lewis was commanding. Steve thereafter went his own way, with scant acknowledgement from his father.

Yet Steve's wartime experiences merited Lewis's approval, indeed wholehearted admiration. Young Lieutenant Hastings had the most gallant war of any member of the family. In March 1941 he landed at Suez, posted to 2nd Scots Guards. Shortly after his twentieth birthday in May, he went into action for the first time as commander of his battalion's 9 Platoon in Libya. He spent the year that followed in the thick of the seesaw desert fighting, during which he was awarded a Military Cross. He formed close friendships with several comrades, but developed a contempt for the higher leadership, from his own company commander upwards. When he heard that David

Stirling was recruiting men for special forces operations with his 'private army', L Detachment, soon to become the Special Air Service, Stephen immediately volunteered. Like other eager young blades, he wanted to escape the shackles of regimental soldiering. Life with Stirling, already a famous figure in North Africa, sounded vastly more rewarding.

From the outset, Steve was delighted with what he found:

> Here was an idiosyncratic collection of people, officers and men with the minimum distinction between them, whose only bond seemed to be a reflection of their extraordinary commander's personality. It was all very different from the enveloping tribal hierarchy of the battalion. Six foot five inches in his desert boots, with a slight stoop, an eager open face with beetling eyebrows beneath a battered service dress cap, David Stirling radiated urgency and confidence. His eyes carried a penetrating directness and hint of impish humour. Here was no welcome for affectation. His expression could shift with bewildering suddenness from an intense, almost puzzled concentration, rather like a schoolboy who ought to know the answer, to one of uproarious irreverence. This change of mood often followed some reference to the doings and denizens of GHQ, whom he held in ribald and more or less permanent contempt. He demanded absolute loyalty and adherence to his own concept of duty, yet one always sensed an underlying kindness and humanity. Here was an inspired and merry warrior whose time had come.

Most of L Detachment's officers had come out from England in the Commando Brigade, now disbanded. They were smart – their social connections contributed decisively to the SAS's ability to secure resources and sponsorship – bright and, it is almost unnecessary to add, brave. There were Fitzroy Maclean and Carol Mather, both of whom later became MPs, as did Steve himself. There was George Jellicoe, son of the admiral; Paddy Mayne, the huge Irish rugby forward, whose drinking bouts 'led to outbursts of berserk proportions' – Mayne once laid out six Australians in a bar brawl; and around twenty others. Most were already veterans of raids on Rommel's airfields.

Steve completed parachute training from a Bombay bomber. Briefing for his first mission with the group, now designated as the SAS, took place in the Cairo flat of Peter Stirling, David's brother, second secretary at the British Embassy:

> In one corner of the large and somewhat battered drawing room a group of SAS officers were poring over a large-scale map of the Western Desert marked 'Top Secret', while George Jellicoe described to them the route they were to take behind enemy lines. Across the room an animated drinks party was in progress, consisting mainly of people going to Gezireh races in the afternoon. It included several pretty girls, and the *'vas et viens'* between the two groups added much spice to the proceedings. The briefing was late, so I subsequently learned, because Mohammed or 'Mo', as Peter's incomparable butler was known, had hidden the secret maps in the bathroom in a praise-worthy if vain attempt to tidy the place up.

The Second World War was probably the last in history in which some members of the British upper class were able to arrange their assignments to suit themselves. In Evelyn Waugh's *Sword of Honour* trilogy, an officer observes in 1940 at the bar of White's club – thinly disguised as 'Bellamy's': 'It's going to be a long war. The great thing is to spend it with friends.' It was in this spirit, and warmly abetted by Winston Churchill, that private armies evolved – SOE, the Commandos, SAS, Long-Range Desert Group, Popski's Private Army, Special Boat Squadron and so on. By the later stages of the war, these organisations were consuming far more resources and high-quality manpower than their achievements justified. The 'Clubland Heroes' atmosphere which Steve's description vividly evokes was funny only up to a point, viewed from the lofty perspective of national interest in a world war. But the exploits of these undoubted heroes contributed mightily to British folklore of the 1939–45 experience, and gave immense pleasure to the participants.

The party in Peter Stirling's flat in Cairo eventually broke up, its guests dispersing variously to the races, and to a column of twenty heavily armed jeeps waiting in the street below. It was 2 July 1942, and Steve found himself embarked on his first SAS operation. They crawled through the dense city traffic towards the Delta, and thence into the desert. At this time the main British army was deployed on the Alamein line, barely forty miles from the Egyptian capital. Four days after setting out, the SAS group was in hiding, and in waiting, at an oasis rendezvous to which they had been guided by the Long-Range Desert Group, sixty miles inland and 150 miles behind the German lines.

Steve's inaugural raid, in three jeeps under George Jellicoe's command, was rudely interrupted by an Italian air attack. All their vehicles were riddled with machine-gun fire, which wrecked two. The third, though badly damaged, somehow carried nine men back to their starting point. There they remained for three weeks, while David Stirling drove back to Cairo to fetch replacement vehicles and supplies. Some thirty men in all, they presented a wild spectacle, burned black by the sun, heavily bearded, intensely bored, and driven mad by the flies. They yearned above all things for the sun to fall each night, 'a great orange ball, its progress eventually perceptible to the human eye as it dropped below the far escarpment, now turned black, the outline of every rock standing sharp against a livid sky. Slowly the hated thing disappeared, leaving the whole desert bathed in colours so rich, hard and brilliant as to defy a painter's brush.' They talked little of home or about the war, but mostly of their fantasies of a day in Cairo which started with a Turkish bath and a shave, and ended among the ravishing belly dancers of the open-air nightclubs.

When Stirling at last returned with a column of vehicles and a plethora of supplies and munitions, they prepared to launch a big airfield raid. Men laboured intently on repairing jeeps and preparing charges with plastic explosive, time pencils and black tape. Then, at dusk, they set forth:

It was easy to see at first. The jeeps kept no particular formation. We picked our own way a little to right or left of the man in front, and following his dust. Occasionally you hit a rock or bad bump; gun mountings rattled, cans and ammo boxes clashed in the back. Mostly we rolled along at a good 20 mph over flat shingle or sand. Every now and again we had to negotiate small escarpments. There was a halt until somebody found a way up or down. The dust rose thicker, engines revved as we changed gear to pull up one after the other, then fanned out again on the level.

At nightfall they hit the airfield, racing their jeeps past lines of German planes at which they emptied machine-gun drums and hurled their charges.

First there was one tentative burst, then the full ear-splitting cacophony roaring and spitting. Streams of red and white colour shot through the darkness, struck the ground and cascaded upwards in a thousand crazy arcs, criss-crossing each other. Some of the incendiary bullets caught fire as they hit the ground and burnt with a brilliant white flame. Figures ran before us, or rather seemed to be lumbering away. Another white stream shot through the night and two of them slumped into the ground ... Our line moved on, leaving the big aircraft crackling and blazing ... My rear gunner said: 'There's two Jerries.' 'Well, shoot at them; go on – shoot.'

One British gunner was killed, several jeeps including those of David Stirling and Steve Hastings were hit. A few miles back on their retreat, Steve's engine subsided into silence. He and his crew somehow crammed onto one of the serviceable vehicles.

On their way home, the group narrowly escaped discovery by successive patrols of searching Stukas. They got lost. There were no more spare tyres, so whenever a wheel was punctured, the jeep had to be abandoned, its passengers being crammed aboard those vehicles which remained. They were utterly exhausted, and down to the last of their water, when somehow they blundered into the rendezvous.

Stirling and a handful of others were flown out to Cairo. Steve was among those who made the slow, painful passage back in jeeps and trucks. They were in the midst of the Qattara Depression when he began to lose consciousness at the wheel, and found himself running a high fever. Back in Egypt, he was sent on extended leave to Beirut to recuperate.

On his return he was flown to the Kufra oasis in southern Libya to join a big SAS operation, decreed by GHQ against David Stirling's better judgement, against Benghazi, some six hundred miles behind the German lines. This proved a disaster. After an epic journey, as they approached the target they met heavy opposition. Turning back, they were repeatedly bombed and strafed by enemy aircraft, losing most of their jeeps and trucks. Steve found himself in a party led by Paddy Mayne, unsure of their position, desperately short of water. 'The next few days were among the most unpleasant in my experience,' he wrote. He and others, stricken by thirst, became delirious and began to fantasise. By a miracle, they eventually reached the Jalo oasis, where they were met by an officer of the Sudan Defence Force. 'My dear chap,' he said solicitously, 'will you have a whisky and soda?' Not surprisingly, Steve's illness recurred. He was diagnosed as suffering from chronic bronchitis, and discharged from active service for six months. It was the end of his time with the SAS. He was glad to have served for nine months under Stirling, and cherished the memories, but he had had enough. He spent the next few months as a staff officer in Cairo, and nobody could doubt that he had earned the break.

Anne, like most women, discovered far fewer compensations in the experience of war than did Mac, Lewis and Stephen. She loved the work she was doing, but never ceased to lament the tragedies, public and personal, that were the common lot. Her mother Violet died of cancer in 1942, aged fifty-nine, though this could scarcely be blamed on Hitler. Among her close friends, one colleague from *Vogue* died when the ship on which she was travelling was torpedoed, another lost her husband, a bomber pilot. A film-director contemporary from Oxford,

Pen Tennyson, was killed in an air crash. Another friend drowned when his warship sank in the Mediterranean. Yet despite the tragedies, Anne learned to marvel at the normality of life between the shocks and dramas. Once in 1944, during the flying-bomb offensive, she was lunching in a restaurant when there was an explosion nearby. Only one patron sought shelter beneath a table, while everyone else continued eating. 'The poor fellow was an American, who had just arrived in England, and he emerged red-faced and apologetic.'

At a time when food was a permanent preoccupation, Anne often found herself writing about it. She collaborated with Constance Spry, then living in an old farmhouse in Kent. Connie had become famous as an arranger of flowers, but turned her wartime energies to promoting healthy eating from the garden. She taught Anne how to cook *petits pois à la française*, then almost unknown in Britain, how to serve cabbage leaves in bundles like asparagus, and sweet corn (likewise unusual at that time) in browned margarine. Anne wrote about another country housewife who had become expert in cooking with weeds: dandelion and wood sorrel salad, elderflower fritters, puree of Good King Henry, rose-hip jam, herb sandwich-spread and stinging nettles on toast were among the recipes she subsequently offered to readers in a pamphlet. She was grateful that the war provided her with an incentive to learn to cook, which she soon did as competently – indeed better than competently – as she did every-thing else in her life. 'I doubt if you *can* cook,' she wrote proudly later, 'until you have made an omelette with margarine, dried eggs and chopped chickweed,' as she had done.

Anne found it hard to keep Rose Cottage going through the war, or indeed to get to Berkshire at all. After a year in which she rented the place to tenants, she lent it to friends, two sisters each with a baby and a husband in the forces, in return for their services in the garden, and a room left free for Anne when she could make the journey from London. This was seldom, and required a three-mile walk up the steep hill from Goring & Streatley station, clutching suit-case and food. It was rare for any car to pass, offering the chance of a lift, for civilian traffic was almost non-existent. In 1943, one of her tenants' husbands, a bomber pilot, was shot down and killed over Germany. The sisters decided to depart for their own home, and Anne took back the cottage.

Anne and Mac began living together that year. In London, they occupied a flat in Swan Court, Chelsea, which Anne inherited when Lesley Blanch went off to marry the French fighter pilot and novelist Romain Gary. Anne said later that she should have understood that Mac's view of marriage was unsympathetic when he employed a fishing figure of speech to propose to her: 'I mean to hook you.' She went ahead anyway, with a simple register office wedding at the beginning of June 1944. The couple set off to honeymoon at Rose Cottage, which had captured Mac's affection as deeply as her own. Two days later, Tom Hopkinson telephoned from *Picture Post* to tell him of the D-Day landings. Within hours, he was on his way to France. The cottage was mothballed for the remainder of the war.

Mac's reports from North-West Europe were examples of fine descriptive journalism. Here is how he began one piece from Normandy in August 1944:

Ask a British soldier, ten years hence, what he remembers best of that famous victory of 1944 in Northern France, and, if he still cares to talk about it, he'll tell you it was the bouquet of smells: the sickly smell in the intestines of a landing craft; the sweaty whiff of damp battledress, the stomach-wrenching stench of dead cattle, the sour air of a blasted village, the peculiar unforgettable odour of a German prisoner.

Ask a German what he remembers best and, for a Teutonic certainty, he'll say it was the horrific orchestra of the Allied instruments of war: the nightmare drumming of the artillery, the wasp-like persistence of the aircraft, the whine of shells, the poop of mortars, the crump of bombs, the unspeakable quavering note of a Typhoon rocket.

Ask a Frenchman, and he'll tell you of the wounded horse that dragged him and whatever was left of his possessions in an overloaded cart to safety; of the crops that were never harvested; of the cows that died for lack of milking; of the litter of tree stumps that was an apple orchard; of the tank track that was a garden; of the graveyard that was a farm.

Ten years hence – if, by that time, you're not too bored with wartime reminiscences to listen, or too young to care – ask me what I remember best of the collapse of the German Seventh Army and, being middle-aged and sentimental about the past as I shall be by then, I'll probably tell you that the magic moment was the beginning of the pursuit, the sight of the columns of the British Second Army riding the road to victory like gods on a cloud of dust. You needn't believe it. War is only romantic in retrospect. The ridiculous truth is that up in the forward infantry areas, we didn't know the battle was won until we heard a rumour that Monty had said so.

The nine-page piece which followed, accompanied by brilliant photographs taken by Leonard McCombe, was probably Mac's best dispatch of the war. *Picture Post*'s writers were usually credited in small print at the foot of their copy, but by that date his byline was appearing at the head of his words. His pieces received star billing through the rest of the campaign in North-West Europe.

In the summer of 1944, Steve Hastings began to feel guilty about his absence from the fighting war. He volunteered for service behind the German lines with Special Operations Executive, and was dispatched first to Algiers, thence to Paris, to await an assignment in the field. There was a long wait, much of it amid the fleshpots, which did nothing to assuage his discomfort about being absent both from his battalion, by now fighting in Italy, and from his old SAS comrades. He was flown to Brindisi, destined to join the Italian partisans. There, more heel-kicking followed, which caused Steve to seek amusement in a characteristic family fashion: 'One day, somebody reported having seen a fox. We spun into action, collected four or five scrawny horses, a mule, and about three couple of assorted mongrels, which we encouraged with bully-beef before setting forth for the chase. The

Brindisi Vale hounds only met twice and, as their Huntsman, I could not claim much success. Several cats were given a nasty turn but escaped. Much abrasive red wine was drunk; we scampered about among the scrub oak, olive and carob trees by the shore, but of the foxes there was no sign.'

On the night of 3 February 1945, Steve and his team were parachuted by American Liberator into the Ligurian Apennines, near San Stefano d'Aveto, thirty miles inland from Portofino. He landed in a pine tree, but was mercifully undamaged, likewise his cockney wireless operator, Sergeant Chalky White. Then they loaded their kit onto mules supplied by the partisans' reception committee, and set off into the mountains. Steve operated under the orders of two other British officers, Basil Davidson and Peter McMullen. As so often with SOE operations, they found themselves struggling with labyrinthine local political complications. All the Italians hated the Germans, but most hated each other almost as bitterly. Two of Steve's bodyguard resigned in disgust because, as good communists, they disliked the British officers' custom of eating separately from the men. McMullen, who trusted the locals not at all, found it difficult to work with Davidson, a professed Marxist, who embraced them. Steve, as a twenty-three-year-old captain then oblivious of politics, was merely bemused by it all. One day he met an elderly partisan leading a mule carrying three 75mm shells. Steve demanded: where was the gun? He received a theatrical shrug: '*Non lo so, io*' – I don't know. Then the old boy brightened up: '*Fa niente, Signor Maggiore*. When we get down there, we'll find a gun that fits.'

In the last weeks of the war, as the German armies in Italy approached collapse, the partisans embarked on ever more daring operations, hitting enemy garrisons wherever they could. At Groppallo, the SOE team appropriated a large German open staff car, loaded a partisan colonel aboard along with themselves, and hastened down the valley towards Bettola. Then they drove on towards Piacenza, which they reached on 25 April. Steve saw before him a pair of great wrought-iron gates protecting a huge Renaissance castle. This belonged, he was told reverently, to that great nobleman the Duke of Grazzano. Steve walked up to the front door, to be greeted by the tall, thin, elegant figure of the duke himself. Steve apologised for the intrusion. 'It is nothing,' shrugged His Grace in impeccable English. 'I am delighted to see you. It has been very difficult here. The Germans requisitioned one wing, and I had the partisans from time to time in the other. Will you have tea or coffee?'

In the last stages of the battle for Piacenza on 29 April, Steve drove to the headquarters of the US 135th Infantry, and explained to a bemused American colonel that the partisans controlled most of the area. Steve was proud of the contribution his Italians made to the capture of the city, fighting harder than ever before. As the Germans were forced out, he drove into Piacenza and commandeered an office in the splendid Palazzo del Commune. A few weeks later, after riotous celebrations, he returned to England.

Lewis's last memorable encounter of the war took place in the spring of 1945 near Hanover, where he entered a large country house to find himself in the presence of Field-Marshal August von Mackensen, a famous German commander of the First World War, by then aged over ninety. The two hoary old veterans enjoyed a long and convivial talk, interpreted by the Field-Marshal's daughter-in-law, who spoke English. The Junker, as Lewis categorised him, welcomed the arrival of the British with warm enthusiasm, having been fearful of the Russians. He would say nothing unflattering about his late Führer, however, except to regret that Hitler had not heeded the General Staff, which might have prompted a different outcome of the war. Mackensen became extremely heated in his denunciation of the Americans, who had no grievance against Germany. 'Why did they want to come and interfere in the war between us and Britain?' the old man demanded crossly. Lewis felt moved to describe some of the scenes he had recently witnessed in Belsen concentration camp. The Field-Marshal lapsed into a sulky silence which persisted until his British visitor departed.

Lewis perceived the war in intensely romantic terms – indeed, he embraced the Churchillian vision that it formed part of a great historic pageant. Watching a British infantry company advancing into an attack through the flickering red and orange light of shellfire in Sicily in 1943, Lewis studied the faces of the men with rapt attention: 'It was England going by – it was Blenheim, it was Salamanca, it was the Heights of Abraham, the Somme, Deville Wood, the Salient. I had seen them all before, the same breed in the same strange illumination. Fathers and sons, they were cut out of the same block, and they were worthy of one another.' Major Hastings finished his war by walking alone into Bremen Town Hall, armed with a walking stick with which he afterwards claimed to have belaboured the resident Nazi officials. Lewis had twenty years left to live, but for him nothing was ever quite as good again. Peace brought the introduction of a permanent close season on Germans, and the old hunter was now too long in the tooth to return to his beloved bush.

In April 1945, Mac delivered a lyrical BBC broadcast to North America about the glories of the English spring:

> What I would like to do this week is to take you down to my cottage and show you the garden. As gardens go, there is nothing very remarkable about it. As I have been in Germany during those vital weeks when I ought to have been mowing the grass, pruning the roses, hoeing the leeks, we are rather behindhand with the vital work. But for all that, I would like to show you my garden because this is the time of year in England when gardens ought to be seen, when their peculiar magic is seen at its best, with a fragile loveliness which the patina of time has a lot to do with.
>
> An English cottage garden is not the work of one man; it is the reward of the loving toil and patience of generations. In my garden, I do not know who planted the daffodils in the bank, put in the hedges, planted the old yew just outside the front door. All I am sure about is that the ghosts of all the dear old gardeners from the time of William the Norman – when another habitation stood where my cottage now stands – from the days of the Crusaders, who are buried in the little church opposite, to the Georgians who built the present cottage – all

I know is that their ghosts – call it the aura of their love, if you like – haunt the cottage now. You can hear them whispering in the gentle spring breeze. You can almost see them lifting the nodding heads of the daffodils and tulips to see how they are coming along. And, at evening time in that wonderful, still air after an April shower, you could almost swear that somebody was moving among the rosebeds.

It is surprising for me to be on this subject, isn't it? I am almost surprised myself. For five and a half years, I have talked and written, broadcast and made speeches, about nothing but war. I have followed a trail of destruction. Nothing else has really seemed important by comparison with war. Yet now, at last, peace is coming into the news again. Funny the way it gets you. I think the first half-conscious thought was during the crossing of the Rhine. I caught myself saying to my neighbour in the boat: 'It would be silly to get killed now.' I do not think he heard what I said through the ear-splitting noise of the barrage; but he sensed the meaning all right, and grinned and smiled.

It is one of the mercies of this terrible war, in which so much of Europe's great heritage has been destroyed, that the riches of the English countryside have survived almost untouched. The descendants of Shakespeare's swans are still gracing the waters of Avon. Wordsworth's dancing daffodils are in full bloom again. Shelley's skylark is nesting. And, to prove that all our memories are not in the past, there are the bomb craters in the rolling wheatfields around Dover, to remind us that we have a present – and a future, too.

Even Mac, with his boundless appetite for sensation, was sated by the experience of war. He now had far more to stay alive for than ever he did in 1939. He prepared to enjoy his own fruits of victory.

SEVEN

The Odd Couple

It is easy to see why Mac married Anne. She was beautiful, clever, witty, effective, a merciless realist. She professed an enthusiasm for the rural life so dear to his heart. It is harder to perceive what Anne saw in Mac. A droll observer might note that he, like Derek Verschoyle, was the enthusiastic and somewhat reckless owner of a .22 rifle, but that can scarcely have been her sole criterion for picking husbands. For all his gifts and charm, Mac was a fantasist of heroic proportions about the society in which he lived, and about his own place in the scheme of things. His aesthetic interests were much slighter than his wife's. She gained an early insight into his priorities when, soon after they were married, she heard him remark loudly at a party: 'I've got the three things I wanted most – a Churchill gun, a Hardy rod and a beautiful wife.' Anne decided that the relationship lacked depth of feeling on her side, and probably also on Mac's. She wrote: 'I strongly resented being counted as a chattel with a gun and a rod, and retreated more and more into my private thoughts.' Mac's taste for self-delusion extended to marriage. He enjoyed the idea of living with a clever woman, but had no intention of changing his habits to accommodate her, to assist in the fulfilment of her own ambitions and needs.

His admiration for Anne's talents was unbounded. Many times later, he said to me, 'You should know that your mother is the most successful woman journalist in Fleet Street.' Whether or not this was true, Mac believed it to be so. But rather than regarding their marriage as a partnership, he perceived himself as having coupled Anne to the engine of his own life, and thus expected her to follow him up whatever lines and branches he chose to explore. In Anne's old age, I asked her to explain the marriage. After a pause, she said: 'Lots of people married the wrong people in the war. Your father cut quite a glamorous figure in battledress. I realised that I was never going to have the sort of great romantic partnership I'd dreamed of. I thought' – further pause for ironic, indeed acid, reflection – 'your father would be *a good parent to children*.'

Soon after they began living together, she gained a foretaste of social difficulties ahead. By an odd chance, Rosamond Lehmann had bought a cottage in Aldworth next door to Anne's. Its location was originally chosen in order for the novelist to be within driving distance of her then lover, Goronwy Rees. She kept Diamond Cottage for five years, latterly much in residence with Rees's successor in her affections, Cecil Day-Lewis, who was once sighted by the Hastingses picking mushrooms in a heavy city overcoat, and carrying an umbrella. To Anne, Lehmann seemed 'as surreal a vision in our quiet village as a magnolia in a cornfield. Rosamond loved the country as a source of aesthetic experience, and appreciated every wisp of pink cloud made rosy by the sunset and every diamond circle frozen by frost on thaw. But she had lived formerly in manor houses with gardeners and cooks to protect her from the harsher realities of village life, and had no more idea how to sow broad beans or pluck a pheasant than I had of how to write a tragic novel.'

Lehmann's visitors were many and lyrical, mostly poets. Exotically beautiful, she was haloed in curls of blue-rinsed hair – it had gone white in her twenties – framing a serious face with enormous eyes, full lips and perfect skin, of which Anne claimed to be envious. She dressed strikingly, even during the war, in cherry-red trousers with an angora sweater outlining her ripe figure. 'Her voice was soft, her *bon-mots*, not always free from malice, uttered almost in gasps. The difficulty about Rosamond as a neighbour was that she was so exquisitely sensitive that she made everyone else feel plain thick.' Lehmann rubbed along well enough with Anne – she had some liking and respect for Rolfe, her father. But, in Anne's words, 'She quickly dismissed Mac as an oaf.' His lack of tact, as well as of plausible literary credentials, created tensions. He was capable, for instance, of articulating in Rosamond's presence, as he often did amid company at large, his belief that the only entirely convincing male literary character created by a woman was Baroness Orczy's Scarlet Pimpernel.

One morning early in their acquaintance, the two were chatting across the boundary hedge. Rosamond professed to apologise for the sorry state of her garden. Mac readily agreed: 'Yes, it is pretty awful. You'll have to dig it all up and weed it from end to end.' This was not well received. One Sunday, the Hastingses were invited to lunch. The day began unpromisingly when Mac apprehended Rosamond's house guest Laurie Lee picking snowdrops in Rose Cottage's garden, and summarily evicted him. When lunchtime came, the guests were presented with a leg of lamb, an almost unheard-of treat, every rationed morsel precious. After the first time around, Rosamond said pointedly, 'Will anyone have some more of these lovely vegetables?' Mac seized the opportunity to take revenge for Laurie Lee's depredations. 'Yes, please,' he said, 'and I'll have more lamb, too.' He was alleged to be the only man in Aldworth impervious to Rosamond's charms.

The careers of both Hastingses were prospering, however. Mac wrote a column under the pseudonym 'Lemuel Gulliver' for *Lilliput*, a notably intelligent pocket magazine of the time, like *Picture Post* owned by Edward Hulton. Soon after the war ended, another publisher, Newnes, invited him to resuscitate the monthly *Strand Magazine*, once the stage for Sherlock Holmes and now fallen upon hard times. He was offered a handsome salary as editor – £5,000 a year – and quit *Picture Post*. Having entered one of his prosperous periods, he indulged a rush of new Savile Row suits, handmade shoes, firearms and other impedimenta indispensable to the man-about-town-and-country. He then addressed *The Strand* with energy and flair. It was a middlebrow illustrated topical magazine, like *Lilliput* published in pocket format. Mac, always possessed of a good eye, had honed this on *Picture Post*. Besides using photographs well, he employed Edward Ardizzone as lead illustrator, and made the magazine a showcase of the best new-generation artistic talent: Le Broquy, Osbert Lancaster, Ronald Searle, Michael Ayrton, Terence Cuneo.

Most months, *The Strand* carried a detective story by the likes of Georges Simenon, Peter Cheyney or John Dickson Carr. Other contributors included Evelyn and Alec Waugh, Somerset Maugham, Anthony Powell – for instance, choosing his thirty books of the year – Graham Greene and Malcolm Muggeridge. James Laver wrote on the future of men's clothes, Nicholas Davenport under the headline 'Has the Rich Man had it?' John Betjeman not only published poems, but wrote prose pieces which included a profile of Evelyn Waugh. Max Beerbohm contributed drawings and an occasional essay, Robert Graves wrote poems. Mac exploited family connections without embarrassment – he persuaded Anne to write articles, and invited Lewis to perform regularly.

Mr. Quill discourses

One of Edward Ardizzone's Mr Quill drawings for *The Strand*

Mac's own work appeared in most issues. He wrote a series of conversations focused upon Mr Quill, habitué of a London pub saloon bar. These were brilliantly illustrated by Ardizzone at his best. Nothing if not versatile, Mac also composed for *The Strand* a dozen charming short stories for children about a magic London cockney bird named Sydney Sparrow and a little girl named Boo, with drawings by Betty Swanwick. One coup came the magazine's way without editorial inspiration. Among the mass of unsolicited manuscripts that arrived at its offices, the editor's secretary, a clever ex-Wren named Angela Mack, noticed a fat collection of papers in early-nineteenth-century handwriting. They had been submitted by a reader who found them in an attic, and wondered if anyone might be interested. Miss Mack glanced, became absorbed, and realised that she was handling treasure trove. These were letters, hundreds of them, written by a soldier who served in Wellington's army through the Peninsula and Waterloo campaigns. Extracts were published in *The Strand*, and later as a book, *The Letters of Private Wheeler*, which is today recognised as the outstanding British ranker's memoir of the Napoleonic Wars.

Betty Swanwick illustration for 'Mr & Mrs Brock and the Awful Fox Family', one of Mac's children's stories for *The Strand*

Mac relished the opportunity which *The Strand* conferred on him to commission some of the finest talents of the day. From the outset, however, he found himself struggling against the economic tide. All publications have a natural span. Once this approaches its end, life-support systems seldom suffice to reverse a steep decline in circulation. *The Strand*, founded in 1891, had prospered most notably during the first thirty years of the twentieth century. Thereafter it became a loss-maker, and remained so throughout Mac's editorship. The only question was how long Newnes, its owners, would go on paying the bills. Meanwhile, Mac enjoyed the ride.

A characteristic letter from Ted Ardizzone to my father during the *Strand* years.

In April 1945, Anne left *Picture Post* to become editor of *Harper's Bazaar*, on a salary of £1,500 a year. Although she enjoyed the glossy magazine world much less than the newsprint one, she made a considerable success of the job. Thinking poorly of English fashion at that period, when there was anyway little in the shops for women to buy, she sought to broaden the magazine's range of general features, commissioning such new writers as Elizabeth David and John Mortimer, as well as rising stars – John Betjeman, Lesley Blanch, Eric Ambler. One of Betjeman's contributions for her was a poem about Christmas. 'You won't like it, old girl,' he said, 'it's rather religious. It's also rather long. In fact, I don't think it's any good at all. Don't feel obliged to use it. How do I look in the snaps? *Such* a nice photographer. I hope he took me out of focus.' I hear John B's voice now, when I read those characteristic words of self-deprecation, preserved by Anne. By an odd twist of fate, sixty years later I found myself asked to read that very poem, which has become one of Betjeman's most celebrated, at a charity carol service in Newbury.

Anne was the first to put Elizabeth David's work into print. As she told David's biographer long after, 'she struck exactly the right moment. There was freedom again and the expectation of holidays once more, without ghastly restrictions or bombs. She wrote beautifully, right from the start. You could smell the shrimps, hear the fishwives talking on the quay. There was this feeling that she wasn't thinking about how to do it, but was always associating it with places – with mountains, ports, beautiful villages. There was a Proustian quality about it.' David's opening piece, in March 1949, was headed 'Rice Again', and celebrated its return to the shops after a long, long absence. She described a recipe for risotto 'which I took down while watching it being cooked by the *padrona* in a quayside restaurant in Alassio'. This was a characteristic David flourish, wildly exotic in the grey, rationed Britain of those days. Nonetheless, Anne found the great cook among the most difficult contributors she used. She wrote: 'For the evocative prose, the scholar's knowledge, the imagination which turned cookery writing into literature, I would put up with almost anything, and indeed did so for a long period. But Elizabeth could never understand that there comes a moment in the birth of any publication when it simply has to go to press.' Anne found David exasperatingly demanding about length – she seemed to assume that a page could be expanded to fit her words – as well as insouciant about meeting deadlines.

Harper's also used the historian Elizabeth Longford's work, and Anne was delighted by her modesty: 'She always seemed pleased to be asked, whereas many contributors would take on a job as a favour.' In Anne's experience as an editor, the most distinguished writers were the easiest and most professional: once they had agreed a fee and a length, their words appeared without fuss. It was the amateurs, famous names who were not professionals, who made heaviest weather of filling a page.

Like most British editors of American parent publications, Anne learned to dread the descents of grandees from New York. Carmel Snow, *Harper's* notoriously awful editor-in-chief, cabled ahead of one visit that she wished to meet Graham Greene, who Anne knew slightly from pre-war days. Anne duly arranged a three-handed lunch with the novelist at the Dorchester, at which she cringed while Snow made heavy-handed literary advances. Greene responded civilly enough, but Anne was wholly unsurprised when he afterwards rejected all offers of commissions, even with lavish cheques attached.

Mac and Anne enjoyed that period when both were running magazines, making good money, and perceived as one of the glamour couples of their trade. Their relationship experienced an interlude of relative stability, though I doubt whether Mother ever experienced a sensation as commonplace as contentment. I was conceived in March 1945, when the approaching end of the war in Europe made parenthood seem a more promising prospect than it had done in years past. Anne found it difficult to cope with her job and pregnancy, especially when maternity clothes were almost unobtainable. She was always hungry, craving meat in those rationed days. I was born on 28 December. She wrote later: 'Max was an impetuous character even at the foetus stage . . . always in a rush, he arrived two weeks early.' While Anne was still in hospital, late one night at their flat in Chelsea, Mac seized a few sheets of paper, on the back of which he had been scribbling ideas and lists of contributors for the redesigned *Strand*. He wrote a letter to his newborn son, sealed it in an envelope, filed it away, and presented it to me on my twenty-first birthday. Its tone reflected all Father's enthusiasm, delusions of family grandeur, and serene assurance that life – in this case, my life – would conform to his own romantic vision.

Monday Dec 31st 1945, 69 Swan Court

My dear boy, I am writing this letter to you on New Year's Eve while you are exactly three days old. I'm alone in our flat. Your mother in the hospital has been put to sleep early because she's become rather overtired with the effort of feeding you. You yourself are lying in your cot in the babies' nursery, with rows of other people's babies all around you, blowing bubbles and working your arms as if your face was covered with cobwebs.

The nurses in the hospital have christened you 'the elephant' because, when you were born, you weighed 8lb 8oz. The surgeon who delivered you was a man named Peel, one of the fashionable and expensive gynaecologists of the day, and the head man at King's College. You were born within a short walk of the place where I was born myself, and within a stone's throw of the house where your great-grandparents lived and your grandfather – my father – was brought up.

By the time you read this, you'll know all about your forebears (or I hope you will) because you spring from distinguished and brilliant families on both sides. And, privately, you can afford to be proud of it, but don't boast about it to too many people. They won't like it and they'll use it against you. If you're a success in the world, they'll say that with such a background, it was only to be expected. If you're a failure, they'll compare you unfavourably with the Scott-James's and the Mac Hastings's who went before.

Because of your background and because it seems possible that you may inherit the literary bent of your mother, your father, both your mother's parents and your father's father, at this moment we're giving serious consideration to your name, which in the literary world means your fortune. Your grandfather on my side was christened Basil, to his lifelong disgust. But it served him right because he christened me Douglas. It didn't matter much because all the world has called us 'Mac'. And your mother and I are thinking that, if you follow in my footsteps, you'll probably be called Mac by your friends too. Your mother's tired of Mac. So our idea at the moment is to compromise and christen you Max; full name Max Hugh Macdonald Hastings. This nomenclature will allow you to adopt any of the following combinations you fancy:

Max Hastings
Hugh Hastings
Macdonald Hastings

You ought to like one of the three. Hugh was the name of your great grandfather on my side, who was a don in classics at London University and fought in the American Civil War [this was characteristic fantasising on Father's part]. Macdonald was the family name of your paternal great-grandmother, who was one of the authentic Macdonalds of Glencoe [more fantasising] – and who died of bad temper. But you'll hear of most of these things in the normal course of growing-up. What I want to put down for you now is what your mother and I almost certainly will have got out of focus by the time this letter comes into your hands – how we're feeling, what we're thinking now, at the beginning of your life.

As I write, your mother is 32 and I'm 36. Your mother, whom I met in the early part of 1941 when she became the Woman's Editor of a magazine called *Picture Post*, is now running a fashion magazine called *Harper's Bazaar,* and the youngest editor in London. So you can say that you were in the editorial chair while you were still in the womb. Everybody has admired your mother's bravery in brilliantly editing a paper at the same time she was carrying you. You should know that she is also regarded as one of the most beautiful women in London.

In my own career, you've arrived in a betwixt and between time. The war is just over and, after five years as a war correspondent, I've got tired of running around the world (at any rate, for the moment). Just now, I'm working on a dummy issue of an entirely new magazine to be based on the old *Strand*. It ought to be published some time next year. But, by the time you read this, whether it's a success or failure won't matter very much. *The Strand* probably won't exist any more.

Financially, we're well off at the present time; which is lucky for you because, as a result of the war, everything is in short supply and what you can buy costs the earth. Your mother has been off her head to get together a layette for you. And I don't know what would have happened if I hadn't mentioned the problem in a broadcast I do every week to America called 'London Letter'. Just a hint that we were having a baby brought parcels of baby clothes from all over the world. So your first wardrobe comes from America, Canada, Chile, New Zealand, Jamaica. Your first hairbrush came from, I think, the Middle West.

We've got two lovely homes for you to come to when you leave the hospital; the flat in Chelsea, littered with your mother's collection of old china (which I imagine you'll have smashed long before you read this) and the cottage in Berkshire. The cottage – Rose Cottage, Aldworth, near Reading – is your mother's property. It's a lovely place in the heart of the Downs and we both hope that it's going to be the address where you spend your childhood. Already, Rose Cottage has hundreds of happy associations for us and I hope that it'll have a lifetime of happy associations for you. We mean never to part with it. We feel especially possessive about the cottage at the moment, because you've come into the world at one of the strangest and most dangerous hours in human history. Believe me, it's needed some courage to bring you into it at all. But we've argued, your mother and I, that as we're not afraid of the future, you won't be afraid either, so here you are.

Europe, at the end of 1945, is back in the Dark Ages. The development of the atom bomb, the first one of which was dropped on

Hiroshima this year, has introduced a new and haunting fear. As I write, nothing is easier to believe than that Russia and America will be at war in the Far East before you read these words. Britain, as a result of two wars, is bankrupt. In my lifetime, this country from being the richest country in the world has become one of the poorest. Now, we're having to negotiate a loan of a thousand million pounds from America to tide us over the years of recovery. But, inevitably, we're going to have an anxious economy which will extend, I'm afraid, right into your own grown-up life.

Nobody will ever forget this year in which you are born. It has marked the end of the Second World War (I was crossing the Rhine with the allied armies only a few months ago); the coming of atomic energy; the election of the first Labour government with an overall majority (your mother voted Labour against my wishes!); the death of Roosevelt and the passing of Churchill from political power.

For your mother and I, this year has meant an important change in both our own careers and, above all, it's meant the coming of you. It's made us very happy. I'm going to fold this letter now, still wet from my pen, unread by anybody, even your mother – and put it away till you're old enough to value it for what it is. Meanwhile, good luck to you, my boy. And a good life.

Your loving father.

I have often reread that letter over the past forty years, and of course it has given me huge pleasure. In many ways, during the decades which followed, its author was a careless father – careless in that, like so many parents, he enjoyed the idea of having children more than the reality, beyond short spasms. But all of us love records of our own heritage. I soon realised my luck in coming from a family which wrote things down. I have often wondered whether Father would have displayed the sensitivity to withhold that letter from me if, as was more than likely, I had disappointed his passionate hope – resembling that of a racehorse breeder who couples two sprinters in search of a Derby winner – that as the son of two writers I would become a writer myself. As it was, of course, at twenty-one I was indeed scraping a living in Grub Street, and thrilled to the knowledge that I had embarked on a path which Father so much wanted for me.

I was christened in the tiny Norman church a stone's throw from Rose Cottage, surrounded at the font by its wonderful twelfth-century knightly effigies, the 'Aldworth giants'. My baptism into the Church of England signalled my father's absolute break with the Catholicism of his own childhood, and indeed with my family's faith as far back as it is recorded. A cynic would say that for both Mac and Anne the christening was a social rather than a religious occasion, as it is for most of the English middle class. Neither, I think, espoused any spiritual belief with conviction.

A woman friend of mine, long afterwards eyeing the photographs of my mother holding me outside the church porch, observed laconically: 'You can see that she's not very comfortable holding a baby.' As Nancy Mitford wrote of Aunt Sadie in *The Pursuit of Love*, one could sense the presence of Nanny lurking just out of shot, ready to take back the bundle as soon as the photographs were over. Ruth Pallant, Father's old girlfriend who became my godmother, presented me with a handsome set of ivory-backed brushes, a last flourish of generosity before her cash ran out, she bolted from husband Bertie and married a handsome but impecunious brigadier. My other godmother was Eileen Dickson, a journalistic colleague of Anne's who by chance also lived in Aldworth. Eileen later succeeded my mother as editor of *Harper's*, but like most godparents soon faded from our lives.

My parents had already embarked upon a domestic routine which persisted through the years that followed. Weekdays were spent in London, where I became a child of Hyde Park and Kensington Gardens. We soon moved from Swan Court to a larger flat in Rutland Gate, just beside the parks, possessed of the day and night nurseries then deemed indispensable to respectable infanthood. On Friday evenings we crowded into the family Austin for a car-sick two-hour ride to west Berkshire, past the perpetually diving neon-lit lady atop the Jantzen swimwear factory in Hounslow, with a pit stop at a road-house (wonderfully 'thirties word, that) named Sidney Foster's outside Maidenhead. At Aldworth, more or less blissful weekends were spent until the time came to return to London, amid sobbings from me which increased in volume with the passage of years.

I loved the country, and the almost unlimited scope for trouble-making it offered, while finding London life pretty dreary, as indeed it was in those immediate post-war years. The urban landscape seemed dominated by bombsites – a yawning vacancy of rubble and weeds stood immediately beside 41 Rutland Gate. There was little to buy in the shops. In Harrods' toy department I peered covetously at the glass cases containing serried ranks of lead soldiers, each surmounted by a printed notice warning that its contents were 'FOR EXPORT ONLY'. It seemed to me that I had missed all the fun of being around during the war, such as Father, Lewis and Stephen had experienced and reminisced so enthusiastically about, while arriving in time to endure rationing, cold and austerity.

Some aspects of London life in the late 1940s would have been more familiar to an Edwardian child than to a twenty-first-century one. Milk was delivered daily by a horse-drawn float, coal dumped in pavement manholes by grimy heavers attired in the manner of Shaw's Alfred Doolittle, with sacks serving as headgear. A gas-lighter with a long pole patrolled the streets each evening, igniting the lamps by a feat of legerdemain which never ceased to delight me. Uniforms were still ubiquitous, both khaki and full-dress, especially where we lived, in exciting proximity to Knightsbridge Barracks. The wares of the jolly fishmonger opposite Harrods were laid out on a great white open slab, and he himself was adorned in striped apron and straw hat. At Christmas, the Edwardian melodrama *Where the Rainbow Ends*, in which St George saves children enslaved by the evil dragon, played to packed houses including my enraptured self. From an early age I walked through Kensington, and likewise the lanes of west Berkshire, alone and without fear. Child molesters and muggers were unthought of.

The parks' congregation of nannies formed the hub of upper-middle-class social life. Invitations to the round of little tea parties in Montpelier Square, Hans Place and Victoria Road were arranged between respective children's custodians, rather than through parents, on the benches beside Rotten Row, or at Miss Ballantine's famous dancing classes for posh toddlers in the Brompton Road, at which I was an exceptionally undistinguished pupil. Mac and Anne's social circle focused on fellow journalists and the rag trade. It was Nanny who, for a limited season, propelled me up the social ladder into the world of get-togethers at the Hyde Park Hotel with little gold chairs and pass-the-parcel; conjurers and dainty sardine sandwiches; sailing boats on the Round Pond; 'tiddlers' – sticklebacks – brought home in jamjars and preserved until their smelly expiry; relentless tours of the Kensington museums.

Nanny picnicking: a drawing by Hugh Casson, who never knew our Jessie Strafford, but who captures her image to the life

Like almost every child of my time and class, I adored Nanny. She came to us when I was six weeks old and stayed for eighteen years, through good times and bad. Her name was Jessie Strafford, and she was already approaching sixty when she signed on. One of eight children of the timekeeper at a Sheffield steelworks, she was Yorkshire through and through, unfailingly clad in grey overalls and sensible round blue felt hat. A comfortably heavy figure, she possessed what Anne described as 'that flat-footed pram-pusher's stance'. She was 'square of figure and a doughty trencherwoman'. Nanny was much grander than the Hastingses, as she was not beyond reminding us from time to time. One of her brothers was a master cutler, in those days a proud profession. She once presented my father with a carving knife of his making, and thereafter it became unthinkable to attack the joint with anything but 'Nanny's knife'. She had found a vocation looking after children, as strong as any which guided others into the Church. She did not like all children – indeed, was balefully sceptical of most: 'That little Henry Johnson doesn't seem very sharp, does he?'; 'I wonder if young Pamela Croome will grow any bigger, madam?'

'Heavens, Nanny, what a sinister idea. Why ever shouldn't she? She's only eight months old, isn't she?'

'*Nine* months, madam. And hasn't put on an ounce for eleven weeks. I should be *very* worried if I were Lady Croome.'

Nanny's affection and enthusiasm were engaged only by her own charges, to whom she was single-mindedly devoted. There had been very few of these. When she joined a family, she stayed until the children were old enough to enter Sandhurst, 'come out' or take over the estate. She was a true imperialist, who after starting 'in service' as a nurserymaid at the age of fourteen had laboured for years under broiling sun in India and Ceylon with an Indian Army colonel; in Kenya under a governor-general; in Trinidad, the West Indies, Egypt and like outposts of British might with other proconsular dignitaries. Her conversation was studded with timeless nursery clichés: 'Who got out of bed the wrong side this morning? . . . A stitch in time saves nine . . . There's no tea for Mr Crosspatch . . . Has the cat got your tongue? . . . That road only goes to Timbuctoo . . . Eat your toast crusts and make your hair curl . . . Wear clean underwear – you might get run over . . . There's no such word as "can't".' She was a fount of stories about the inadequacies of black servants, tiresome domestic intrusions of zebras, perils of drink, sterling qualities of the Tommy. At bathtime she regaled me with snatches of old music-hall songs, almost invariably imperialistic: 'Goodbye Dolly, I must leave you, though it breaks my heart to go . . .'

When Mac committed some social crime, Nanny would drop a prim remark which emphasised how far down in the world she found herself, amid the Hastings household: 'Sir Edward' – her former employer in Kenya – 'was buried at sea off the *Ajax*.' The unspoken corollary was that Father's remains, far from attaining the glories of submersion from a cruiser of the Royal Navy, would be fortunate to secure disposal from a tramp steamer. Nanny's decades of service in official residences imbued her with a natural authority which won the deference of the park sisterhood. Whatever the deficiencies of the Hastings family's pedigree, housing arrangements and bank accounts, her eminence secured brevet promotion for me, and later my sister, with consequent access to Kensington and Chelsea parties, birthday Punch-and-Judys, sticky cakes and musical chairs. My first girlfriend, met at Miss Ballantine's when I was four, possessed the unsurpassable name of Merelina Ponsonby.

Hugh Casson's vivid representation of the Hyde Park sorority

Rather than of my parents, almost all my memories of early child-hood are of Nanny, who never took days off and seldom holidays. Father's appearances were most readily identified with the presents he brought home from far-flung places: an authentic cowboy outfit from America; model soldiers which he showed me how to array into a British fighting square; toy guns of many shapes and sizes; smelly Bedouin robes from Jordan; the mounted hoof of a bison he had shot in India; a Norwegian model of the balsa raft *Kon-Tiki*, in which Thor Heyerdahl had recently crossed the Pacific, and which Father himself constructed with extraordinary dexterity from a kit of logs and string. For the most part, however, he was more frequently observed going than coming: to shoots and fishing expeditions, assignments abroad, his beloved Savage Club.

How I yearned to accompany him on these trips, and how romantic he made even the most commonplace destinations sound! When he spoke portentously of taking 'the Great West Road' and 'the Bath Road' to Berkshire, the journey seemed vastly more promising than a mere drive down the dreary old A4. He represented the Highlands of Scotland, by no means mistakenly, as an earthly paradise to which good Englishmen were admitted at intervals equipped with rod and gun, as a reward for exceptional merit. From my earliest years he seemed possessed of superhuman powers to make exciting things happen. It was in his gift to provide stars' autographs, fix meetings with comedians, privileged backstage visits to the circus. I did not then grasp that these are the sort of petty perks made available to journalists to compensate for lack of more substantial power and rewards. When once we took the Golden Arrow to Dover, en route for the Côte d'Azur, I threw a shocking scene because my request to travel on the engine footplate was denied. It seemed likewise monstrous that, when we saw Len Hutton lunching at a nearby table in the Oval restaurant during a match, Father admitted that he lacked the acquaintance necessary to introduce me to the great cricketer. I had taken it for granted that if Father chose to command a boon, it would be conferred. At a time when Sir Jimmy Savile was still a Bevin Boy, for me Mac, during his spasmodic lunges into playing the good parent, conducted a perpetual *Jim'll Fix It*.

Once in a while, he took me to watch him broadcast from the BBC's studios in Portland Place. I stood with face pressed against the glass wall of the control room, peering at his elegantly suited figure, addressing the microphone in impeccably modulated tones. Mac attributed his beautiful speaking voice to the Jesuits' training in Rhetoric, for which he had won prizes at Stonyhurst. It is surely true that all schoolchildren should be taught to speak, just as they are taught to write. The gift of self-expression is priceless. Even in casual conversation, and even when he was talking nonsense, Mac's diction commanded as much admiration as his tailoring.

One day in December 1948 Father, with his usual surfeit of optimism, decided that I was ready to make my own broadcasting debut. He arrived at the BBC studio for his weekly turn accompanied by offspring and a visibly disapproving Nanny. The sceptical Australian producer, Peggie Broadhead, was assured that I was fully rehearsed to tell the US audience on cue: 'This is Max Hastings from London town. Happy Christmas.' In the event, alas, in the midst of the live transmission my usual restlessness asserted itself. Bored by Mac's peroration to the American public, I clambered down from my seat and began exploring beneath the studio table. Mac was driven to follow, crawling on all fours with a roving microphone, cajoling me to deliver my line while Nanny and the production staff looked on in mingled hysterics and despair. At last I pronounced: 'Max wants potty.' Father, forever the professional, improvised heroically to persuade his transatlantic audience that this demand was scripted. Thereafter, however, I had to endure a longish wait before again being offered access to the BBC's airwaves.

From my earliest days, I was captivated by Mac's gifts as a raconteur. There were lots of war stories, of course, told with the gusto which he brought to all his memories of 1939–45: how Monty stood by the dusty roadside in Normandy in August 1944, urging his armoured columns, 'On to the kill!'; how cocky captured German officers could be cut down to size by removing their jackboots; how he once ate a dog when rations were short. There were shooting yarns, fishing anecdotes, tales of journeys on the transatlantic *Queens*, of London restaurants and wartime bivouacs. It seemed to me a miracle of social alpinism that he was invited to the annual London Christmas lunch of Bertram Mills's circus. He represented the model I yearned to emulate.

I swallowed some of his prejudices only temporarily, but adopted others for life – for instance, a suspicion of beards and bow ties, a loathing for cats and football, which he declared to be played by brutes for the amusement of other brutes. He told me that team activities were mere games, while anything worthy to be dignified as sport must involve individual exertion – shooting, fishing, riding and suchlike. The unworthy thought did not then dawn on me that the Hastings distaste for ball games is rooted in our gross incompetence at them.

Father's life seemed the pattern of what I wanted for myself, so that as soon as I started to buy my own clothes, I dressed in imitation of him. When I was old enough to choose my own holidays, I hastened to destinations which he loved, mostly Scottish. When I wanted to test myself against physical danger, which he persuaded me that every right-thinking Englishman should do, I addressed the same perils he had confronted, regretting only that the Germans were unavailable (temporarily, anyway) to play their usual forty-five minutes each way on the other side.

In only one respect did his personal record disappoint me. From an early age, I was an eager and somewhat credulous reader of P.G. Wodehouse, whose works formed my image of how young English gentlemen comported themselves. One day I asked Father how many times he had spent the night in chokey after, say, stealing a policeman's helmet or being discovered dancing in the fountains of Trafalgar Square. He assured me with some asperity that he had never served even an hour behind prison bars. This was a blow to my image of him as a man-about-town, a role which in all other respects he seemed to fill with assurance.

I was equally awed by my mother, but in a different way. For a start, she was dauntingly tall, near enough six feet. Though she liked to perceive herself as a shy, fawnlike slip of a girl, in truth she possessed the habit of command, and an absolute intolerance of fools. She seemed a pattern of glamour and fluency, never less than flawlessly turned out, seldom at a loss for the *mot juste*, not infrequently acidulous. I often attended Mother's bedside early in the morning, where she sat surrounded by newspapers – we took them all, of course –

telephone and breakfast tray prepared by our faithful London daily, Mrs Elmer. There was the ritual of telephoning Harrods, to provide a list of groceries for delivery. In those, its elegant pre-Fayed days, I grew up supposing that it was natural to purchase all commodities, from stamps to underclothes, writing paper to toys, at the great Knightsbridge emporium. We met in its banking hall, my hair was cut in its barber's shop, tea was taken in its restaurant, school uniforms were ordered from its menswear department. The delusion that Harrods was the only possible place for a properly conducted London household to do its shopping later precipitated my first financial crisis, when I attempted to adopt the practice at my own expense.

Even in my childhood, Anne not infrequently gave vent to a disobliging remark or two about Mac before setting off for work. Brisk, concise instructions were given to Nanny and Mrs Elmer, a peck on the cheek was administered to me, then she swept out in a haze of scent and high purpose. Although my ideas were sketchy about how she spent her working hours, I gained occasional insights by being conscripted as an extra for fashion shoots. In those days, as never thereafter, my appearance was thought appealing. Decked in tweed cap and coat or more casual attire, I was photographed beside breathtakingly arrayed, formidably painted models in Bond Street, Markham Square, Pall Mall, or attending a supposed family picnic – enlivened with a primitive barbecue – in Richmond Park, which did duty as a rustic location. There was no money and not much glory in these assignments, in the days when models earned two guineas for a shoot, maybe three if they were stars. But in me they assuaged a craving for attention which already dismayed my critics. Early experience established my conviction that everything interesting and agreeable in London happened within two miles of St James's Square. The rest of the great metropolis was tiger country.

Ours was the last generation to learn to eat with a silver spoon and pusher before graduating to adult dining equipment. 'Nursery food' has become a modern term of contempt, but oh my, as Mole would have said, it was delicious. Nanny's expertise at gratifying small palates, not to mention her own, had been refined over half a century on three continents. A modern nutritionist would recoil in horror from the fattening treats which she put before us. Anne complained that she was obliged to resort to serious black-marketeering to keep Nanny supplied with rationed tea. Even in the worst days of post-war austerity, I remember every nursery meal with delight. Sardine and cress sandwiches, Shippam's meat paste, bread and butter with hundreds-and-thousands, meringues, treacle sponges, Swiss rolls – we gorged on them all. On red-letter days, we had chocolate cake from Fuller's. When I devoured an entire example in a couple of sittings, Mummy expostulated crossly that it cost six shillings and ninepence. To this day, I think of Fuller's cakes as the supreme delicacies of childhood, and mourn their passing.

Mummy's return from the office was the signal for me to bound into the drawing room for a few minutes' exchange of pleasantries, and sometimes a game. However modest the flats which we inhabited in London, and even though Mac and Anne had no 'good' furniture, thanks to her taste the main rooms were invariably elegant. Their tone was raised by some fine old china inherited from Violet Scott-James, and a few striking pictures: an Augustus John watercolour; a magnificent Ardizzone originally painted to illustrate Mac's Mr Quill stories for *The Strand*; the odd Rowlandson drawing. The drawing room and its contents mercifully escaped my childish depredations, which were confined to the nursery end of the premises.

Anne later commented balefully upon 'that awful final round of Ludo before bed, varied occasionally with Snakes and Ladders'. My remorseless demands for the same game day after day reminded her, she said, of the fate of Tony Last in Evelyn Waugh's *A Handful of Dust*, condemned in perpetuity to read Dickens to the maniac Mr Todd. Television did not enter our lives until a set was bought in 1953, at the same moment half the country did the same, in order to watch the Coronation. Until that date, and the pleasures of *Muffin the Mule* and *Whirligig* which followed, my cultural horizons were bordered by radio, comics and books, to which I was addicted from the moment I could read. Perhaps the only periods of childhood in which I could be thought profitably employed were those during which I was engrossed in *The Sword in the Stone*, *Children of the New Forest* and a relentless procession of adventure stories, many by G.A. Henty and H. Rider Haggard. I became intimately familiar with Athos, Porthos and Aramis, while remaining complacently ignorant of the names of any footballers. I developed a passionate allegiance to *The Wind in the Willows*, and an equally violent hostility towards deluded little souls who preferred *Winnie the Pooh*. Ugh!

Having sought to describe my mother, it is only just to acknowledge her perception of me. She wrote:

I have always been slightly afraid of Max, whose audacious nature overpowers my cautious one, and afraid *for* Max . . . He was not the usual wrinkly baby, but a completely finished product with a purposeful expression. He looked quite at home in the world, firmly demanding what he wanted. At eighteen months, sitting up in his high chair at a seaside hotel, an admiring elderly lady said to me, 'He does enjoy his food, doesn't he?' There was no chucking his egg around or leaving his food unfinished. At two he spoke so fluently that he could have made a political speech. At five, when we took him for an interview at his pre-prep school, the headmaster's wife said, without admiration: 'I have never seen such a self-possessed child.' I am sorry to say that when our party left the study for the schoolroom, he had pushed her aside and gone through the door first.

It was a black day when my education began. I attended Wagner's in Queen's Gate, one of those smart London day schools which did so much to mould little imperialists – yes, even at that late stage – and taught us a little. Schools and I never prospered together, though Wagner's was less beastly than those which came afterwards. I began to discover how bad I was at making friends, to learn that self-absorption is no more plausible a formula for social success at five than at twenty or thirty. The only relationship I remember well from that period was with Merlin Holland, Oscar Wilde's grandson, whose father Vyvyan knew my parents. For the most part, I was an outsider. I lacked any self-corrective mechanism. I adored Nanny because she spoilt me rotten. My will was much stronger than hers. Discipline was entirely lacking from my rompers regime, never mind afterwards. It required years of marriage for me to learn some basic manners which I should have acquired in the nursery, had I been a more receptive pupil, and Nanny less malleable to my demands.

With a modicum of cunning, I easily circumvented her attempts to impose rules. Since my parents were seldom in evidence, I acquired the early habit of doing exactly what I liked, and found it hard to vary this practice merely to appease teachers in the classrooms of 90 Queen's Gate. Mr Lefroy, the headmaster of Wagner's, observed at a prize-giving (though I never myself won a prize at any school): 'Max Hastings resembles a Chinese firecracker, which we expect to explode at any moment.' While this sally raised a laugh, it was not intended as a compliment.

In my irritation at Mummy's absences, I lacked any perception of the difficulties every woman then faced if she attempted to combine marriage and motherhood with a career. The more significant her professional role, the greater were the dilemmas which she encountered. '[Anne Scott-James's] editorship of *Harper's*,' in the words of one of Elizabeth David's biographers, 'established her as part of that brisk, well-educated, increasingly powerful, yet still rather embattled breed of women journalist-editors.' Her generation were pioneers, and suffered fearfully in consequence. As she left in the morning, I pleaded, 'Mummy, *try* and get back for tea,' adding resignedly: 'But I know you'll be late. Shall I see you in my bath? Anyway, mind you're home before I go to sleep.' Nanny said: 'Now, do be early, today, madam. We'll keep you a meringue till half-past five, and not a minute after.' But half-past five found madam with a queue of people still waiting outside the editor's door, and letters to sign. Anne recorded later the spasm of regret which she experienced as she thought: 'Bang goes my meringue,' and everything it stood for. She described a typical schedule on days when she accompanied us to do clothes shopping:

2.00 Buy Chilprufe vests and Shetland cardigan at Hayfords.

2.45 Winter coat and leggings, Debenham & Freebody

3.30 Business appointment in Grosvenor Street. Nanny and Max wait in car reading *Peter Rabbit*.

4.00 Socks, shoes and blouses at Harrods. Nanny pays while I
hurry to telephone couturier who is only in between 4 and
4.30, when he leaves for America.

4.30 We divide forces. I take a taxi back to the office, and send
Nanny and Max home in the car.

Likewise on birthday party days, her notebook was scribbled with
memos to herself about a confusion of matters professional and
domestic: 'Speak printers re May colour pages. Write April lead. Plan
2-colour section for June. Order birthday cake at Green Lizard.
Twenty-one presents, 12 boys, 9 girls. See Judy about photographing
Oliviers for New York. Candles, balloons, records, Nuts in May and
Mulberry Bush. Fix advertising meeting. Separate table for nannies?'
When party day came, there was always a phone call from her secretary in the midst of 'Happy Birthday':

'I won't keep you five seconds, Miss Scott-James. There's a cable
in saying will you be in Paris the first collection week or the second?
What shall I say?'

'Better say the second week.'

'Bye.'

At summer holiday time, Mummy usually drove us down to Devon,
Cornwall or whatever other little paradise had been booked. She
stayed through the first couple of days, then raced back to the office,
leaving me on the sands with Nanny, her thermos flask and sewing,
and later my sister Clare. Anne wrote:

I found those lazy days by the sea piercingly sad. Perhaps because the
English summer is so short, there is always a dreadful nostalgia about
a summer's day, marguerites and poppies in a dusty field, or white cliffs
throwing long evening shadows. In your mind, your child's mind becomes
all mixed up with your own, and the pathos of innocence become an
agony which keeps the tears welling in your eyes.

I used to sit half-choking on the beach as I watched that touching
back view: little Max in blue mackintosh waders hand in hand with
stalwart Nanny, both paddling inch-deep in the tiny breakers of low

tide, Max clutching a hopeful bucket in his free hand, Nanny holding up her skirts above her varicose legs.

'Oh God, make it last, make it last for ever,' you mumble mournfully. But hell and damnation, you are driving up to London late tonight and coming back for just one day to fetch them. It is not the mild regret of leaving any ordinary pleasant occasion; it is the splitting of the heart, the butchery of one's own youth.

'Mummy, mummy, watch me cut a crab in half,' calls Max from the water's edge. He, at least, was not troubled by sentiment.

Yet by Anne's own admission, her emotions were confused about how long her patience could have endured the simple pleasures of sandcastles and West Country teashops. She nibbled without enthusiasm at pink and green dainties, topped with synthetic cream.

'Could you eat my share of cake, Nanny? I don't really feel like it.'

'Well, I'll be greedy, madam, and have just the tiniest bit. *Bite* it, Max, *bite* it. What do you think your teeth are for?'

'I'll order some more toast, Nanny. I'm sure you're hungry after all that sea air.'

'Well, it *is* nice toast, isn't it? Perhaps just one more slice. Give over pawing that cake, Max. Either take it or leave it, but don't just pick the nuts off the top.'

Anne sobbed through the first few minutes of her lonely drive home, but found that as the miles went by, her mind began once more to turn to, and then to race about, her beloved magazine. She was planning a new feature as she reached Hammersmith, 'tossing it about in my mind as in a butter-churn'. She thought: 'I must phone Frances tonight and get her to chew it over, and we'll get started on it tomorrow.' By midday next day she was again absorbed in her work. Like most clever women, the tiny world of the nursery could never have satisfied her. Even as a child, I sensed her impatience with it.

Today, this is all familiar stuff. The world has changed dramatically to meet women's needs and aspirations. But in Anne's day there was no accommodation, no pity for a woman who chose to try to do it all. She felt overwhelming social pressure to look like a 'proper' mummy as well as a committed magazine editor, and went through the motions with dogged, desperate deliberation. She never filled the domestic role with conviction, and I came to despise her efforts as mere masquerade. She tried to behave as mummies were supposed to behave, but the outcome resembled an amateur dramatic performance.

All these years later, I see that my scorn was unmerited, and I sympathise with her dilemmas. She deserved professional fulfilment. There is also the small matter that without her income my upbringing would have been incomparably less comfortable. Father's means could not alone have sustained the lifestyle we enjoyed, the social pretensions to which I grew accustomed. But it was hard to see those things half a century ago, when Mummy's impatience with 'Happy Families' was manifest, her sophistication sorely tried by bedtime stories. She inspired respect and fear, but uncertain affection. None of us in our family were great kissers. I scarcely remember physically embracing either of my parents, far less seeing them indulge such a gesture towards each other. In part, this reflected the scepticism of the times – the English times, anyway – towards exhibitions of emotion. But the Hastingses carried undemonstrativeness farther than most.

Anne's outbursts of anger were alarming, often provoked by displays of incompetence, especially those perpetrated by Mac, of which allowing the car to run out of petrol was the most commonplace. She seldom smacked me – public opinion thought her forbearance mistaken – and Father never did. Neither used any swearword stronger than 'bloody' or 'damn'. But I trembled before her wrath. I can still conjure vividly the image of a night when she burst into my room in a rage and transparent negligee, to catch me reading by torchlight under the bedclothes. Until the day of her death, she perceived herself as a mild, gentle, much-put-upon little creature of the forest. I, by contrast, saw her as possessing many of the characteristics of a Sherman tank. In the school holidays, knowing how much I preferred Berkshire to London, she early adopted the practice of depositing me at the cottage for weeks on end with Nanny, and later with my sister Clare. I danced a ritual jig as she disappeared down the path en route to the city and the office. I knew that the way was thus cleared for a blissful interlude, doing exactly what I chose.

EIGHT

Success Stories

The Strand Magazine closed in 1950. Father received a pay-off from the publishers of a year's salary, £5,000, which caused him to feel prosperous. At forty, he embarked on a career as a freelance writer and journalist that made the ensuing decade by far the most successful of his life. He contributed hundreds of articles to a range of newspapers, continued to broadcast, edited a magazine – and published ten books. In 1950 he wrote the first of a series of detective thrillers about Montague Cork, an insurance company boss who was modelled on a friend and country neighbour named Claude Wilson. The five 'Mr Cork' stories which appeared in the next fifteen years sold well, even if they did not attain best-sellerdom. The first, *Cork on the Water*, set the tone. Mr Cork, a Bentley-driving, stiff-collared, late-middle-aged pillar of the City of London, investigates a dubious insurance claim following the discovery of a body in a Scottish salmon river. His inquiries take him behind the scenes at the ballet (like most of his generation Father was in love with Moira Shearer, whom he knew slightly), then into the Highlands.

The cast of characters was liberally endowed with ex-commandos and Nazi veterans, the plot with deadly duels on the heather-clad hills using stalking rifles. Mr Cork caps his triumphant resolution of the case by catching a giant salmon. More than one reviewer compared Father's fiction debut to John Buchan's thrillers. Almost two decades later, the book was filmed – embarrassingly badly – for BBC TV. Father wrote of a world of officers and gentlemen, sportsmen and deferential servants, which was already almost defunct. Yet he loved this milieu, and threw into the Cork books the absolute belief in his own plot-lines and characters that is indispensable to success as a creator of fiction. The next tale, *Cork in Bottle*, focused upon a mysterious shooting on a remote Norfolk estate, where incest was the principal hobby and the squire still exercised dominant power in a community without indoor sanitation or much taste for strangers.

Cork in the Doghouse was written around the world of illegal dogfighting, 'the fancy', and a Staffordshire bull terrier named Honey. *Cork and the Serpent* was the least convincing of the series. It dealt with the racing world, which Father knew much less well than he supposed, and portrayed aristocrats, about whom his ideas were formed by West End stage caricature rather than personal intimacy. Nancy Mitford once said that she could not imagine how Trollope wrote so convincingly about dukes, when he did not know any. She would have withheld that accolade from Mac's portraits of rural grandees. Nonetheless, Mr Cork was a delightfully original fictional creation. I love the books for the echoes they provide of their begetter. I hear Mac speak through every page, and cherish his evocation of the countryside in the post-war period.

The Highland fishing drama in *Cork on the Water*, for instance, is beautifully done:

> When the great salmon took his fly on July 4th, 1949, Colonel Johnson, perched on his matchstick legs on the edge of a granite rock, was nearly tilted into the river. Another man would have been broken in the fish's first rush. A lesser angler, under the driving pressure on the tackle, would have lost control immediately in the snag-strewn broken water. Even Colonel Johnson, unprepared for the fish's cannonball strike, nearly botched it. For a breathtaking moment, in the salmon's first upstream rush, his rod point was dipping in the river . . .

Likewise, Mac's picture of romantic but wretched old East Anglia for *Cork in Bottle* remains a delight. When he wrote of such things, of places he knew and thrills he had experienced for himself, few writers did it better. The Cork books sold modestly well in America, and were widely translated in Europe, for audiences who embraced their quintessential Englishness.

Mac's second string, indeed one of his principal activities for most of the decade, was equally charming, yet was commercially disastrous for the family. His spell at *The Strand* had whetted his appetite for editorship. He yearned for a platform from which to proclaim his passion for rural Britain. In 1951, with financial support from optimistic friends, he launched a monthly magazine entitled *Country Fair*. He acquired offices in Lowndes Street behind Knightsbridge, a Land Rover adorned with the magazine's logo, and persuaded Angela Mack to follow him from *The Strand* as his secretary. He enlisted some splendid names as contributors: 'B.B.' on shooting, Roy Beddington on fishing, Constance Spry on gardening, James Robertson Justice on falconry, A.G. Street on farming. Arthur Street, a robust Wiltshire farmer whose country writings were already famous, was credited as co-editor, to give credibility to the new creation among genuine rustics.

The magazine looked enchanting. Its covers were adorned with animal caricatures drawn by Hanna. Its photographs reflected the eye for an image which Father had developed on *Picture Post*, and honed at *The Strand*. He wrote all the captions himself, and wonderfully wry and witty they were. Each month the magazine carried a long essay on a chosen English county, written by one of its most prominent literary residents – H.E. Bates on Kent, Anthony Armstrong on Sussex, John Betjeman on Berkshire and suchlike. Over the seven years of Mac's stewardship, *Country Fair* created a portrait of a vanishing rural England, its ways and personalities. It provided a showcase for his prejudices, whimsies and enthusiasms.

Yet, like most such self-indulgent ventures, it never made money. By 1954 it had accumulated a loss of £17,000, which increased annually thereafter. Having pushed his own overdraft to the limit to fund the magazine, and exhausted Arthur Street's cautious willingness to invest, Mac dunned friends for support in a fashion that embarrassed and irked Anne. 'You know perfectly well that Connie Spry doesn't have much money. How can you take £500 off her?' she rebuked him bitterly.

In some respects Mac was the least ruthless of men, but his passion to keep *Country Fair* afloat swept aside his scruples. He solicited cheques for the magazine wherever he could get them, always believing that one more heave at sales and advertising would secure his creation's future. He loved the magazine like a baby – more, indeed, than any baby in our family – as a blissful expression of his own personality. It was a bitter blow when at last in 1957 the magazine had to be sold for a song.

Anne referred for years afterwards to 'that awful *Country Fair*', a drain on the family finances. For the first few issues she herself contributed a jolly column under the heading 'The Weekender'. But when she perceived the magazine's commercial failure, she turned away to get on with making her own living. Many things progressively poisoned her marriage to Mac, but *Country Fair* was prominent among them. Anne, a tough realist, felt increasing disgust that Father's self-indulgence threatened to ruin the family, as well as to squander his own talents for no reward. Mac's travails as a magazine publisher exercised a powerful influence on my own career. They convinced me that God is with the big battalions. Almost every journalist, and indeed editor, is best advised to attach himself to the payroll of the richest possible press lord, rather than strike out bravely on his own. Few writers have commercial gifts capable of carrying them beyond the manufacture of expense claims.

Mac, always prolific, contributed regularly to other people's magazines such as *Woman* and *John Bull*. His greatest success of the early 1950s, however, was the most surprising. One day he was summoned to a meeting at the Savoy with the Reverend Marcus Morris. Morris was an implausible parson, who fathered four children by his beautiful wife, an actress, while pursuing one of the more energetic and exotic love lives in contemporary London. He also possessed remarkable gifts of salesmanship, which enabled him to persuade the publisher of *Picture Post*, Sir Edward Hulton, that he could create an entirely new kind of children's publication, which preached virtue and godliness alongside top-quality strip cartoon stories and journalism. He would bring class to comics. Part of the vision of Morris, a near-genius in his brief season, was that his weekly paper should include real-life adventure reporting. Teddy Hulton, who had formed an admiration for Mac's courage as well as his reporting abilities during their *Picture Post* years together, suggested his name to Morris. At *The Strand*, Mac had penned the Sydney Sparrow stories for children. He had the gift of addressing a young audience without condescension, indeed with confiding frankness, together with a breathless delight in novelty that transmitted itself to his readers. Sydney Sparrow had been part of my infancy. Now, Father's exploits for the new Hulton 'comic' began to loom large in my boyhood.

When Marcus Morris's boys' paper *Eagle* burst upon the news stands in 1951, from its first issue Mac was a star contributor, with the title of '*Eagle* Special Investigator'. While the front page was dominated by the doings of Dan Dare, a fantasy cartoon spaceman, inside Mac described each week a real-life venture into some job or experience likely to capture the imagination of children. Through the early years of *Eagle*'s stunning success, he recounted how he learned to scuba dive, became a 'living firework', joined the fire brigade, traversed Arctic wastes with the Canadian Mounties, explored London's sewers, caught a salmon, trained with the Household Cavalry, submerged in a submarine, drove a coach and six, rode with the great jockey Gordon Richards, survived St Moritz's Cresta Run, tried to be a cowboy in Calgary, helmed a motor torpedo boat, drove a racing car under Stirling Moss's tuition, rode a camel with the Arab Legion and many other sensations besides.

His feature prospered mightily, making him a hero to a generation of schoolboys, and of course to me. His collected articles sold well as books – *Eagle Special Investigator* and *Adventure Calling*. Marcus Morris's paper for some years maintained a huge circulation, and spawned a brood of sister publications catering to different target groups of children – *Girl*, *Swift* and *Robin*. Collectively, they represented an extraordinary achievement by Teddy Hulton. It was a tragedy that their packages of history, potted biography, adventure and skilfully presented morality tales for children, brilliantly edited, written and illustrated, survived only until the knowing, cynical, and in most respects deeply nasty 'sixties.

Many journalists would have been mortally embarrassed to perform pantomime stunts for the amusement of children. Never so Mac. In print as in life, his brand of innocence rendered him impervious to blushes. His success in the role was rooted in the fact that his readers could perceive that he loved every moment of being paid to fulfil his own fantasies. He was taught to fly a Tiger Moth biplane by Joan Hughes, an instructor who had been one of the wartime stars of the Women's Air Transport Auxiliary, and who said 'Jolly good show' when they met. On their first flight together, at 2,000 feet Joan said: 'OK – you've got her.' Mac wrote: 'Suddenly, the thing which, in Joan's hands, had behaved like a tame swallow, began to bucket in the air. The wings swayed drunkenly, the nose reared up and down and the needles on the bank and turn indicator swung about in agonised protest. I wobbled the stick, I fiddled about with the trimmer and, finally, I put my foot hard down on the rudder, in the hope that it might work like a brake.' He eventually mastered the plane, of course, and after eighteen hours' dual instruction at White Waltham airfield near Maidenhead, graduated to flying solo, dressed in the approved manner of Biggles, with leather helmet and sheepskin flying jacket.

As a circus knife-thrower's target, 'Stripped to the waist I stood against the board in the darkness, feeling exactly like any paleface in a Redskin encampment. Hal swung the flaming hatchets in the air and performed a sort of war dance. I pressed my bare back against the splintered board and held my hands locked together in front of me as tightly as if I were bound at the wrists. I shall never forget the swish of those hatchets. They flew towards me, spinning through the air in flaming arcs, and the blades bit into the wood with force enough to fell a tree.' On the Cresta Run a few weeks later, 'I was hanging on for dear life and we were swinging round a bank of ice like a wall of death. I completely forgot to change the position of my hands as I'd been told to. I just dug in my rakes and held on for dear life as the toboggan made another knife-edged turn underneath me. I was out of Battledore and sizzling up the steep banking of Shuttlecock, on the second leg of an S-turn.'

His grinning features became famous to a generation of schoolboys,

142

peering from a tank turret, the cab of a Canadian Pacific locomotive, the cockpit of a racing car, the back of a camel and the 'box' of a husky-drawn dogsled in the Arctic. He was the forerunner of a legion of modern television hosts who perform stunts in the same fashion, though I doubt whether any gains as much pleasure from his experiences as Mac did. *Eagle* also paid well: in 1952 he was making almost £5,000 a year from Hulton – a retainer of £2,000, plus fifty guineas an article.

As a child, my awe of Father was rooted in his fame as *Eagle* Special Investigator. Schoolmates teased me mercilessly about the chasm between my own physical clumsiness, most notable on the games field, and Mac's weekly masquerade as Superman. I read his accounts of derring-do with painful consciousness of my own inability to match them. This helps to explain why, after leaving school, I lavished so much of my energy on overcoming terror, and myself learned to parachute, ride the Cresta Run, steeplejack and otherwise make terms with the demons conjured by Father's doings.

The combination of *Eagle*, *Country Fair*, Mr Cork, regular broadcasting and occasional contributions to newspapers made Mac a widely recognised figure in the early 1950s. Though his heart was in the countryside, he also enjoyed the world of London clubs and restaurants. He lived upon a principle that was the antithesis of Groucho Marx's. Any club that would admit Mac became, in his eyes, the cynosure of exclusivity and excellence. He shared Basil's enthusiasm for the Savage, then in Carlton House Terrace, with its matey and – from a less roseate perspective than his own – somewhat *passé* congregation of writers, artists, actors and publishers. He also patronised the Beefsteak, in its weird Gothic timbered hall at the foot of Leicester Square. He was a faithful attendee at the twice-yearly dinners of the Saintsbury, a mixture of writers and wine buffs who sampled prodigious quantities of great vintages at the Vintners' Hall. When he worked in an office off Knightsbridge, for a few years he patronised the nearby Royal Thames Yacht Club, an odd choice for a Hastings, since we are a landlubbing tribe.

Most favoured of all by Mac was the Thursday Club, whose

thirty-odd members met each week in a private room on the top floor of his favourite London restaurant, Wheeler's in Old Compton Street. Its principal luminaries were actors Peter Ustinov and James Robertson Justice, *Daily Express* editor Arthur Christiansen, Larry Adler, Baron the fashionable photographer, the Marquess of Milford Haven and, not infrequently, Prince Philip. Lurid gossip-column speculation surrounded the Thursday Club's gatherings, because of its royal connection. In truth, I fancy that its chief extravagance was drunkenness on a scale that would have impressed Evelyn Waugh. The company seldom broke up before four or five, and provided Father for days afterwards with exotic anecdotage, on which I was an avid eavesdropper. The club was subsidised by Bernard Walsh, Wheeler's genial proprietor, who presided annually over a gala spring meeting at Colchester, to greet the arrival of the new season's oysters. It eventually collapsed in the 1970s, by which time its most prominent members had either resigned – like Prince Philip – or died. Even the open-handed Bernard became weary of tolerating the unpaid bills of the surviving hangers-on. I was entered for membership at birth, but attended only a couple of meetings as a teenage guest.

Mac forged a self-image as the gentleman journalist, in the maintenance of which no vulgar monetary consideration was permitted to interfere. His suits came in profusion from John Walls of Savile Row. There were shoes and boots from Codners to fit every venue from the ballroom to the hunting field, though he hated dancing and rode to hounds only a dozen times in his life. There were lots of guns, about which more later, together with fitted cartridge magazines and bags, shooting brogues, silver sandwich-cases, saddlery, leather luggage, swordsticks. A passing introduction to some activity investigated on behalf of *Eagle* often induced Mac to equip himself as a practitioner in a fashion that would have impressed Mr Toad. Jammed into cupboards in London and Berkshire were archers' bows and arrows, falconers' hoods and gauntlets, ferreters' nets and lines, lassos and cowboy chaps, driving whips and top hats. Most of these accessories were used or worn but once, until I got my sticky and unauthorised little fingers on them.

Mac seldom received invitations to shoot or fish for free, because he numbered few landed grandees among his acquaintance. But he paid for his share of an occasional grouse day or salmon week, and dined out off the memories for months afterwards. Indeed, he talked so much about his sporting experiences that for years I cherished a delusion that he filled his diary with weekends at great houses and on famous rivers. In a school essay on 'The Ideal Parent', I wrote at ten: 'Nearly all parents enjoy sport and often take their lunch and go shooting on the Downs or fish if they can. Some are not lucky enough to be able to do this, as they live in town and can seldom get a day off in the country. Some cannot afford train journeys and if they have not got a car have to stay in London.' Only much later did I understand that the reality of Father's sporting life was much more modest than I had supposed, and contributed grievously to his overdraft.

In 1953, when I first departed sobbing towards boarding school – in my case, a football-fixated punishment camp near Newbury named Horris Hill – Father initiated a custom which he maintained through the years which followed. On the first day of term, before we left for the station he took me to lunch, occasionally accompanied by my mother, at one of his favourite London restaurants. We started with the Caprice, then as now in Arlington Street, but incomparably plusher in its 'fifties guise. Father introduced me, aged eight, to the head waiter, solemnly assuring me that Mario would become one of the most important people in my life. He pointed out David Niven, Noël Coward and other stars at neighbouring tables. None of this spoiling treatment prevented me from bursting into tears when confronted by a sorbet in place of the ice cream I had ordered. I recognised an attempt to bribe me into acquiescence about boarding the grimy school puffer at Paddington, and was not to be suborned out of richly justified sulks.

On subsequent last days before incarceration, we ate fish at Wheeler's; beef from the trolley at Simpson's in the Strand; smoked salmon at the Savoy; lamb at the Ivy, where Father pointed out all manner of writers and publishers whose names meant nothing to me. The gastronomic round had two consequences. First, in conjunction with the rest of Father's programme of conspicuous consumption, it convinced me that we must be pretty rich, a delusion which went uncorrected until I was sixteen or seventeen. Second, and more usefully, it supplied motivation. I became imbued with determination that as an adult I would enjoy the same standard of living, whatever drastic measures were needed to achieve it.

When Father, in conversation, wove a pattern of dreams for my future, such an outcome was taken for granted. He talked with unflinching assurance about 'when you play your first salmon . . . when you find yourself standing in a grouse butt in a gale . . . when you join the Beefsteak . . . when you're taking an open ditch in Leicestershire'. He cautioned me about the etiquette of never signing my name in any book which I might give as a gift, until I could do so as its author. He introduced me to tailors, bootmakers and head waiters as a future customer, to editors and publishers as a prospective contributor. He provided in ample measure what every child seeks most passionately from a parent – complete belief. My mother by contrast, incomparably more realistic, made plain her fear that I was born to be hanged. From an early age she treated me in the same fashion as did my schoolmasters: as a habitual criminal rashly granted probation, but certain soon to reoffend. The evidence was on her side. She loved me sure enough, but in her determination not to succumb to foolish delusions, she expected the worst and usually got it. Father, however, even without benefit of a couple of drinks, and more vigorously thereafter, prophesied: 'You'll end up as Sir Max Hastings, editing a national newspaper and writing better books than I've done.' The tears come even now, at the memory.

In 1951 Anne resigned the editorship of *Harper's*, partly to have another baby – my sister Clare, born later that year – and partly to write *In the Mink*, a professed novel, in truth a memoir, about her experience of the fashion business. There is a chapter in it entitled 'Nanny', which represented one of Anne's wittiest and most observant feats of portraiture. Unfortunately, however, it depicted Miss Strafford with withering condescension: 'Her mind was a pinhead, her world the smallest imaginable. But she was complete master of it, placid, appreciated, content.' Anne never contemplated the impact her words would have on the park sorority, who read and debated them avidly. 'Nanny Johnson says I ought to sue Mrs Hastings,' Nanny Hastings – nannies always referred to each other by the names of their employers, not their own – told me in high dudgeon, pursing her finely moustached lips. I do not think she ever thereafter liked my mother. But she had become too deeply rooted in our household, and perhaps also felt herself too old, conveniently to decamp. She swallowed her employer's casual dollop of contempt.

In the Mink was well received. A year or two later Sandy Wilson, then at the height of his fame as author of the West End hit *The Boy Friend*, tried to turn the book into a stage musical, though it was never performed. Anne found herself increasingly in demand as a newspaper contributor. Early in 1953 the *Sunday Express* asked her at short notice to write an article on Queen Mary, who had just died. Harold Keeble, the paper's editor, liked it so much that he invited her to become a regular columnist. Each week thereafter, she filled 'the Anne Scott-James Page', which was about anything she chose – fashion, politics, topical controversy. At the outset she was not lavishly paid – £3,000 a year – but this was doubled after eighteen months, when she began receiving generous offers from rivals. 'I cannot overstress the pleasure of being a star writer on a successful newspaper,' she wrote. 'The Beaverbrook Press in those days when Lord Beaverbrook himself was still alive and a hyperactive proprietor, had a mystique which impressed all journalists except those who could not stomach Beaverbrook's mischievous – but to my mind harmless, because lunatic – politics.'

She came to love Harold Keeble, one of her best mentors: brilliant, creative, witty, mendacious, treacherous. Dispatching her to, say, Rome, he would announce reassuringly that he had briefed the paper's local correspondent: 'I've told Tom to give you all his time in Rome and to meet you with a car and cash.' More likely, she well knew, Keeble had told 'Tom': 'Don't let Anne bother you when she comes out.' After some shameless piece of back-stabbing, she said to

Anne Edwards, her opposite number at the *Daily Express*: 'If I saw Harold drowning in a pond and I had a pole, I wouldn't fish him out.' Anne Edwards said: 'I'd push him under.' My mother learned, as all journalists must, to shrug off the double-dealing as part of the game, and enjoy the ride. 'Harold made life so entertaining that I looked forward to every day in the office,' she said. She loved the challenges of last-minute deadlines, pages torn up and rewritten at lightning speed.

Beaverbrook's titles were rich at that time, possessed of huge resources and facilities. Their names sufficed to open almost every door, to persuade the most implausible people to accept calls. Later, Anne found 'the non-stop turmoil' of the *Daily Express* too much of a good thing. But she loved her time on the *Sunday*, and later on the *Sunday Dispatch*, sister paper of the *Daily Mail*, to which she moved for the usual reasons – more money and intense dislike of the reptilian John Junor, who succeeded to the *Express* editorship when Harold Keeble was fired. Always meticulous, she checked every comma of her copy, which meant lingering in Fleet Street – this was the period when she forsook forty years of water-drinking – until 10 o'clock on Friday nights. She recalled one oddity of this period – the only lesbian proposal she ever received, from the *Daily Express* star writer Nancy Spain. Miss Spain took Anne for what was supposedly a 'get to know you' lunch at Wheeler's. To the unconcealed mirth of waiters, the hostess proved unable to keep her hands off her guest, who was more bewildered than cross.

Anne became, in those years, one of the most celebrated woman journalists in Fleet Street, combining acerbic wit with a brilliant eye for fashions – not merely the couture kind – and for controversy. I was not the only one in whom she inspired fear as well as respect. She was formidable, sometimes unyielding, not above tantrums. 'You see this trench in my shoulder?' Harold Keeble said to me years later. 'It was made by your mother crying on it.' There were many evenings when I sat in a dressing gown before bed, playing with my soldiers in a corner of our sitting room, listening avidly to my parents exchanging Fleet Street gossip. El Vino's wine bar, the Savoy Grill and the Cheshire Cheese became imbued in my eyes with infinite romance. Mac and Anne mercilessly dissected editors and executives, retailed their jokes and follies. My mother said with deep conviction: 'Never listen to anyone who says what a wonderful character Max Beaverbrook was. He may have been a newspaper genius, but he was a horrible, horrible man.'

In the eyes of the media world, Mac and Anne were a glamour couple, sharing success. Yet the divide between them continued to widen. Mac was an essayist with a feather-light touch, and a superb descriptive writer. However, his views on any serious subject – politics, the arts, world affairs – were those of a retired cavalry colonel. Like Dr Johnson without the sagacity, he was 'a true-born Englishman, and fully prejudiced against all other nations'. He and Uncle Lewis agreed that Africa south of the Zambezi would always remain white-dominated. He regarded Americans with disdain, and relished the Thursday Club convention whereby transatlantic guests were obliged to write 'lost colonial' after their names in its book. He believed passionately in the superiority of all things English to those of anywhere else.

Although he read widely, his favourites were comfortable home-grown middlebrow writers – Dickens, Cobbett, W.H. Hudson, Kipling. He had no patience with Jane Austen; had never, I think, read George Eliot, and certainly not Proust; found Hardy unacceptably bleak. More surprisingly, I never recall him speaking of Trollope. He loathed opera and ballet, and though a discerning judge of a photograph or drawing, took little interest in paintings and none in music. He professed an enthusiasm for gardening, but seldom himself wielded a trowel. Though he loved animals, his own record as a pet-owner was uniformly disastrous. His knowledge of the countryside, of trees and birds, was considerable, but most of his enthusiasms were philistine. His literary gifts and eye for whimsy were not matched by judgement. Anne said in old age: 'Your father wrote brilliantly on slight subjects, but the more serious the issue, the less sensible his view of it.'

She was a lot cleverer. It was irksome for her to be denied the pleasures of music, unless a friend invited her to Covent Garden. She found it hard to drag Mac to the theatre for anything more demanding than a Noël Coward play or *My Fair Lady*. Her more cultured acquaintances quickly wearied of Mac's sporting stories, his serenely confident and usually wildly mistaken political forecasts. Anne afterwards claimed that the moment when she realised she could not indefinitely endure Mac's society came in 1956, during the Suez crisis. 'Your father proclaimed: "In a decade, people will see that Eden is as great a man as Churchill,"' she recalled with infinite disgust.

Impatient of perceived folly or inadequacy in the world at large, Anne was unlikely to tolerate it indefinitely in a husband. If she had met Tolstoy, she could well have told him that his books would be improved by judicious pruning. Had she encountered Winston Churchill at a dinner party in the 1950s, before pudding came she might have suggested that he would have best served his own reputation by retiring from politics at the end of the war. It was not that her observations and judgements were foolish – until the day she died, they remained acutely penetrating. But they were of a severity which caused victims, not least members of the family, to quail before her tongue.

When marriages turn sour, sexual infidelity may be a proximate grievance, but the root cause is most often loss of respect on one side or both. While Mac sustained a deep admiration for Anne, he was far too selfish about his own enthusiasms to take much heed of her desires. He was shameless in allowing her income to take the strain for his own financial follies, *Country Fair* prominent among them. He made no attempt to adjust his lifestyle to his fluctuating fortunes, and merely passed an increasing proportion of school bills across the dinner table to his wife.

The couple gave occasional little media dinner parties at the flat, impeccably arranged by Anne and catered by her German cook, Martha, whose pastry I remember with veneration. The Hastingses were broke in a very English upper-middle-class way. There might be lobster for dinner guests, but the flats were always rented. In the early post-war years it never occurred to them to buy property. By the mid-1950s, for all their celebrity and relatively large incomes – at least £12,000 a year between them – in those days of high taxation they lacked ready cash to buy a London home. They continued to sustain a pretence of partnership, but seldom slept under the same roof. Though each was photographed constantly in the course of their professional lives, scarcely a single image exists of them posing together as a couple. There is no shot of them with Clare and me, their children, because the four of us never functioned as a unit save for the occasional viewing of an old Fred Astaire and Ginger Rogers movie on Christmas TV, or a weekend game of mahjong.

'My relations with your father worsened as it became increasingly clear that we had few interests or beliefs in common,' Anne acknowledged to Clare in an open letter which she published in 1993. I often wondered why my parents did not separate in the mid-1950s, when the relationship had already become loveless, on my mother's side anyway. In part, I think, it was that divorce in those times was perceived as a much graver step than it is considered today – and also that each of them had already racked up one failed marriage. Apart, they would have been even more stretched financially than they were together, with school fees to be paid. Above all, rightly or wrongly, they perceived an unhappily shared household as better for Clare and me than a broken one. Anne wrote: 'For years I fostered the conventional hope that our children would be a sufficient bond, but in this I was disappointed.'

The consequence was that the marriage stumbled on, in an atmosphere of sustained rancour which we all came to take for granted. Long after, Mother observed sardonically: 'There was nothing wrong with your father that a good psychiatrist could not have sorted out.' This was her perception from a relatively early stage of their marriage, and unlikely to form a basis for happiness or even a tenable truce. She asserted that 'If our marriage was inwardly barren, it was rarely acrimonious.' But gestures of love, or even goodwill, were never discernible between her and Mac. Their relationship was sterile. Clare and I accepted it for the usual reason that children do: we knew nothing else.

NINE

Rural Idylls

'The cottage', as we always called it, was our haven from every childhood trouble, the scene of almost all my own happiness – and of some dramas and misfortunes. It was a modest enough place, built into the side of a chalk slope some fifty miles west of London, a brisk walk from the escarpment where the Berkshire Downs fall away steeply towards the Thames at Goring. When my mother first acquired it in 1938, it was an unimproved farmworker's dwelling with earthen floor and outdoor sanitation. Over the years that followed it was rebuilt, extended and furnished with her usual excellent taste. It had three small bedrooms above, one of them Mother's, and one downstairs for Father. This arrangement seemed at the time perfectly normal, but prompts a sigh from me now. There was a single low-beamed living space, created by knocking together the former parlour and sitting room, and a little kitchen with a coke-fired Esse cooker. The garden was tended by Dobson, a neighbouring farmworker, invariably clad in an old beret, battledress jacket and aura of grumpiness. His wife, Mrs Dobson, acted as housekeeper, did the cleaning and a little cooking.

In the early years of my childhood, when food rationing was severe, the grass tennis court was given over to chickens. It was rehabilitated for white flannels and the kiss of racquets on balls only during a brief phase around 1950 when Mac and Anne attempted to make some show of conducting conventional country social life together. The court then again sank into decay, in step with their relationship. We owned a pretty Guernsey cow named Carmen which grazed a neighbouring field, providing milk and butter until she ran dry and was pronounced too old to calve again. Mother had designed the garden with some flair. In 1945 she added a mildly exotic touch by enlisting the services of local German prisoners-of-war, then readily available as cheap labour, to dig and pave a sunken garden, as well as build some pleasing walls. The vegetable garden was taken seriously as a source of supplies. We ate a lot of shot pigeons and ferreted rabbits (I have had no appetite for them since) to supplement the meat ration.

The village shop, McQuhae's, an emporium identical to that in Miss Marple's St Mary Mead, with blue blinds to signal its closure and old-fashioned scales on the wooden counter in its charmingly musty interior, provided groceries. For these, an account was submitted every year or two, of an accumulated immensity which horrified Mother. When she could bring herself to study its sheaves of itemised bills, there was always trouble about a range of goods which I had debited illicitly. Mr McQuhae also presided over the poky little neighbouring pub, the Bell, its taproom unaltered for a century or two, at the back door of which I made demands which became more pressing when, aged ten, I developed a taste for Babycham. I feared Mr McQuhae, an elderly Scots misanthrope, but he was happy to accept shillings from any of us.

It is extraordinary to remember how primitive were those little Berkshire villages, so close to London and yet utterly remote from it, even after the Second World War. Most of Aldworth's inhabitants worked on the land. Few had ever visited the capital, or wished to. I once chatted to an old man who told me that he had only twice been to Reading, ten miles distant – once when he got married, and again to register his wife's death. Almost everyone travelled by bicycle, and a few farms still used horses. Corn cut by the binder was threshed by a giant machine almost identical with those of Tess of the d'Urbervilles' era. Partridges flourished in high stubble, cows had horns, meadows untainted with chemicals were rich in September mushrooms. Most of the farmers I knew seemed permanently cross, sometimes with me. A succession of increasingly weird vicars, one of whom liked to ring the church bells in the middle of the night, inhabited Aldworth's spacious Georgian parsonage. An enchanting little steam train puffed its way from Didcot to Newbury through the local villages – Compton, Hampstead Norris, Hermitage. I was occasionally put aboard at Compton for the journey to prep school. If Nanny, Clare and I wanted to visit the shops in Newbury, we caught the daily bus.

Some of my rural pleasures were entirely innocent: picking blue-bells, picnics with Nanny, early essays in gardening and rearing ducks. Other diversions led to trouble, however. Oscar Wilde was quite mistaken in suggesting that it is difficult to misbehave in the country. For a child Rose Cottage and its environs, equipped with tools and weapons of all kinds, offered infinitely greater latitude for mischief than London. I achieved an early disgrace one Friday evening when we were disembarking from the family Austin on the steepish decline where we offloaded. As Nanny emerged, on a whim I released the handbrake. This set the car rolling briskly downhill, and caused Nanny to break her leg. Amazingly, she displayed not the slightest ill will about her subsequent fortnight in hospital. Possessed of infinite benevolence towards her charges, if not to the wider world, she rejected any notion of holding me blameworthy.

Not long afterwards I was racing down the same hill on my tricycle, with a small neighbour named John Ferrant standing on the back clinging to my shoulders. He slipped, fell off and broke a collarbone. As driver of the vehicle, I was deemed responsible for his mishap, somewhat unjustly as it seemed to me. Although I never extended my depredations outside the family, I regarded any piece of my parents' property – cars, tools, clothes, technology, valuables – as legitimate booty, an attitude which persisted into my twenties. An eager entrepreneur, at the age of eight on a hot day I manufactured ice-lollies in the fridge, and walked to a motorcycle scramble on the Downs to sell my melting products for tuppence each.

I loved cooking with Nanny, and in rather the same mode I found explosives irresistible. Father had large reserves of both modern powder and shot for loading his own cartridges, and black powder for his nineteenth-century flintlock guns. These offered a child of an enquiring disposition plentiful scope for experiment, and I achieved some impressive bangs in neighbouring spinneys. Testing the efficacy of a bow and arrow, and perhaps with some precocious Cupid image in mind, I loosed an idle shot at the chest of the little girl in next door's garden – that once owned by Rosamond Lehmann – and scored a palpable hit. My great-grandfather, oddly enough, was whipped for doing something similar at Harper's Ferry in 1861, as I discovered from family correspondence, but I was too slow-witted to plead ancestral example in my defence. In Aldworth, the girl's mother made a fuss – what enlightened modern opinion would call a disproportionate response. The bow was confiscated.

It would be mistaken to suggest that others were always the victims of my activities. Most often, they impacted on myself. Dispatched one day to my bedroom for a rest after lunch, I decided to escape irksome captivity by emulating Hopalong Cassidy. I reasoned that if he could leap nimbly from a moving stagecoach, it would be simplicity itself for me to vault from a first-floor window. I suffered a badly sprained ankle. Out on my first bike with Nanny and Clare, I sought to terrorise them by careering full tilt towards the pushchair down a steep slope, with the anticlimactic consequence that I was thrown off, and fell sobbing at Nanny's feet nursing multiple abrasions.

A year or so later, out from prep school, as we walked into the cottage Father drew my attention to a large collection of fireworks. These, he said, were assembled for a forthcoming Thursday Club party. On no account was I to touch them. I spent the next hour in my bedroom, dissecting the largest rocket. Curiosity then prompted me to apply a match to its heaped entrails. For some hours after-wards, fearful of recriminations, I concealed the frightful burns on my hand until, in the midst of tea, the pain became unbearable and I burst into tears. I returned to school in heavy bandages and disgrace, after a visit to the Streatley doctor. Any sense of guilt was moder-ated, however, by learning that a week later the Thursday Clubbers, liberally oiled, had burnt half the thatch off a nearby cottage roof while participating exuberantly in Father's firework display. It could be argued – indeed often was, by my mother – that Father and his friends displayed a talent for idiocy to match my own, their excesses being rendered less excusable by age.

I knew that I was badly behaved and accident-prone, and the village agreed. Mrs Dobson, the housekeeper, an important cog in the domestic machine for sustaining Rose Cottage, mutinied and eventually jumped ship. She declared that she would take no further responsibility for the place if I was planted there without proper supervision, which did not mean that of Nanny. News of my unsuitability travelled. Invitations to local children's houses, always sparse, were seldom extended more than once. The local grandee, Lord Iliffe, organised a boys' cricket match at Yattendon, to which I was invited on the strength of his acquaintance with my parents. Hopelessly incompetent with bat or ball, and thus uninterested, I lay dozing prostrate in the outfield until noticed, bawled out, and sent home in disgrace.

Why do children misbehave? Some years later, when the scale of outrages with local friends escalated, an angry villager said to us one night: 'If your parents weren't who they are, they'd call you lot delinquents.' It was as if I was determined to undo in a single childhood all the virtue so laboriously banked by Hastingses and Scott-Jameses over the previous century. Looking back, I still cannot explain myself. It was not that being naughty made me happy. On the contrary, social failure rendered me miserable for twenty years and more. I was anything but fearless, trembling before the prospect of my misdeeds' discovery and the retribution that would follow. Never one of those cunning trouble-makers who escape punishment, I was always found out. With hindsight, most of my misdeeds were too trivial to confer heroic status, sufficing only to provoke dismay and anger amid those who had to live with me. Yet I felt no inclination to reform. If I could not be the best best, I would be the best worst. An obsessive curiosity about the consequences of courses of action impelled me to crime after crime.

I 'borrowed' binoculars, cameras, shooting sticks, and forgetfully abandoned them on the Downs. I tested firearms, roamed beyond any stipulated boundary, disobeyed the sternest and most sensible injunctions. We seldom entertained other children at the cottage, partly because few wanted to come, partly because Mother never encouraged them. For years I nursed a grievance that her punishment for my little escapade in jumping out of the bedroom window was to cancel the planned visit of a small acquaintance, a rare and thus eagerly anticipated occurrence. Yet it would be unjust to blame my parents for my narrow social circle. I simply lacked the gift of making friends – as also, in considerable degree, did Mac and Anne themselves.

Both possessed a large acquaintance, but Father had no intimate friends and Mother few. Part of the trouble with their social life was that they were so ill-assorted a pair. The aesthetes and fashionistas most sympathetic to Anne could find little to say to Mac, the outdoorsman red in tooth and claw. This was almost literally the case, since he cherished a theory, imparted to him by some aged rustic, that the most humane means of dispatching a wounded pheasant was to crush the back of its skull between his teeth. Father was a better talker than listener. His shooting friends were amused by his extravagances, but frightened of my mother, who did not disguise her contempt for them.

Anne always professed to be a countrywoman, and indeed had a notable knowledge of wildflowers and a gift for gardening, which she later turned to good account in her writings. But she was swiftly bored by farmers moaning about the crops, or worse still by red-faced men who returned with Mac from a September partridge day, drank prodigious quantities of gin, and exchanged noisy recollections of the third drive. Anne liked to see animals grazing in the fields, but had no intimate interest in them beyond that afforded by their enhancement of the view. She actively disliked dogs. 'The truth,' she once acknowledged, 'is that though I love the country, and am good with plants, I was brought up a London child.' She enjoyed the ideal of rural life much more than its social manifestations, a confusion which has sometimes extended into my own experience.

They saw something of John and Penelope Betjeman, who then lived a few miles over the Downs at Farnborough. 'Betch' or 'John B', as he was always known, was already celebrated, and both Anne and Mac, as editors, had often commissioned his work. But Betjeman was not remotely the type to find Mac a soulmate, given his own abhorrence of shooting – remember his verse about the Porkers and their pheasant massacres. Anne, who adored John B and later became a close friend, was nonetheless bewildered in those early days by the harshness, verging upon sadism, with which she watched him treat his son Paul. When the boy appeared in the drawing room one day, and they began to discuss his future, his father exclaimed gleefully: 'I wonder if he's going to be queer. Oh, I do hope so. Wouldn't that be fun?' Anne, like most of Betjeman's acquaintance, was baffled by the manner in which he could display such kindness to a host of outsiders – including me, not many years later – while tormenting his own offspring.

They saw a lot of Nicholas Davenport, City journalist and a successful investor on his own account, though not, alas, on that of my parents. He lived with his painter wife Olga at Hinton, a pretty Georgian house near Oxford. One wintry day when I professed seven-year-old boredom, my parents took me with them to a Davenport drinks party. Failing to receive the attention which I thought appropriate, I drifted outside, packed a snowball, and precipitated it through the window into the crowded drawing room. Why, why? I still cannot say.

One day after a Davenport lunch, Mac and Anne gave their fellow guests, the Labour politician Douglas Jay and his wife Peggy, a lift to Oxford station. As they stood gossiping on the platform awaiting the London train, Douglas suddenly vanished. After some confusion, it was discovered that he had spotted a pretty girl on a train halted at the opposite platform, dashed over the bridge and was last seen disappearing towards Birmingham. This was not untypical, and surprised only Anne and Mac.

One of the few neighbouring couples both my parents liked were the Wysards, who occupied a large house of which even as a child I was envious, not far from Bradfield. Tony Wysard, a pillar of the Thursday Club, had established a pre-war reputation as a caricaturist for glossy magazines. He spared himself further exertion, however, and wasted a significant talent, by marrying the heiress to the McDougalls flour fortune, an agreeable but highly strung and scatty woman named Ruth. Tony emerged from the war a major in the Rifle Brigade, a rank which he affected until his death. With his impeccable tailoring, twinkling eye, boisterous charm and fine regimental moustache, he looked every inch the hero.

He liked to describe how, in the days after Dunkirk when everyone was preparing to repel the invaders with Molotov cocktails, he insisted on uniformity among each of his platoons, arming one with petrol-filled champagne bottles, a second with hock bottles, a third with claret and so on. His house was filled with military memorabilia. It came as a shock to me, when once I asked a mutual friend whether 'Uncle Tony' had served in the desert or North-West Europe, to receive the disarming response: 'Oh, Tony never got nearer a battlefield than Dover.' Thus did one discover that a fine military bearing can be quite unrelated to military achievement. Tony was, however, the most convivial and generous company, seldom quitting Rose Cottage without slipping me a ten-shilling note, sure path to my heart. A splendid raconteur, eyes glittering with genial mischief, he lifted a bushy eyebrow theatrically to emphasise his climaxes. He laughed heartily at the antics of both Mac and myself. But privately, I think, he was himself too cautious a character not to be alarmed and sometimes appalled by our excesses.

Mac and Anne's relationships with their extended families were tenuous. Marie and John Scott-James, Anne's siblings, died at fifty and forty respectively. The sisters were never close, though Marie had sufficient literary bent to review novels for the *Observer*. Anne's father, Rolfe Scott-James, continued to live in his cottage, The Forge at Upper Basildon. Five years after Violet's death in 1942, he married a French academic named Paule Lagarde, who taught at the London School of Economics. Anne detested her stepmother, whom she described as 'hard as nails, the sort who gives the French *bourgeois* a bad name'. Occasional family teas at The Forge took place in an atmosphere of icy formality, sometimes obvious rancour. As a child, I perceived grandfather Rolfe merely as old, grave, crusty. He died, aged eighty, in 1959. The charmless Paule inherited his modest estate, a source of further bitterness to Anne, for it eventually passed to her stepmother's French nephews and nieces.

We saw something of Mac's mother and sister, Billie and Beryl, at the restaurant which they then owned in Marlborough with Beryl's husband Leslie Scott. The dread hand of snobbery reared its head here. I knew Beryl and Leslie only as a jolly and generous couple, without children themselves, who occasionally took me to London productions of Gilbert and Sullivan. My father, however, was underwhelmed by Leslie's cheerful vulgarity and shortage of aitches. After his brother-in-law died suddenly in 1959 and Mac failed to attend the funeral, his relations with Beryl were never again close. She remained a mightily kind figure in my life, however, and often regaled me with stories of Mac's childhood disgraces, which strengthened my hand in excusing my own.

Grandmother Billie Hastings, Basil's widow, was likewise sweet to Clare and me, but never concealed her dismay about her son's improvidence, my behaviour, Mac and Anne's incompatibility. Granny was a great worrier, and life had given her plenty to worry about. A good Catholic until her death in 1960, worshipping for forty years at the Brompton Oratory until she left London for Wiltshire, she was distressed by the absolute lack of religion in my parents' lives – and in Clare's and mine. It all seemed to her a sad falling-off from the days when Basil and his brothers and sisters were pillars of South London's St Vincent de Paul Society. A Victorian sceptic once proposed that all churches should bear a sign: 'Important – *If True*'. Mac retained a primitive, non-churchgoing belief in a Deity, but Anne lacked even that.

Lewis was the only one of Basil's brothers and sisters whom Mac broke bread with, or indeed of whom I knew anything. The rest of 'the Tribe' of his aunts and uncles played no part in our lives. Mac met Lewis regularly in London, and made sure that I got to know him. Anne, rather surprisingly, found the old boy immensely attractive and loved his rich, booming voice. I was captivated by him. He told war stories, occasionally took me to see war movies, and once terrified me by an attempt to teach me to swim through plunging me headlong into the surf of a Cornish cove. But there was no shared contact involving Marigold. Neither Lewis nor Mac saw anything of Stephen, and I scarcely met him until I was in my teens. When I enquired about my cousin – seeing his name in the paper as an MP and suchlike – Father merely said priggishly: 'Lewis has never thought Stephen quite the thing.'

This was unjust, but reflected enduring tensions between father and son. After the war, Steve joined the Secret Intelligence Service, with which he served for more than a decade in Finland, France and Cyprus, becoming an ardent Cold Warrior. He entered the House of Commons as Member for Mid-Bedfordshire in 1960, and served as a Conservative MP for the next twenty-three years, espousing causes and enthusiasms right-wing even by the standards of Lewis and Mac. Steve contrived to move in much grander circles than other Hastingses, and eventually married into a stately home, Milton in Cambridgeshire. A notable horseman, he became something of a hero in Leicestershire hunting circles, especially after once winning its famous cross-country race, the Harborough Ride. He recoiled from acknowledging to himself, still more to the world, that his own family antecedents were humble, even slightly disreputable. Though without personal fortune or indeed earned income, Steve loved to play the aristocrat, which no other representative of our branch of the family has pretended to be. Lewis and Mac were impatient of his snobbery, treated him as a lounge lizard and indeed cad, and reciprocated his disdain. Anne detested him, both for his politics and his pretensions. The consequence was that Clare and I met no circle of cousins on either side of the family, save occasionally Marie Scott-James's daughter Clarissa, some years older than ourselves.

My parents resolved their irreconcilable tastes in conversation, as in so much else, by meeting most of their acquaintances separately, on neutral turf. Anne pursued a social life in London, where Mac embraced his clubs. In the country, he periodically disappeared alone on sporting expeditions, a source of much chagrin to me, who yearned to accompany him. I received riding lessons at the Chieveley stables of a leathery old retired cavalry officer named Major Glover, which neither convinced my instructor of my talent, nor imbued me with much enthusiasm for horses. What I wanted was to be taken shooting and fishing. Father, however, seemed more eager to spin yarns about moors and rivers than to show them to me. At the time I thought he was selfish, which he certainly was. Later, however, I realised that he also lacked scope or cash for getting me started as a country sportsman. He had a gun for some years in the Iliffe Estate syndicate, near the cottage at Yattendon. For a few seasons he ran a wild little shoot on the Downs above Compton, on a farm owned by Claude Wilson's insurance company. His part-time keeper, Mr Allright, occupied a cottage in Aldworth and boarded ferrets, one of Mac's brief enthusiasms. I was sometimes taken to join the guns for lunch in the pub, and to follow along for a drive or two. But his game book suggests that he shot only a dozen times a year, even when he was in funds.

Almost the only shared fishing expedition I can remember was undertaken one Sunday, on a stretch of Piscatorial Society water near Newbury. We went equipped with the wherewithal for catching roach and perch. When we set off along the riverbank, I was entrusted with a large ball of breadpaste. In a careless moment I deposited the bait in the grass, then could not for the life of me remember where. In those days of rigid rural sabbatarianism, there were no shops open from which to buy fresh supplies. 'Well, that's the end of that, then,' said Father crossly, and took me home. Years later, he once took me on a holiday to the Shetland Islands in pursuit of sea-trout, but we caught nothing all week, and never looked like doing so.

What did I want from my parents, which I did not get? I still find it hard to answer the question. Materially, I had a pretty comfortable middle-class childhood. No one was ever cruel to me – my mother seldom intended to generate the fear which she inspired. Nanny indulged her charges disgracefully, not infrequently offering Clare and me little subsidies from her own purse, a habit which persisted until her death. Some of our happiest hours with Nanny were spent completing football pools coupons together. Like her shrewd stock exchange investments, her pools entries prospered with surprising frequency. Occasionally she would take me to stay for a few days at the little terraced house she owned in Sheffield, trips which I enjoyed hugely.

Both Clare and I owed much to Nanny's love, to the fond smiles which beamed from her kind old face. I can see now how desperately lonely was her life. She possessed a scanty acquaintance even among her own kind, never took a holiday, seldom even a day off. Almost everything she owned in the world reposed in her musty little bedroom at our London flat. She claimed just one friend, a Sheffield neighbour named Mrs Green, to whom she often wrote painstaking screeds, and whose doings formed a staple of her conversation. Yet, even to my childish eye, Mrs Green never seemed as keen on Nanny as was Nanny on her. Nanny clung to us as desperately as we clung to her. Poor, dear woman, she had nothing else.

I was fearful of being accident-prone, a sensation which took forty years to subside, and which was obviously rooted in experience. Why was it that, even when not bent on mischief, I had to smash my fishing net through the glass front door of our holiday hotel on Jersey, incurring a hostility from the management which persisted through our stay? How could it be that my passion for bonfires, which a generous infusion of petrol was obviously indispensable to ignite, so often precipitated major conflagrations? I also yearned to discover how to relate successfully to other people, and blamed my parents for my inability to do so.

One of the great boons of middle age is that most of us stop being jealous. We cease to envy other people's greater wealth, fame or apparent happiness, and better understand the sorrows which almost every family harbours. My wife Penny likes to quote a Jewish saying: 'If you make all those round the table lay their troubles down upon it, you take a look at everybody else's, pick up your own and walk away.' In adulthood, one learns so much about the horrors of other people's childhoods that the shortcomings of one's own recede into insignificance. This has certainly been so for me. A friend not long ago told us of his boyhood, during which his mother was married six times, and he was dispatched to spend holidays from Eton in children's homes. His experiences, he said, have rendered him incapable of intimacy with either sex ever since. By any objective measure, and certainly by such a formidable standard of misery as he achieved,

I had little to complain of. But fifty years ago, my sorrows and frustrations seemed real enough.

Lacking talent for ball games or companionship, I wanted to get on with growing up, to escape from my own social failure. At school I fared reasonably well academically, but was the last to be picked for any team. Popularity eluded me, with both masters and boys. In my awe of my parents' achievements, which seemed so great because they were trumpeted in print, I was full of fear that I could never match them. I was irked that we seemed less rich than we deserved to be, and occupied more modest homes than other boys. We seldom did anything together, as a family. Not only did I form few friendships, but I seldom received invitations through children of my parents' friends, because they had almost none in common.

Many of my misdemeanours arose from being a solitary, with only my sister to exploit as a plaything. Clare was six years younger than me, and I blush to remember how poorly I repaid her sweetness and loyalty. She was often the sole witness of my crimes, sworn to secrecy: 'You won't tell Mummy and Daddy, will you?' She saw me drop Father's lovely Walther .22 rifle from a treetop house, smashing the stock, then glue the pieces together again, so that discovery of its destruction was postponed until the weapon was lifted from its rack. Clare was often an innocent accessory, sometimes indeed victim, during and after my crimes. When I was eight, Father penned a magazine piece entitled 'Conversation with my Son'. Here is how it went:

'Can I have some nails for my hammer, Daddy?'

'It isn't your hammer; it's mine. And what do you intend doing with the nails?'

'I'm making a soap box car.'

'Where?'

'Up at the toolshed. It's quite all right, Daddy, I'm not doing any damage to your things. Really I'm not.'

'What's that stuff on your hands?'

'Just paint.'

'Just paint? You've got some on your face, too. No, don't rub it off on your sleeve. Haven't you got a handkerchief?'

'It's in my other trousers.'

'Now, where did you get this paint?'

'It isn't any good to anybody, really, Daddy.'

'I didn't ask you whether it was any good. I asked you where you found it.'

'Somebody had thrown it away with the junk in the toolshed.'

'What led you to suppose that somebody had thrown it away?'

'The tin was jolly rusty.'

'What have you been doing with it?'

'Just painting.'

'That's self-evident. I want to know what you've been painting.'

'The kiddie-car.'

'Clare's kiddie-car?'

'I asked her if she'd like it in another colour, and she said she would.'

'So you did it to oblige your little sister? Where is she now?'

'Up at the toolshed.'

'What's she doing?'

'Riding the kiddie-car.'

'The one you've just painted?'

'I told her it was wet paint; but she wouldn't wait, Daddy.'

'Just you wait till your mother hears about this. I thought you two seemed suspiciously quiet this morning.'

'Where are you going, Daddy?'

'Where do you think I'm going?'

'If you're going to the toolshed, there's something I want to say to you.'

'Go on.'

'I've spilt a bit of paint – only a little bit, mind – on the door.'

'Don't tell me you've painted the door as well.'

'Only half of it, Daddy. I couldn't reach the top. I wanted to make it all nice before you came up the garden.'

'That was thoughtful of you.'

'Do you want to go inside the toolshed, Daddy?'

'Certainly. Why not?'

'Well, it might be a bit difficult at the moment. You see, Clare was very naughty and I thought she was going to take her kiddie-car on the road.'

'Well?'

'Well, Daddy, I used some of those old bricks up the garden. I knew you wouldn't mind because they weren't any good anyhow, to make a barricade.'

'Let's get this clear. Since you have been up the garden this morning, you've found a pot of paint and spread it over yourself, the toolshed door and the kiddie-car.'

'Yes, Daddy.'

'You have now bricked up your sister in the toolshed, where she is riding the kiddie-car you have just painted.'

'I told her not to, Daddy.'

'So you've already assured me. As a matter of interest, since you've bricked up the door, how have you yourself been getting in and out of the toolshed?'

'Through the window.'

'But that window won't open.'

'It's open now, Daddy.'

'Do you mean you've broken it?'

'I was coming to that, Daddy. It was an accident. It wasn't me. The boy next door cracked it with his bow and arrow. I told him you'd be very angry.'

'So the boy next door is involved, too?'

'No, Daddy, he's gone home now.'

'And the cracked window?'

'Well, I thought it wasn't much use having a cracked window . . .'

'So you've done the job properly?'

'You can hardly notice it's missing now, Daddy.'

'Is there anything else you want to tell me before I inspect for myself what you've been up to?'

'Oh no, Daddy.'

'You haven't been in the garage, have you?'

'Only to get the oilcan.'

'The oilcan?'

'The kiddie-car needed oil badly.'

'Did Clare go with you into the garage?'

'Yes, but I sent her out at once because she climbed into the car.'

'Did this happen before the painting of the kiddie-car, or afterwards?'

'Afterwards, Daddy.'

'And after Clare started riding it?'

'Yes, Daddy.'

'Go down to the house immediately and ask your mother for some turpentine.'

'It's O.K., Daddy. I thought you might want it, so I took it up to the toolshed for you.'

I suggest that this passage shows how ponderous Father could be. Others say, however, that it displays his acute ear as a reporter. The family drove back to London that night in heavy silence. On arrival in Kensington, I scuttled gratefully away to my room and toys, and stayed in hiding from all save Nanny.

Granny, my father's mother, recorded gloomily in her diary one weekend: 'Anne brought nannie and the children to lunch. A nightmare. Children worse behaved than ever.' This was hard on Clare, an exemplarily nice child, but accurately reflected the family's mood of despair about the new generation. A growing number of my letters home from prep school referred to crimes alleged, denied, committed, or for which absolution was sought: 'Dear Mummy and Daddy, I'm afraid I have no idea where the brown tape-measure is, *and I have absolutely nothing to do with its disappearance*' . . . 'I am sorry about stealing your little pistol and will never do such a thing again' . . . 'I *know* quite well I don't deserve it but please let me start "*les vacances*" with a clean slate. I will place the money to pay for those Flit guns on your dressing-table as soon as I get back.' Here is a *Sunday Dispatch* column my mother wrote in the mid-'fifties:

So it's goodbye to the dear, gay school holidays and the tranquil pleasure of family life. It's pleasant to recall how one sweet, romping day succeeded another. Take the first week with our little lot. My son got the mumps and other children staying in the house were hurriedly withdrawn in closed carriages by reproachful parents; when my daughter fell in the river (Father was in charge) and ran a temperature of 105 while the house was tense with recrimination; when I had to cancel two parties and tickets for the theatre; when the stove got a mood and I couldn't get the oven hot; when 250 rose bushes and sweet pea plants, ordered in January, arrived in a crate with a note advising immediate planting.

Take the second pleasure-laden week, the week of the thrush's funeral. When there was a sad little coffin and a funeral cortege and a tombstone movingly inscribed 'May his little soul rest in peace' and some good singing and everyone crying like mad. Crocodiles' tears, really, because of course the children had murdered the bird. Convinced that they were St Francis of Assisi and Joan of Arc respectively ('even the wild creatures would come and sit in her lap'), they had been unsuccessfully rearing nestlings on the kitchen stove. Left to itself, that fluffy chick would have lived to steal my strawberries in July. It was the week when the budgerigar got out and the car conked and we received a meaningless but disquieting bill from the income tax.

Take the third week, when my daughter got mumps, my son fell out of a tree (pushed, some say) and my husband hopped it to the Continent. When my best friends arrived on a flying visit from abroad, and I was stuck in the country, and they had a marvellous time without me. That was the week of too many Easter eggs eaten by too few people, with punishing consequences.

Take the fourth, climactic week of this idyllic season, when I went to London and got the mumps ('Can you beat it, our beauty queen's mumpy,' my son reported laconically) and I wondered why people who permanently have small pig eyes in large criminal faces bother to live. When I had to keep getting up and posting cabbages to the country contingent, because in all country places there's a chronic

168

shortage of fresh vegetables. When I had a breeze with the office, who couldn't see why I couldn't interview lots of sparkling people with a temperature of 101 – 'Only don't come near us,' they said. 'What about the sparkling people?' I said, 'they may not want it either.' 'Find some who've had the thing,' they suggested. 'That narrows the field,' I said crossly, and went back to bed.

When my son took my daughter, well wrapped up, on a few minutes' stroll in the sun, and brought her home, stumbling blindly, two hours later, gloves, cap and muffler gone. 'We went a little too far,' he explained. 'For the last two miles, I had to prop her eyelids open with matchsticks to keep her awake.' When I had to check a school clothing list of 86 items, making replacements to the tune of £20. Yes, they've been wonderful, enchanting holidays, though I use the word 'holiday' with a merry laugh.

My parents' habit, endemic among journalists, of exploiting family life as column-fodder was a source of much embarrassment to me at school. Anne's pieces reflected her vision of herself as a benign, harassed, multi-skilled housewife-career woman. In this she was the forerunner of an entire generation of female journalists who write columns from this perspective today. Years later, my own children reproached me for alleged parental shortcomings. I pointed out that I was never absent from the bucket-and-spade round. 'Maybe,' said my daughter tartly, 'but you never looked as if you enjoyed it much.' Here was a powerful echo of my own memories of Anne about the house – eagle-eyed, efficient, occasionally jolly, but seldom looking as if she relished the domestic bit, however often she professed in print that she did so. She did, however, have a notable capacity for retaining the loyalty of staff. Her cook Martha, as well as Nanny and our daily Elsie Elmer, stuck around for decades. Mummy possessed the virtue most important in relating to employees: with Mrs Hastings, everybody knew exactly where they were.

So, likewise, did I. In childhood and indeed adolescence, I lived in an almost permanent state of apprehension when she was about the place, lest the latest of my depredations should be discovered. An objective observer might suggest that this attitude merely represented the usual professional distaste of the criminal classes for the proximity of the law, which reflects poorly on the malefactor, rather than upon the constabulary. Be that as it may, tensions relaxed dramatically when Mummy disappeared out of the door and I could resume whatever project I had in hand, safe under Nanny's all-unseeing eye.

I loved to listen to Father, however. A significant part of his romantic nature, as well as of his peculiar brand of conceit, was to assume that any product, establishment or artist patronised by himself was the best of its kind imaginable. When he bought an Armstrong-Siddeley car, he declared authoritatively: 'People who really know about motors regard this machine as better than a Bentley.' He persuaded himself that Churchill shotguns were superior to those of Purdey or Holland, simply because he had struck up a friendship – on his side verging on hero-worship – with the gunmaker Robert Churchill. He asserted the literary superiority of Surtees to Dickens. He thought Noël Coward the finest playwright of the twentieth century, and Kipling the greatest poet of all time.

Impressed by Lewis's 1917 Military Cross, he would assert to me in perfect earnest: 'Some soldiers reckon a really good MC worth more than a VC, you know.' He discovered a weird white Irish tweed named borneen, from which he had a summer jacket tailored that in due course, as an act of filial piety, I copied for myself. Each generation of politicians yielded to Mac a predictable hate-figure. Lloyd George was succeeded in his satanic gallery by Aneurin Bevan; Bevan by Tony Benn. He was captivated by the cleverness of a farmer in the pub who said of Benn: 'If I had a dog with eyes like that, I'd shoot it.' Mac's views on politics and the arts could scarcely be described as nuanced, but he advanced them with a confidence unencumbered by doubt.

He sought to imbue his son with his own passion for the ancients – he came from the last generation of educated Englishmen for whom the classics were a dominant force. He pressed upon me his favourite musty old Edwardian works – J.C. Stobart's *The Glory that was Greece* and *The Grandeur that was Rome*. When first I went to prep school, he gave me an exam crib on all things Roman, entitled *Res Romanae*.

He wrote solemnly in the flyleaf: 'Don't lend this or lose it. It helped me to love and understand the ancients as I hope it will help you.' I am not sure that the tattered little brown volume did any such thing for me, but I cherished it totemically, and still do, because it meant so much to Father.

He blossomed most eloquently and convincingly when speaking of the English countryside and its history. 'Turnip' Townsend and Coke of Norfolk vied for supremacy in his pantheon with Marlborough and Wellington. He perceived the development of English agriculture as a glorious pageant that persisted into his own days. He welcomed every advance in rural mechanisation and science with an enthusiasm which made him a darling of the industry. Until the 1970s, when he belatedly awoke to the environmental horrors unleashed during the preceding generation, his writing and TV films unstintingly celebrated the achievement of British farming. He loved men who worked the land, and spent many of his happiest hours in their company. His whimsical reflections on the countryside were among his best writing. 'Foreigners give the English credit for three things,' he mused in a characteristic passage. 'The beauty of our children, the lushness of our pasture and the mettle of our horses. Why is it, then, that when all three are brought together, we who speak Shakespeare's tongue call the occasion a gymkhana?'

By the mid-1950s, for all his success Mac harboured one notable unfulfilled ambition: for Africa. Though, metaphorically speaking, he had lived more than forty years at the feet of Lewis, absorbing his uncle's yarns of adventure amid bush and beasts, he had never experienced these things for himself. He yearned to emulate Lewis's rambles through great wildernesses under the sun, rifle shouldered and faithful servant at his side. Now he set about translating this dream into reality.

TEN

Bush Fever

The success of *Eagle*, and of its Special Investigator column, offered Mac a splendid opportunity. He had almost exhausted the scope for undertaking *Boy's Own* adventures close to home, and had little difficulty convincing the editor, Marcus Morris, that he should head for the Dark Continent in search of more extravagant excitements. He spent hours in earnest conclave with Lewis beside the library fire of the Savage Club in Carlton House Terrace. 'Always remember,' said the old hunter, 'wild Africa is not on your side – you are irrelevant, at best.' After much musing, Mac devised a challenge which might justify in print the expenditure of a significant amount of Hulton Press's money. He would cross the Kalahari Desert in British Bechuanaland – modern Botswana – to search out the last of the ancient bushmen of the region, by then hunted and persecuted to the brink of extinction. He christened his quest 'The Search for the Little Yellow Men'. One morning in 1954, accompanied by his favourite photographer Chris Ware and Lewis's old big-game rifles, he embarked for Salisbury, Rhodesia, on a BOAC flight which in those exotic days stopped en route at Rome, Cairo, Khartoum, Entebbe and Nairobi, before landing at what was still the heart of Britain's African empire.

Arrived in southern Rhodesia, where he proposed to outfit himself for his expedition across the Kalahari, he was undismayed by the disbelief of the locals, who recognised a greenhorn when they saw one. Father had a serene, endearing conviction that if he defined a purpose, however vaguely, it would be fulfilled. In those days it was deemed foolish to attempt a passage across Bechuanaland's roadless

172

wasteland without a big truck and an accompanying Land Rover to extricate it from sand when it became bogged, as was sure to happen. When Laurens van der Post, viewed in Africa even in those days as something of a charlatan, conducted an expedition not dissimilar to Father's a few months earlier, his equipage would not have disgraced a royal safari. Mac's trip, by contrast, was entirely DIY, the austerity of its outfitting determined by *Eagle*'s modest budget. His hopes of enlisting the services of a game warden to accompany him were swiftly dashed: the professionals were all either too busy or too expensive.

After days of enquiry, in Bulawayo he at last located an old Chevrolet 1½-ton truck of wartime vintage, the property of 'a huge beef of an Afrikaner with a drainy laugh and a chest like a tribal tom-tom'. He also met a twenty-year-old local named John Currye, who offered his services as driver and mechanic. Currye was no old bush hand, but a restless city boy who fancied an adventure, the perils of which he scarcely recognised. Mac gratefully enlisted him. They bought a water tank, spare drum of fuel, tarpaulin, spade, pick and spares. Chris Ware stocked up with a Primus stove, tin plates and eating irons, cans of meat and sardines, biscuits, fruit and a first-aid kit. At 5 o'clock one morning, they loaded the vehicle. Mac laid his rifles – a seven-millimetre for soft-skinned game and a .404 that would stop an elephant – on the rack behind the front seats. Then the truck ground fitfully westwards out of town on the first leg of a 1,500-mile marathon, towards the end of the metalled road at the Bechuanaland frontier.

Mac was often at his best writing for children. For their entertainment he could give full play to his sense of romance, as he did on the road to Maun that morning in 1954, setting out to seek the bushmen:

Men can keep on redrawing the maps; but Africa's heart today remains as savage and untamed as when Lobengula ravaged the country with his Matabele impis. The *Panda-ma-tenka*, the old elephant hunters' trail, is no more a road now than it was when Selous lumbered through with his ox-wagons to shoot for ivory with a Martini or a muzzle-loader. The elephant, the buffalo, the lion, the crocodile and the black mamba remain to dispute millions of miles of undeveloped territory with their old enemy, man. In the southern interior, there is still a race of human beings, left behind in the struggle for progress, who exist now just as our ancestors used to live in the Stone Age.

Mac was the merest tyro in Africa, yet within days of landing in the continent he was driving unguided into its wildest regions. He felt himself at home because he had vicariously voyaged there for years, through the tales of his adored uncle. Lewis once met a bushman, when soldiering in German South-West Africa in 1914. He came upon the little man asleep beside the carcass of a giraffe which he had killed with a poisoned arrow. They conducted a halting exchange through the medium of Lewis's local tracker, who spoke the bushman's curious clicking tongue. The hunter said he was resting before going to meet his family, a day's march distant. He would then bring them to the kill. Lewis speculated with a shudder upon the likely state of the meat, exposed to merciless sun, by the time the bushman brought his clan to eat it.

Forty years later, Lewis waxed lyrical to Mac about the joys of Bechuanaland, six times larger than Britain, and of the Kalahari Desert: 'Its most important inhabitants are the buffalo; it's still the private hunting territory of lion and leopard, the stamping ground of a million antelope, and all the better for that. It's a place which man has never conquered and where even nature has never made up its mind.' A fortnight after that conversation, Mac crossed the border into Bechuanaland, stopping at a police post to buy a licence to shoot game for the pot. 'Oddly enough,' he wrote, 'I had no prescience of possible failure. Before we set out, I was gloomy and apprehensive. But, once we were moving in the old truck, I felt the way I used to feel as a war correspondent. It was waiting for the raid, the battle, to begin that was tough. Once the bomb went up, one felt exhilarated and carefree.'

Here he was, once more enacting in reality a childhood fantasy. I know exactly how he felt, because thirty years later I often experienced the same joyous sensation myself, setting forth in search of adventure at somebody else's expense. For three generations of

Hastingses, Africa has proved the most intoxicating place on earth. In Mac's day there was much less game than there had been in Lewis's era, but the continent had not yet experienced the stunning human population explosion that was to come in the second half of the century. If Bechuanaland in 1954 was no longer a very dangerous place, it was still a wilderness dominated by animals, not people. Mac found himself in a personal paradise, memories of which he cherished until the end of his days.

Under the Union flag outside the District Commissioner's headquarters in the tiny settlement of Francistown, DC George Atkinson studied Father's truck.

'How much petrol have you got?'

'About sixty-seven gallons.'

'Water?'

'Twenty-four gallons.'

'Guns?'

'One .404, one 7-mill and a shotgun.'

'Plenty of spares?'

'Yes.'

'I think you'll get through all right.'

Atkinson told him that his best chance of finding bushmen lay far south-westwards, in the Ghanzi district. 'If you find the real yellow bushmen, remember that they're still pretty wild. It wasn't long ago that four airmen who made a forced landing in the Kalahari were killed by them. Not long either since one of our District Officers was shot dead with their poisoned arrows. If you come up with them, don't frighten them. It's when they're frightened that they tend to be dangerous.' To get to Ghanzi, Mac needed to cross a bridge at Toteng which had been wrecked by floods, and was only now being rebuilt. Atkinson lent him the doubtful services of two local African 'boys' under detention, who would cook for him in return for their passage to Maun, where the local DC would provide replacements. Stay on the east side of the Okavanga basin, he was told. He could shoot his meat, and buy eggs and goats from native villages. They would reach the next waterhole in a hundred miles.

Atkinson waved them off. Mac loaded the seven-millimetre, and they began their long, painfully slow rollercoaster ride along what they quickly decided was the worst road in the world. It was not a road at all, of course, but a mere spoor through the bush. After three hours, during which they advanced about twenty miles, Father decreed that they should make camp in the shade of a big merula tree. They began to learn a little about John Currye. He had been born in the Congo, son of a Lancashire mother and Scottish father, and had never cared much for schools. In consequence, he proved a poor hand at the mathematics for working out quantities of fuel, water, miles. But this shortcoming was entirely outweighed by the fact that he was an enthusiastic companion, apparently untroubled by Mac's inexperience, and a superb mechanic. That first night they extended their tarpaulin overhead from the roof of the truck, and slept beneath it. Thereafter, they learned better – using the canvas as a groundsheet, to restrain the worst of the myriad insects underfoot. The boys, named Wilson and Habana, were a trifle sulky as they cooked their mealies, because Mac had flinched on aesthetic grounds from shooting an ostrich which they had passed. 'Ostrich very good to eat!' urged Habana. John tried sleeping on the roof of the truck, but only once. During the night a merula branch collapsed on him. He awoke to find that a baby owl which had fallen from its nest was sharing his blanket.

The rest of the 320 miles to Maun proved an ordeal chiefly by heat. 'Our eyes were half-closed with a rime of fine grey dust,' wrote Mac. 'Our noses were blocked, our lips cracked, and our tongues stuck to the roofs of our mouths like biltong. Our clothes were so sticky and stained with sweat that we couldn't force our hands into our pockets. Our ribs were so sore from the pummelling we were taking in the truck, that every shattering bump punched a gasp out of us. The wind licked over arid plain and vast white saltpans like the breath of a furnace. At intervals whirlwinds, which we could see coming, spiralled into us and enveloped us, as we buried our heads in our arms, in a choking cloud of hot dust. All about us were bush fires, laying blankets of murky smoke along the skyline.' The truck's speed fell below 4 mph. Its radiator boiled constantly. Mac reflected on the consequences of a breakdown, which seemed increasingly likely. Their water tank was soon more than half-empty. They drank often, but never enough.

Mac, however. was enchanted. Great herds of game roamed everywhere – wildebeest, springbok, gazelle, giraffe, in a profusion that, had they but known it, no successor generation of travellers would see. He gazed with delight on the birds, butterflies, monkeys. His first attempt to shoot a buck for the pot failed. He missed the shot because his hands were shaking so much from the lurching of the truck. Their baggage rolled and juddered in a hopeless chaos that tore the labels off food tins, smashed everything breakable including the glass of the hurricane lamp. Cartridges littered the floor. The reserve petrol drum broke loose, almost crushing Chris Ware. They were travelling along the fringe of a vast saltpan named the Makarakari, following faint truck tracks in the sand. When these were lost, they climbed anthills to scour the horizon through binoculars until they spotted the trail again.

Then they glimpsed a sudden patch of livid greenery ahead, and knew they had found Nata, the next waterhole. Just short of it, a flock of guinea fowl chattered in the scrub. Mac jumped down with his shotgun, stalked the birds until they rose clumsily into the air, then dropped three with two shots. They filled the truck's water tank from a thin stream pumped up from the well, ate a little, and pushed on. A few miles beyond Nata, Mac stopped near a herd of wildebeest, and set out alone to stalk one with his rifle. As he plunged through high grass rearing above his head, he tried to remember Lewis's advice, and carefully loaded and cocked the rifle. He could see only fifteen yards or so ahead. Within a few minutes, he realised that the wildebeest had winded him, and were gone. More dismaying, he had lost his bearings, and had no idea which way the truck lay. He shouted, and was rewarded only by silence. He suffered some minutes of near-panic as he pushed blindly through the thick cover. Then he became more methodical. Fixing on a clearly identifiable tall tree, he circled this in widening spirals until at last he found the truck. It was a sharp lesson. Never again did he wander on foot without taking bearings.

They bounced and clattered on. Chris Ware observed that Mac at the wheel resembled a golliwog on the end of a spring wire. Chris was excused driving duty, because his pictures were the priority. It was hard for him to keep his cameras, caked in dust, fit for use. At that night's camp, all three men were almost too exhausted to eat. John Currye waxed lyrical about the joys of home in Bulawayo, racing his motorbike, drinking with the boys, listening to 'jizz'. He said: 'I may be a rough Rhodesian, but this is too rough for me.' Father was optimist enough to assume that he didn't mean it. Chris Ware observed with some feeling that properly organised safaris travelled with fridges and white hunters who knew what they were doing. Here, he remarked, he was at the mercy of a team leader who had never seen a lion outside a zoo. Fried guinea fowl failed to raise morale. Mac concealed from the others the fact that his bowels were in a state of mutiny.

Next day, however, everything got better. Mac shot a springbok from the cab of the truck, and found his spirits soaring: 'I was learning the ways of Africa; and I began to get the fever of it in my blood.' Writing afterwards for his audience of schoolchildren, he asserted his own idea of what life should be about: 'You'll find that there's very little fun in playing safe. There is not much that I have come across that is worth doing without the zest of danger; the thought that you can so easily come a glorious cropper; the hope that if you keep your head, you'll save your hide. In the arid, pitiless land of the Kalahari, I was saving my hide.' After an apparent eternity of emptiness, they met a sudden outcrop of lush green vegetation. Rounding a bend, they saw a river before them, and after crossing a rough timber bridge they found themselves in the little town of Maun. This was the showpiece of what passed for civilisation in the Kalahari, complete with swimming pool, golf course and tennis courts. Within half an hour they were drinking beer from the fridge of Riley's Hotel.

Their chief problem now was time. In just a fortnight the rains were due. When these came, movement in the wilderness would be impossible. If Mac was to find his bushmen, he needed to do it quickly. As with all such media assignments, adventures must be telescoped to fit time and budgets. They set about buying equipment to replace all the stuff smashed on the drive from Francistown. John Currye laboured beneath the Chevy, fearful that its clutch was stripped. There was doubt whether the broken bridge at Toteng, the only place where they could cross the river to get to the south-west, was repaired for traffic. Their boys, Wilson and Habana, were surrendered to the Maun DC as instructed. Replacements were needed. Father quizzed the DC's wife, Mrs Allison, about three lions she had shot. He experienced a spasm of envy, since he yearned for a chance at one himself.

Things started to look better for the expedition. John Currye reported that he had mended the clutch. News came that the bridge at Toteng was passable, though no vehicle had tried it yet. The DC found them a new boy, named Malenga. They bought a lot of leaf tobacco, Transvaal Special No.1, to offer the bushmen if they found them. They set off again into the bush. Conditions were worse, though they had not thought it possible, than those they had met earlier. Within a few hours, Mac at the wheel – never a skilful driver – almost ditched the truck. It careered headlong down a steep decline, apparently bent on overturning. The whole load, including the big petrol drum, broke loose and crashed about inside, creating a mad cacophony. At last, to their surprise, the Chevy lurched to a halt, hot metal ticking, in the midst of a thorn bush. They repeated that experience half a dozen times before reaching the bridge at Toteng, where they made the inaugural passage past a sign warning: 'ALL TRAFFIC CROSSES ENTIRELY AT OWNER'S RISK'.

Once over the river, they refilled the water tanks and headed for their next camp, in a huge soured saltpan still marked on their map as Lake N'Gami, though it was almost dry. To Mac's weary irritation, a crowd of local villagers squatted round the truck, begging tobacco and declining bribes and threats to make them go away. Bushmen were the only people the visitors wanted to meet just then. No other Africans would do. They heard a leopard as they ate their guinea-fowl stew, but felt too weary to become excited.

At the next waterhole, Tswai, about a hundred miles from Maun, they found a lonely white trader's store, remote as that which John Buchan invented for Prester John. Its owner, whose name was Gower, said that it was months since he had seen a visitor. Would they like a cup of tea? They told him about their quest. 'There's a bushman here now in the camp,' he said. 'The boys call him Big Guts. His family are out there somewhere in the *bundu* about twenty miles from here. Do you want to see him?'

Big Guts proved to be a little man with a swollen belly lined with deep creases, clad in a ragged pair of oversized shorts which clung precariously to his narrow loins. He was one among a sad host of his people who had abandoned bush life to attach themselves to the coat-tails of white man's life, without discovering much comfort or satisfaction. He chattered volubly in his clicking tongue, which the explorers were thrilled to hear for the first time. His family were out there sure enough, he said: '*Kwa! Kwa!*' Gower said: 'I think he can lead you to them.' The ramshackle expedition 'welcomed Big Guts as if he were Father Christmas'.

There was no track where they were going, the trader warned. It was virgin bush. At the first sign of rain they should turn back fast, or they would never get out at all. Father unloaded all their spare rations and the extra fuel drum, replacing it with a further fifty gallons of water. Then they set off westwards, Big Guts at intervals pointing convincingly. Hour after hour the truck battered a path through the scrub. Mac shot a gazelle, which they skinned and ate round the fire that night. His bowels were still in revolt, so the hunter himself abstained, watching in disbelief as Big Guts ate two entire legs of meat, laughing manically in a fashion which he sustained through the days that followed.

They awoke to find a giraffe a few yards away, peering curiously down at them. Big Guts, still convulsed with mirth as well he might be, ate several more pounds of meat while the others made do with mealie porridge. That day the going got much worse. Again and again they foundered in the sand and were obliged to reverse, make a rush, and smash a passage through the vegetation blocking their course. Father noted with alarm that they were using a gallon of petrol every two miles. At that rate they could not long pursue their search. '*Kwa!*' urged Big Guts merrily, gesturing them on. '*Kwa!*' They were approaching a huge kopje, which he promised was their destination, when the truck lurched into soft sand and bogged. Mac took his guide, a waterbag and rifle, and prepared to complete the distance on foot. Leaving Malenga and John digging, he trudged away into the bush. He covered barely a mile before admitting defeat. It was far too hot to walk. He suffered a moment of panic at the discovery that he had once again lost the truck. Then, mercifully, he glimpsed Chris Ware standing like a fingerpost on its roof, pointing the way back.

Many hours of digging later, together with more hours of grinding at a bare walking pace through the bush, they reached the kopje. They found only the tattered remains of two grass huts – skerms, as they are known. The bushmen were gone. Big Guts sniffed the blackened remains of a fire and gestured onwards. They asked him: how far? 'Three days.' John Currye shrugged: 'We haven't the fuel.' Father said they would push on as far as they dared. Some hours later, Chris Ware drew attention to Big Guts's behaviour. He pointed first left, then right, then laid a skinny arm across his mouth and giggled. Chris said, 'I think he's taking us for a joy ride.' John said, 'I'm bloody sure he is.' Malenga and the bushman chattered to each other. Big Guts eventually climbed down from the truck, sniffed the air and laughed again. Mac remembered someone telling him that bushmen laugh when they are frightened.

They abandoned the quest, turned the truck in its tracks, and set off on the gloomy path back to trader Gower's. There was little talking in the camp that night, only more laughter from Big Guts. Chris Ware was stung by a bee swarm. A tyre punctured. One of the big, heavy wheels had to be changed. The radiator boiled every half-hour. John blocked an oil leak in the engine with a splinter of wood. There was a rainstorm, which they knew was the harbinger of more, much more, to come. Back at Gower's, after drinking a mug of tea they were thankful to offload Big Guts. The bushman was still laughing as they drove away. The morale of the little expedition was at rock bottom.

Two days later they reached Ghanzi. This was a wired compound in the midst of the bush which housed a small police detachment and Ernest Midgeley, the DC who administered the surrounding 69,000 square miles of nothingness. Sitting on the verandah of

Midgeley's quarters, Mac, weary and unshaven, listened as the DC quizzed one of his policemen about the nearest bushmen. Ba'phuti, the constable, stood at attention as he reported that he knew where to find a family of Makokas.

'Can you lead this *marena* to the Makokas?' demanded Midgeley. 'I think so.'

'Are you quite sure, Ba'phuti?'

'Quite sure, *marena*.'

First, however, they had to repair their transport. A front spring of the truck was gone. There were no spares within a hundred miles, except a few designed for a Ford. John Currye asked: was there a welding kit anywhere? Yes, indeed, a mere twenty-six miles away. The tough, infinitely resourceful young man set off immediately in the police inspector's truck, to weld a Ford leafspring into something that might fit a Chevrolet. Late, very late that night, there was a tap on the wire mesh of the rest hut where Mac, sleepless, was writing his notes by the light of an oil lamp. 'It's John, Mr Hastings. We've done the job. It was pretty rough. I had to drive there and back without lights – the circuit on the truck had gone. But I can fit the new spring in a couple of hours tomorrow morning.' 'Good boy.'

At dawn, as Currye worked on the spring Ba'phuti arrived, trailed by womenfolk carrying his bedroll and pack with suitable dignity. Midgeley had ordered the constable to travel in plain shorts rather than uniform, to avoid alarming the bushmen. Soon after, they headed once more into the heat haze. They stopped at a ranch, Ramsden's, to drink tea. The two English farmers, Frank and Bert, said they had plenty of tame bushmen about the place, but were more doubtful about finding the wild ones, the Makokas. 'You might find them, you might not. One day they're about the place; the next you hear they're eighty miles away.' They warned Father to carry his rifle if he met them: 'They know what it is, and that way they're less likely to stick a poisoned arrow into you. They'll tell you they haven't got any bows and arrows. You needn't believe them. You can be sure they've got them hidden somewhere about. But they don't like producing them because they're afraid the white man will take them away.'

The author sanitised to serve as an extra in a fashion shoot for *Harper's Bazaar*; and more in character, failing to enter into the party spirit, while Nanny looks on balefully.

ABOVE At a Butlin's holiday camp in 1956, when I was ten and my sister four. Clare looks characteristically uneasy about what enormity I might be planning to perpetrate next.

Mac's happy masquerade as Action Man ABOVE AND RIGHT circus performer Hal Denver throws the knives, while *Eagle* Special Investigator acts as target.

As a Bedouin in the Jordanian desert.

ABOVE Mac learning to fly a Tiger Moth.

LEFT As a cowboy in Alberta.

OPPOSITE Practising the snake charmer's art in southern India.

THIS PAGE AND OPPOSITE
Mac's 1956 adventure
in the Kalahari Desert,
where he sought out
some of the last wild
bushmen.

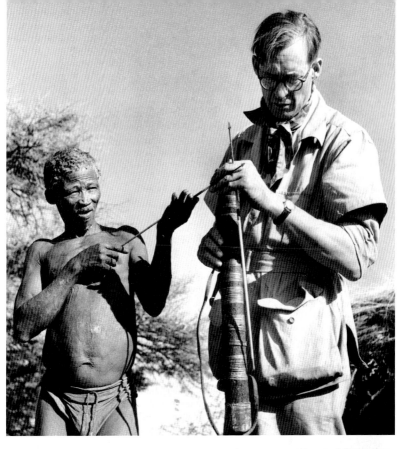

LEFT The author in a rare moment of childhood ecstasy, escaping from boarding school for the holidays.

BELOW Father purporting to take an interest in my steam engine.

ABOVE AND RIGHT Anne on assignment for the *Daily Mail* among Masai in Kenya, 1960.

LEFT One of the few occasions on which the fractious Hastings men assembled, at Brown's Farm in 1964 for the christening of my half-sister Harriet. Left to right: the author (then eighteen), Mac, Lewis and Stephen.

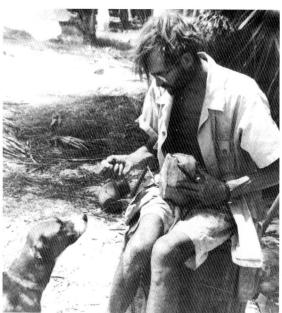

Mac's last and craziest adventure, making himself a castaway on an uninhabited Indian Ocean atoll in 1960
ABOVE Arrival on Ressource, with Dog Friday and scanty possessions.

LEFT Feeding Friday, when hardship had started to tell.

OPPOSITE TOP Near to despair, with pitifully little in the pot.

OPPOSITE BOTTOM Signalling for rescue, just before he collapsed.

Mac on the telly

BELOW With presenter Cliff Michelmore and producer Donald Baverstock on the floor of the BBC *Tonight* studio.

BOTTOM Costumed for the dream sequence of his film about a makeover of Rose Cottage's garden. Clare peers behind the camera, a 35mm Newman.

ABOVE A weekend party at Rose Cottage in its 1968 post-Mac incarnation: my sister Clare stands with John Piper, Osbert Lancaster and his daughter Cara, while Penelope Betjeman sits on the grass and John B reads an improving book. The seat was that into which I once emptied a Luger automatic.

RIGHT Osbert's perception of Maudie Littlehampton and Anne in cocktail party conversation. Socially ubiquitous publisher George Weidenfeld lurks behind.

ABOVE Anne poses at Rose Cottage in the 1970s – a publicity shot for one of her first gardening books.

BELOW Anne with Osbert at the launch of *The Pleasure Garden*, which he illustrated.

Late editions
ABOVE Mac at Brown's Farm, looking healthier than was usual in his final decade.

RIGHT Anne at ninety, apparently indestructible.

The author begins the long struggle to follow in the family footsteps: aged twenty-one in 1967, steeplejacking on a South London chimney for the *Evening Standard*.

'I'll remember.'

On and on they drove.

It was country in which I would have said that a jackal couldn't find cover. I was overwhelmed by a sense of utter helplessness at the sheer enormity of the search that I had set myself so lightly by the fireside of a London club. Then Ba'phuti pointed. Slinging my rifle on my shoulder and dropping out of the truck, I stumbled over the hot, soft sand and threaded my way through the maze of tangled scrub. Loping towards me, raising his knees with a springing lift like an antelope, was a wizened little man with a distended belly and hair that grew in pepperpot tufts. Where he had sprung from I couldn't guess. The landscape seemed quite empty. All I cared was that he was nothing like any of the Africans I had ever seen. He wasn't black; his skin was yellow. The only clothing he wore was a loincloth made of antelope hide. My long quest was ended. I had crossed the Kalahari Desert to within twenty-five miles of the South-West border. I had bashed the stuffing out of a truck. I had pretty well bashed the stuffing out of myself and my faithful companions. But we'd done it. By all the black mambas in Africa, we'd done it. I had found the Stone Age Man.

A cynic might say that what Mac had achieved was not very remarkable. In Bechuanaland in those days, white men not infrequently encountered bushmen. His own astonishment and wonder was that of a tourist, seeing for the first time something familiar to those who made their lives in south-west Africa. His principal feat was to have overcome the hazards created by the inadequacy of his own crazy little expedition. But Mac possessed a gift, which lay at the heart of my own devotion to him, of imbuing with romance even a journey to the Highlands of Scotland. He loved to create melodrama in his life, to cast himself in the role of a character out of Buchan or Rider Haggard. His innocent, breathless delight in the adventures he devised for himself was infectious, and he conveyed it brilliantly to a generation of schoolboy readers, who thrilled to his exploits because he was so sincerely thrilled by them himself. A journey across a few hundred miles of wilderness which would have been commonplace to an old Africa hand became an epic when performed by a novice who, until three weeks earlier, had never donned a bush jacket. Mac cast himself as the gentleman amateur explorer, a pose which would have invited derision from the Royal Geographical Society. Some mirth must indeed have trailed in his wake across Rhodesia and Bechuanaland, at the notion of a journalist straight out from Britain renting a truck and setting forth to conquer the Kalahari in the service of a boys' comic. But to a million young readers of *Eagle*, and to his son now as then, the performance was irresistible.

Not surprisingly his new acquaintance, barely four feet tall, looked nervous. Mac offered a cigarette, which was eagerly received. The little man pointed to a clump of marula trees, took his guest by the hand, and led him away towards them, Chris Ware and his clicking cameras scurrying close behind. Mac had told the rest of the party to stay in the truck, to avoid overwhelming the bushman. He got as far as asking his name, which sounded like Xa-ou, but then needed Ba'phuti to interpret. The constable came up just as they approached Xa-ou's family, squatting in a circle in the scrub. There were nineteen of them there – nine women, six children and four men. Another nine men, they said, were away hunting. Their five skerms were shaped like molehills, with low entrances which even the bushmen had to crawl into. Only the sick and the old, Father knew, used the skerms. Fit adults slept in a circle around the fire. Their bodies often bore burn-marks, where they had rolled into the embers on a cold night.

The atmosphere among the group was tense. Xa-ou seemed friendly enough, but others trembled when Mac spoke to them. Some slipped away to hide. Like so many others of Africa's wild species, they had suffered such appalling persecution at the hands of man, who had hunted and harassed them to the verge of extinction, that their wariness represented common prudence. Things improved when Father proffered tobacco. They all began to smoke, some using pipes carved from antelope bones. Bert Ramsden had told Mac that the bushmen were always baffled by white men's carelessness about throwing away the tins in which their meat came. To these people tins were price-less, for they had learned to forge arrowheads from them.

Mac groped presumptuously in a skerm. 'It seemed inconceivable that a family of human beings could exist with so little property. They had one or two bone knives, an animal skin with some liquid (probably milk) in it, a few ostrich-egg shells.' Everything else they owned hung in little antelope-hide dilly bags which hung on their hips. Possessions would imply permanence. These bushmen were still nomadic hunters, each family cherishing its traditional territory into which others ventured at their peril. Their only valuables were their weapons – the bows and arrows on which they depended for exis-tence. At last Mac found a quiver, two feet long, made from a hollowed length of tree branch, capped with hide. He examined the arrows, each in two pieces. The shaft was a reed, bound with animal sinew. The head was made of sharpened bone, to which was attached a tiny barb, hammered out of tinplate. There were no feathers to steady its flight. Mac reckoned that, to be effective, it would need to be fired at a range of no more than ten or twenty yards.

When he emerged from the skerm carrying the quiver, a chill fell on the gathering. Xa-ou crouched with his head sunk on his shoul-ders. Another hunter, whose name sounded like 'No', slipped round behind the human predator. As Father fingered the arrows, he did not know that their poison, which can kill a giraffe, was smeared on the boneshaft, not the barb. It was made from a beetle's larvae, stiff-ened with gum from the t'lopi tree. In his ignorance, Mac was living very dangerously. When he handed the quiver back to Xa-ou, the tension relaxed sharply. Xa-ou accepted another cigarette, and No produced his bow for examination.

Mac looked curiously at it, reflecting that a schoolboy could have made a much more efficient instrument – yet could not have used it half so well. No mimed the firing of an arrow, holding the bow against his chest at an angle. None of the white visitors had ever seen a weapon so oddly aimed and used, yet No then demonstrated that he could place an arrow accurately at a range of thirty yards, whether standing, kneeling or lying prone. Even after achieving a hit on a quarry, a bushman hunter was obliged to follow the spoor for hours, some-times days, before the poisoned shaft did its work. When he reached the carcass, it was too heavy to carry, so it was necessary to travel for many hours more to fetch his family, a race with the vultures. Some-times others of the clan could be summoned to the kill by smoke signals. Yet bushmen often went hungry, and at the end of the dry season when Father met them, Xa-ou's family was very hungry indeed. They seemed to lack even the roots and berries which supplemented game in their diet. Mac gave them all the spare rations in the truck.

At that time it was estimated that ten thousand bushmen remained in Bechuanaland, Angola and South-West Africa – modern Namibia. Most of these had already succumbed to the white man's dominance, becoming more or less literally scavengers beneath his tables. Only a very few thousand of the Makokas lived as Xa-ou's family did, in the manner that had remained almost unchanged for half a million years. Mac, Chris Ware and John Currye were the most privileged of tourists. They encountered one of the last communities in a society which has now vanished for ever.

Chris photographed every aspect of the family's doings until he sagged with exhaustion. They were fascinated to see one man start a fire by rubbing two sticks, in a fashion which they had supposed mere Boy Scout legend. Within one of the women's dilly bags, Mac came upon a small tortoise-shell. Inside this, in turn, lay lamb's wool and a green aromatic powder. He realised that he had found her beauty box. In their hair, on their legs, around their necks, all the women wore exquisite beans worked from shell.

They stored their water in hollowed ostrich-egg shells. With the aid of Ba'phuti as interpreter, Xa-ou's people told Mac about 'eat-all-day' beans, of which a handful could sustain a man – or at least a bushman – from sunrise to sunset. They described the *tsamma*, seeds of a watermelon which Europeans disdain but the bushmen prize, roasting them then grinding them between flat stones into meal.

When Mac asked No how they lived when game ran out, the little hunter led him a few yards into the bush, and pointed out a plant like a tiny green vine. He dug furiously with a sharpened stick, and at last pulled up a tuber the size of a turnip. Scraping off the skin, he offered it to his visitor: 'It was rather like eating something between celery and parsnip, full of cool, refreshing juices; enough to save a man's life who was in dire need of water.' The family rejected Chris Ware's urgings to dance. Midgeley, the District Commissioner, later explained that they danced only at full moon, when they often played pantomime games all night, acting out a lion hunt, or a hawk swooping on its prey, or dogs running down a gemsbok.

Hour after hour, white visitors and bushmen talked. 'We kept at it,' said Mac, 'because it was no use going away and expecting to find them in the same place tomorrow.' Indeed, next day Mac learned from Ba'phuti that Xa-ou's family had already moved on, perhaps alarmed by their visit. He reflected on one point which seemed to him significant. During their encounter, all the curiosity was displayed by the white men. Maybe, Mac thought, this was why bushmen had advanced so little for so long. 'Curiosity is the human quality which moves the rest of us to experiment, to improvise, to explore, to invent and to develop. I fancy that the Makokas gazed without surprise at our cameras, our watches, our rifles, our clothes, all the ingenious impedimenta of civilised man, because they were mentally incapable of being interested. Like the animals about them, their ruling quality is only the negative emotion of fear.'

When the time came to go, with grave courtesy the bushmen accepted presents of tobacco. The two groups waved, one from the truck, the other from the fireside, until they were out of sight of each other. Father, Chris and John felt a sense of awe about what they had seen, which remained with them for the rest of their lives. Next day, as they headed north-east once more, they were told of another bushmen's camp nearby, and drove to it. There, however, instead of authentic hunter-gatherers, they found a sad cluster of half-tame pygmies, already collecting kitchen utensils and using matches in place of tinder, as well as being obviously diseased. The family had chickens and goats. These were not bushmen such as Mac had travelled so far to see, but a sub-group on a tragic, squalid path towards 'civilisation'.

On their return to Ghanzi, DC Midgeley cut short their excited account of what was to them a remarkable encounter. He urged his visitors that they had better get a move on if they wanted to get out of Bechuanaland before the rains. John Currye said: 'I've seen enough sand.' The battered old Chevy started to wend its way north once more across the Kalahari, on a course towards Victoria Falls. They had barely started before the first storms came: 'The black velvet of the African night split open like an over-ripe fruit,' wrote Mac. 'A jagged red fork of lightning ripped through the skin of the sky. Thunder sounded like the crash of war drums. With a whoosh, the clouds bucketed a cataract.' The truck was soon ploughing through heavy mud, struggling to make ten miles an hour. They drove all night now, John Currye fearful that the Chevy was on its last legs. Chris Ware gave a sudden exclamation, causing Father to wake from a doze in time to glimpse a big leopard in the headlights. He groped for his rifle, eager for a trophy, but the beast was gone.

They risked a bathe in the river at Toteng to wash away some of the filth in which they were coated. This provoked the DC's subsequent wrath. He told them that by rights, the local crocodiles should have had them. They fractured another spring on the truck just as they approached Maun. But by now Mac, triumphant, did not care. That night Chris Ware pumped a forge's bellows while John used a heavy hammer to temper a new leafspring to replace the broken part. Chris paused for a moment, walked round the truck in the darkness – and fell headlong into the concrete inspection pit. The expedition's luck, which had favoured it brilliantly for so long, had at last broken. Chris smashed five ribs. He was obliged to remain in hospital until an aircraft could be found to fly him to Livingstone.

Now there were just Mac and John Currye, pushing onward in the truck. Instead of desert, they found themselves in green and marshy game country, amid hippo and elephants, cranes and herons, paradise flycatchers, kingfishers, squawking louries. Again and again the Chevrolet had to detour off the track to avoid tree trunks thrown down by elephants. Amid the rain, the flies became almost unbearable. When Mac walked into the bush to shoot a buck, their boy Malenga followed him, pumping a cloud of DDT around his head. There was water everywhere, and many moments at which they feared the truck irretrievably bogged. They stopped to watch the passage of a great herd of wilde-beest, hastening south. Mac shot one for the pot. Suddenly, right by the trackside, they glimpsed a huge, black-maned lion, no more than five yards away. It turned and trotted off into the bush.

Mac decided that the moment had come to enjoy himself, and to fulfil a lifelong ambition. Ignoring a display of eye-rolling alarm from Malenga, he and John set off in pursuit. They had stalked some way, Mac increasingly confident that they must come upon the great animal, when John touched him on the shoulder and breathed: 'Behind you. The lioness is behind you.' Mac turned, glimpsed a crouching form fifty yards distant, and fired. His quarry fell. 'You've got her!' cried John exultantly. It seemed one of the great moments of Mac's life, when at last he joined the brotherhood of Uncle Lewis and all those generations of African hunters he admired and envied so much. 'Now let's go after the old man,' said Currye. They hastened onwards – and found nothing. The shot must have hastened the lion's flight into the bush. They returned to the carcass – and instead of a dead lioness found a huge hyena. It was a crushing disappointment, the nearest Mac would ever come to acquiring the rug of his dreams.

That night they camped beside the Chobe river, within easy reach of Vic Falls. Mac shot a brace of duck for dinner, and while the boys cooked them the two white men stripped and scrubbed in the river, then sat listening to the hippos 'clearing their throats like elderly colonels'. Night fell, and the mosquitoes descended. When the trav-ellers finally slipped into fitful sleep, they were wakened by more torrential rain. They sat, sodden, drinking coffee brewed on the Primus, waiting for dawn. At first light Mac potted crocodiles, dreaming of handbags. Every beast he hit disappeared into the river, however, its tail thrashing. They pushed on to Victoria Falls. That evening they had to waken a slumbering policeman to open the barrier that marked Bechuanaland's border with Rhodesia. As the truck touched a metalled road for the first time in weeks, they felt as if they had begun to drive on a carpet. At Vic Falls Hotel, Mac threw himself on a bed and fell asleep without taking off his clothes.

Next day, a little plane from Maun brought in Chris Ware, scarcely able to walk. They divided the remaining stores between their two boys. John Currye agreed to drive the truck back to Bulawayo, and kept the Primus stove as a souvenir. Mac and Chris caught the BOAC plane home, their only souvenir a baby crocodile which the intrepid explorers presented to the London Zoo. It was christened Marcus, in honour of *Eagle*'s editor, and survived for years.

When Mac's children's book about the experience appeared, entitled *The Search for the Little Yellow Men*, it was inevitably dedicated to Uncle Lewis, who sent a characteristic letter:

> I was struck by the contrast between your story and the series of 'adventures' in the Kalahari recently given on TV by [Laurens] Van Der Post: the same scene, and achievements no more than yours, but blown up by VdP into a saga of original and death-defying exploration of the unknown. And stuffed with tear-jerking sentiment about the savage way we – the British and Dutch and the Bantu – have deprived the Bushman of his heritage in the African continent. What falldoodle it was!!

Mac was pleased when a *Sunday Times* reviewer, quite unknown to him, made the same comparison: 'What is so remarkable is that (unlike Mr Van der Post who last year took a carefully-equipped expedition into the same hazardous country) Mr Hastings had never been in Africa before.' The difference, of course, was that Mac was a shameless journalist-adventurer, while Van der Post possessed a lifelong gift for mystic waffle which sustained a reputation until after his death, when some of his deceits and exaggerations were exposed.

Mac's experience in the Kalahari was among the happiest of his life, fulfilment of a family dream. His narrative gained him less celebrity than he deserved, for it described one of his finest hours as a journalist-adventurer. I have cherished ever since a photograph of him dirty and grim-faced, standing amid the great wilderness in his bush jacket, rifle shouldered. There was Father in the heroic guise in which I loved to see him – and in which, of course, he best liked to perceive himself.

ELEVEN

Mac on the Telly

Towards the end of 1956 a BBC television producer whom Mac had never heard of, Donald Baverstock, rang and said he wanted to meet. Donald, a volatile and impassioned little Welshman in his early thirties, had energy, originality and talent, as well as the financial good fortune to be married to Enid Blyton's daughter. He liked to act the part of a Chicago gang boss, striding into the BBC Club, an entourage of loyal acolytes trailing in his wake, with the strutting aggression of a man who expects a shoot-out, and welcomes the prospect. A staccato talker, Baverstock hired and fired in lunges, launching dramatic creative thrusts of which the most spectacular was now imminent. At his first meeting with Mac, in a smoke-filled pub in Notting Hill, the BBC man disclosed that he had been commissioned to start a new weekday magazine programme, which would be broadcast at early evening for the next few weeks. Would Mac be interested in contributing some short film items about the countryside? Donald was explicitly recruiting among old *Picture Post* hands – the magazine had just folded. He believed that they had the gift for smart, snappy, witty, irreverent photo-journalism, even if they had never worked in television.

The embryo programme was, of course, the legendary *Tonight*, which first burst upon the airwaves in February 1957. Its begetter, BBC's Head of Talks Grace Wyndham-Goldie, said that her vision was of a programme 'which looked at those in power from the perspective of the powerless'. Transmitted five evenings a week, in the years that followed *Tonight* acquired an audience of eight million, and became one of the sensations of that first British TV generation. Presented by Cliff Michelmore, a veteran of the radio music programme *Two Way Family Favourites*, it featured as reporters Fyfe Robertson, Alan Whicker, Derek Hart, Trevor Philpott, Slim Hewitt – and Macdonald Hastings. It had a resident topical calypso performer, Cy Grant, later replaced by Robin Hall and Jimmy MacGregor. Many of the young turks among its directors and producers rose to the top of the BBC – Donald's deputy, Alasdair Milne, would become director-general. Donald himself had a journalistic genius which flourished dazzlingly on *Tonight*. One night Mac took me, a boy of eleven, to the temporary studio off Kensington High Street from which the first programmes were transmitted – nobody then imagined that the show would become a fixture. Amid the cameras, cabling and dazzling lights, the tension in the gallery and relentless sense of crisis, I watched enthralled as *Tonight* was transmitted. I shook the hand of Cy Grant – the first black man I had ever met – secured the autographs of Baverstock, Milne and the rest, and went home starstruck.

Like every successful news impresario, Donald made up the story as he went along, flying each programme by the seat of his pants. A later *Daily Mail* boss, David English, once observed to me that all great editors are obsessives. So it was with Baverstock. He intervened in everything, tore up running orders without warning, threw tantrums and sometimes drunken scenes worthy of a Hollywood diva, and produced a programme which delighted and enthralled the nation. It was sharp, newsy, brave, whimsical, funny. From the outset, Mac Hastings's weekly turn was perceived as comedy by most of the Baverstock mafia, pavement types to a man. Mac, however, treated his mission with the earnestness of a true believer. He sought to educate a vast urban and suburban audience – for *Tonight* soon dominated the nation's airwaves in a fashion unthinkable in today's multi-channel world – about rural Britain.

He revisited much of the repertoire which he had performed for *Picture Post* back in 1938. He made little films, initially between four and six minutes long, later more protracted, about pheasant-shooting, salmon-fishing, cattle-farming, sheepdogs, remote Wiltshire villages and Scottish trawlermen. Today, when television has been everywhere and filmed everything, it is hard to believe that in the late 1950s Mac was a pioneer, but so he was. Indeed, all the *Tonight* reporters were. They did things which are now wearily familiar, but were then excitingly new.

Mac shot a piece with the Household Cavalry in which he traversed the jumps in their Knightsbridge riding school, describing through a primitive radio microphone the sensations as he rode. He created a 'dream' film about making over the garden at Rose Cottage, which for some years had been sorely neglected. Standing amidst its weedy borders in old trousers, he fantasised before the camera about transforming his plot. He persuaded every manufacturer of garden machinery in the country to dispatch tools and men to west Berkshire. The boxy old Newman camera filmed a great advancing column of cultivators, hedge-trimmers, flame-throwers, mowers, watched by Father in 'dream' white jacket and flannels as they introduced perfect order to the little garden. Then Mac did his 'pay-off', back in the wilderness in old trousers, looking around with a shrug and saying, 'What a pity it was all a dream.' In those innocent days, when millions of people swallowed at face value *Panorama*'s 1 April film of Italy's spaghetti harvest, few viewers worked out that Mac filmed his closing shot alongside his 'intro', before the machines moved in. Instead, they perceived him as making magic.

He had been a well-known journalist for almost two decades, but *Tonight* made Mac, like all its regular contributors, a star for a season. He achieved a street recognition which of course he adored, as did I. In school holidays he often took me on location. There was a memorable occasion, during the great frozen winter of 1962, when I flew with him by chartered helicopter to a snowbound farm in the West Country, to describe a weather siege which persisted for more than two months. I loved the chopper trip, of course, but was already so absurdly tall that both Father and I found it an ordeal to share the farmer's bed, while the camera crew dossed down on sofas.

Once, filming at the village of Castle Combe in Wiltshire, he sent me to buy cigarettes for him. Walking back through the little crowd which always gathered where a TV camera appeared, I heard one woman say to another, 'Ooh, there's that Macdonald Hastings.' At that moment, I reflected very consciously that when I grew up I wanted people to say, 'Ooh, there's that Max Hastings,' though at fourteen I had not the slightest conception of how such a miracle might be achieved. During the garden filming I staged a shameful display of pique because my sister Clare featured in the film, and I did not.

On other occasions I witnessed some of Mac's embarrassments – or rather, what might have been embarrassments, if he had possessed any grain of self-awareness. Part of his success as a TV presenter stemmed from an absolute lack of it. Like all genuine eccentrics, he was oblivious of the impact his actions had on others. Nonsenses on film which reduced the Baverstock gang to hysterical laughter in the viewing theatre at Lime Grove – whence the programme moved once its longevity became assured – left Mac serenely unmoved. There was the occasion when he filmed Kenzie, a rascally old Lincolnshire poacher whom Mac helped to make a celebrity, supposedly calling geese. We lay for hours in a freezing ditch with the camera crew, Kenzie calling for all he was worth, while the geese resolutely declined to respond. The film was transmitted anyway, Mac alone failing to perceive its comic quality.

Gin made him accident-prone. One day in a pub whose landlord was initially thrilled to have on his premises Macdonald Hastings, TV celeb (though the ghastly word had not been invented in those days), he stood on a chair to examine a glass case containing a magnificent painted plaster fish in a case. In a scene recalling *Three Men in a Boat*, he toppled the case and was left standing in the ruins, clutching fragments of the fish. The landlord's enthusiasm for celebrity customers vanished like winter sunshine.

On another occasion, Father decided to make a film about a cottage in Sussex where a headsman – supposedly the executioner of Charles I – had lived. As a gesture of bravado, in the seventeenth century this character had carved a headsman's axe into the lintel inside his front door. Mac knew the story, because the estate on which the cottage stood had once belonged to his pre-war friends the Pallants. They had long ago sold up, but Mac rang the new owners. He arranged to undertake a reconnaissance for the film, and was invited to lunch, collecting me from school at Charterhouse along the way. Roast lamb and apple crumble with this unknown and un-interesting but obviously prosperous banker and his wife went well enough, and afterwards we all trooped down to the cottage, now occupied by a farmworker. The cowman himself was absent at work, and his wife, deferential and nervous, admitted us with much apron-wiping. Horror of horrors, the interior of the cottage had been replastered. The axe was no longer visible. Mac called for a sharp knife, and tentatively picked at the plaster. A chunk or two fell away, revealing timber, but no axe.

He chipped away a trifle further, watched with increasing anxiety by the cowman's wife, and with some dismay by her landlord. Father decided that more professional measures were called for. Praying in aid the estate office, a plasterer – or rather, unplasterer – was summoned from Haslemere. By 5 p.m., most of the wall around the front door lay on the floor. At that point the cowman walked in. After a brief survey of the situation, he launched into a peroration which began, 'I may not know much about my rights, but I do know that . . .' At 5.15 an elderly neighbour stopped by, and announced jovially, 'I hear you'se looking for that old axe thing. Why, it were taken away to the museum these twenty year back.' At 5.30 we drove away, Mac the only member of the party oblivious of the trail of outrage in his wake. When I suggested that our hosts felt injured, he waved a dismissive hand and said, 'It's nothing, boy. I shall send them flowers.' Flowers? Lifetime invitations to the Chelsea Gala would not have restored harmony to that devastated corner of west Sussex.

Even in my teens I perceived the perils of Mac's cavalier attitude to money. The fee for his early five-minute films for *Tonight*, each of which required three or four days to recce, shoot, edit and dub commentary for, was thirty-five guineas. As late as 1962, the BBC was paying him only £3,500 a year for his half-time services, less than he had earned from *Eagle* a decade earlier. In those days presenters were modestly rewarded by the parsimonious Beeb. On location with a four- or five-man crew, Mac bought round upon round of drinks not only for the BBC team, but for half the occupants of whatever hotel bar they found themselves in. I discovered that he seldom, if ever, troubled to submit expense claims for entertaining. A gentleman journalist, he thought, should rise above scrabbling for petty cash. Thus, even when in the eyes of the world he achieved some fame, he made little out of it. The lesson stayed with me all my life. Not a farthing spent on my own assignments has ever gone unclaimed for.

As *Tonight*'s fortunes boomed, Mac's horizons widened. He undertook film tours for the programme in Kenya and India. He was commissioned to make several series of fifty-minute documentaries about the countryside, which proved hugely popular – notably *Riverbeat* and *In Deepest England*. He was always impeccably tailored on camera, and viewers became fascinated by his endless changes of clothes. Eventually *Tonight* ran an item about his wardrobe, arraying racks of suits and shoes across the studio floor. His speaking voice was a model of what was then admired as 'BBC English'. When the time came that I made my own first film for television, in Vietnam in 1970, when I was twenty-four, Father wrote me a long letter about the shortcomings of my performance. I resented this not at all, because I knew that his strictures were just, and prompted by love. His remarks are worth quoting not in the context of my own career, but because they reflected his shrewd understanding of what broadcasting is – or at least then was – all about:

> Better to put my comments on your programme in *24 Hours* last night in writing because you can consider it again, and the impression on your memory is likely to be stronger. You made two major mistakes which I beg you never to make again. You RANTED, especially in your wildtrack. The law is that, in television, you are not addressing a mass audience. You are talking to a small family group relaxing in their sitting rooms at an hour when they are thinking of bed. They are simple people whose interest must be won, to concern them with an exotic 'spot' on a subject they can't even place on the map. Between you and me, you talked last night like an anonymous newscaster. What you said was sense. But you will never be a TV personality until you inject warmth into your voice, a more confidential 'avuncular' manner.

The lens of the camera isn't ten million people; it's Mrs Jones thinking about groceries, doing her knitting and waiting to be interested. TV is the most confidential of all mediums of communication. Even more confidential than a feature film, when actors accustomed to the stage offer a grimace or a gesture which might be necessary to reach the gallery at Drury Lane, but which is quite unnecessary on a big screen where the flicker of an eyebrow is enough. On the little screen, the relationship with the audience is even more intimate than that . . . God knows, it's a difficult act, especially in the sort of conditions in which you have been working lately. But you mustn't think of yourself, you must think of 'them' sitting around the box in their homes. You must give an appearance, whatever the strain under which you are working, of complete, flattering and good-humoured relaxation.

You must think, not so much of hot news, but of the things that *they* might want to know. Play it cool, and as intimately as you know how. An appearance of wisdom is born of a soft, unexcited voice. Your second mistake was to talk to camera with sunglasses on. It is as bad manners to talk to Mrs Jones from behind sunglasses as it would be to enter her house smoking a cigarette. If you must wear them, what you should have done was to take them off as you addressed the camera. The gesture would have been valuable to enable you to get the juice up for the piece to camera, and as a courtesy, like raising a hat. You would have got the message across that you were talking under a blazing sun, without presenting yourself with dead man's eyes.

All this was true, and reflected wisdom born of Mac's mastery of the medium as it was at that time. As a reporter on *Tonight* he achieved his greatest popular success. He was a superb television presenter in the manner of those days, imbued with a passion for his subject – the English countryside – which he conveyed to his viewers. His scripts were famously word-perfect. Unfortunately, however, not only was he not making serious money from the BBC, nor was he from anywhere else. He had quit *Eagle*, which after its dazzling early success was in terminal decline. The remains of *Country Fair* were sold off in 1957. He was still writing books – he produced several manuals on game shooting which sold well, but into a small market. He published a delightful rural anthology, *Macdonald Hastings's Country Book*, but few anthologies make much money for their compilers.

He was often seized by extravagant financial hopes for unlikely projects. His 1960 novel *A Glimpse of Arcadia* was set in Victorian London. It tells the story of a river urchin who catches the last salmon to run up the Thames. It is a pleasant enough little yarn, with minor-key echoes of Hemingway's *The Old Man and the Sea*. But Mac convinced himself that it had Dickensian merits and selling potential, and formed a company to shield the huge royalties he expected to earn from the book. In the event, *A Glimpse of Arcadia* never even 'earned out' the £200 advance he was paid for it. He sometimes embraced ideas for inventions which would make his fortune – I remember in particular a children's board game named 'Rat Race', of which he had a prototype printed. But his commercial instincts were non-existent. On the rare occasions when he or Anne was solvent, and invested a little money in shares, they invariably plunged. Such people as the Hastingses do best to stick to what we understand – which means journalism. By the end of the 1950s, Mac's earnings barely sufficed to pay his share of a town and country lifestyle, never mind fund the education of two children.

Without Anne's income, the family would have been shipwrecked. After leaving the *Sunday Dispatch* in 1959, she accepted a glamorous-sounding title and large salary to become women's editor of Beaverbrook Newspapers. This proved a false step. She hated the chronically rancorous atmosphere at the summit of the Express Group, and found male chauvinism institutionalised in Beaverbrook's great black building at the bottom of Fleet Street. Her control of space and appointments was ill-defined, a fatal weakness for a newspaper executive. She found herself with no real power, and precious little influence.

One of her quirkier memories of that period was of commissioning an article from Margaret Thatcher, then the newly elected

MP for Finchley. Anne invited her to write about the experience of motherhood while serving in the Commons, and offered a fee of £100. Uniquely in Anne's experience, Thatcher accepted the commission but rejected the terms as over-generous: 'The fee is too high,' said Thatcher, peremptory as always. 'The current rate for a short article in a national newspaper is £50.' Bemused, Anne took the deal, but was less confident she had got a bargain when she received Thatcher's words, which were entirely banal. Anne took against The Lady after that experience, and maintained her scepticism throughout Thatcher's premiership: 'Except on matters of economics, Mrs Thatcher was never, to my mind, a woman of ideas.'

After two miserable years at the *Express*, Anne moved to become a columnist at the *Daily Mail*, an incomparably happier experience, not least because she shared an office with Bernard Levin, whom she admired prodigiously. Though I think Bernard returned the compliment, he professed to treat her as a near-imbecile, especially when she was struggling for inspiration: 'Anne Scott-James, how you ever got into Fleet Street I cannot imagine. You never seem to have an idea in your head, but nonetheless, I do not like to see a woman in distress without lifting a finger to help her, and I would commend you to page five of today's *Financial Times*, which you are too feather-brained to read, where there is a promising paragraph about the new industry of breeding miniature fish for fish fingers.' Anne said 'Thank you' with unfeigned gratitude, and opened the *FT*.

The only episode which caused Bernard to display apparently genuine anger towards her took place when she found in her morning mail a charming drawing by Augustus John. It had been sent by John's widow Dorelia after reading Anne's published interview with Edward Heath, then the new Tory leader. Anne had mentioned in the piece how much she envied Heath the John drawings on the walls of his flat. Dorelia said she would much prefer that Anne acquired a further example of her husband's work than that Heath did, and enclosed this handsome present. Bernard, mad with envy, said to their shared secretary: 'Carole, I will dictate a letter to Mrs John on Anne's behalf to save her the trouble. Are you ready? "Dear

Mrs John, It is extremely kind of you to send me the delightful drawing by your late husband – as you know, I am a great admirer of his work. Unfortunately, journalists on the *Daily Mail* are not allowed to accept perquisites, and I must regretfully send it back."' Even after Anne had countermanded Bernard's instructions, rancour persisted for the rest of the day.

The first assignment she undertook for the *Mail* proved one of the most exciting and rewarding she ever fulfilled – a series of big descriptive pieces about the game parks of Kenya and Tanzania, then still British-ruled, and places of mystery and enchantment for British newspaper writers as well as readers. Anne produced fine work from the trip – big interviews with Joy Adamson, the lion queen, and David Sheldrick, famous for his intimacy with elephants.

Thereafter, she flourished as a weekly controversialist. Indeed, her *Mail* column represented probably the best journalistic work she ever did. Newspaper columns are designed to provoke reaction, to inspire popular echoes. Here is a typical sample of her efforts:

> When parliament reassembles tomorrow I ask every man and woman in the House, from the Prime Minister to the youngest member, to emerge from their personal fog of lethargy, cynicism and laissez-faire and to attack politics this year with fire and spirit. The sickness of the British nation is not due to our war effort, loss of Empire or insuperable economic weakness. *Britain is dying of boredom*. The world is crackling with new ideas, some cheerful, some terrifying. But what do we hear from our leaders? Bromides, clichés, and announcements which fade into yawns on the languid parliamentary air . . . Spike your dim little speeches and give us a clarion call.

Likewise, on the limitations of British Railways:

> Why did the heating fail on the 8.10 p.m. diesel train from Paddington to Wolverhampton on Tuesday, the coldest night of the winter, so that frozen passengers wrapped themselves in newspapers or stamped in

the corridors? *Nobody knows*. Why is the 7.56 a.m. train from Maidstone West to Charing Cross consistently late, but never rescheduled? *Nobody knows*. Why was a main-line train from Paddington to Swindon totally unheated last Friday? *Nobody knows*. Is there no way of putting some blood into our consumptive railways system? What's needed now is something constructive. *What the railway bosses have got to do is to put some stuffing into the railway staff.* The telephone inquiry system should be ripped open from end to end. Ticket collectors should be more choosy about whom they eye as a criminal – one can't help arriving without a ticket when one's departure station has carried a placard saying 'Please pay the other end'. The funny thing is, I love railways. When the train is punctual, the carriage warm, the refreshments good, a train journey is more relaxing and more beautiful than the same journey by car. I long to see the railways revitalised, for myself as well as for the country, and with strong leadership I believe it's possible.

This was scarcely prose of Tolstoyan significance, and Anne herself would never have pretended that it was. Like all such journalism, it was designed to earn a cheer at the nation's breakfast tables, then ignite next day's bonfires. But indignation is more difficult to sustain than it sounds, popular themes harder to identify than they appear. Many journalists share a delusion that they are born to become columnists. A weekly fixed space in which to sound off about personal hobbyhorses seems to represent Shangri-La, the summit of a reporter's ambitions. In truth, however gifted they may be, only a tiny minority of writers possess the special gifts to flourish as columnists.

In her pages, Anne campaigned vigorously for better design – especially of buildings, and for preserving the best old ones. If her judgements were sometimes wrong-headed (she described the disastrous new Cumbernauld estate outside Glasgow as 'the most exciting place in the whole of Britain', never having had the misfortune to live there), she was utterly right to denounce the cult of the highrise. She castigated Oriana Fallaci's cult 1961 book *The Useless Sex*, which to her offered too bleak and one-dimensional a view of the predicament of women, and of the sterility of domestic life: 'To me,' wrote Anne, 'a woman is happy who has found a man with whom she can fully communicate. A woman is happy if she is deeply interested in anything, whether it is people, work, art or just running a home.' Fallaci, she argued, mistakenly translated discontent with her own personal predicament into a universal female predicament.

She denounced boarding schools, and said she thought eight too young to send children away from home. How I wished she had reached the same conclusion back in 1953! I sometimes wonder what *Mail* readers, even in 1961, made of a characteristic Scott-James touch, in a piece offering advice about entertaining. She described the botheration of being obliged to use a stand-in cook when Martha, her usual wizard, was in hospital. The newcomer demanded more help, 'so I borrowed a parlour maid from my only rich friend', who brought a butler too. She added: 'Never ask an MP to dinner – he will be kept late at the House and ruin your timetable . . . Never get helpers you haven't tried out before.' Though Anne supposed herself down-to-earth, she could act pretty grand, in print as in life.

In her old age, she often asserted that there are nowadays far too many newspaper columns, retracing the same ground on the same day in the same title. As a former editor, I agree wholeheartedly. Every national title today boasts twice as many columnists as their talents deserve space. She also thought that, individually, my generation of journalists write too much. No professional controversialist, she argued, can produce first-class work more than once a week. Indeed, when there came a time that I myself sometimes contributed to two or three national titles on different subjects, she chastised me for excessive output: 'Beaverbrook would never allow his people to write for more than one paper,' she said, 'and he was right.'

I pointed out that few proprietors are nowadays prepared to pay any journalist, however successful, sufficient money to monopolise his or her services. She stuck to her guns, writing in her autobiography: 'Today it is not uncommon for a writer to publish almost identical columns in a Sunday paper, a daily, and a weekly

202

magazine. This helps to pay the school fees, at the price of yawns from the reader.' Yet I sometimes heard her old colleagues express scepticism about her own working practices, arguing that she made a mighty prima-donna fuss about producing a single piece a week. She was sufficiently valued to earn a good salary – the *Mail* was paying her £8,000 a year in 1963 – for a small output. Most of us have to write much more to match her income in today's money.

She was right, however, in asserting that for a columnist the generation of ideas is a far more challenging task than their expression on paper. Bernard Levin was prodigious in this respect. He was also a master of that indispensable journalistic art, getting one's first and last sentences right. Anne once heard him say, 'I like to start with a paradox and end with a platitude.' She also acknowledged the importance of being in touch. No columnist can produce top-class work without meeting people. A star performer, she said, 'will know Wigan as well as Westminster . . . The writing must be sincere and go straight to the point.' Many practitioners fall into the beartrap of verbosity. Levin, again, did some of his best work in a column for the *Mail* which was no more than nine hundred words long, the same length as most of Anne's pieces. Today, many columnists occupy space of twelve or even fifteen hundred words. This is almost invariably too much. Some of Levin's later work for *The Times* suffered grievously from overwriting, especially when he bored for Britain about Wagner.

If the careers of both Mac and Anne appeared to be flying high, their domestic life became increasingly wretched. They lived almost entirely separate existences. Once, we all went on holiday together with the Wysards in the South of France – Tony Wysard was Clare's godfather. I revelled in the luxuries of the Blue Train, but otherwise the trip was not a success. Whatever the wilful delusions of parents, few small children enjoy Nice as much as Newquay. English sand is miles better than foreign muck, as I told the parents frankly after our trip to Cavalière. Thereafter a new summer routine was adopted. Our parents went their own separate ways, while Nanny was dispatched with Clare and me to Frinton, Broadstairs, or – in red-letter years – to a Butlin's holiday camp.

To this day, friends dissolve into hoots of laughter at this notion. Butlin's is perceived as the acme of vulgarity. I leap passionately to its defence. Camp life perfectly suited the young Hastingses, along with millions of their generation. Clacton, Filey, Margate – we tried all of them, and were entranced. The food was great, the pools and boating lakes and mini-railways free and impeccably supervised. I roamed at will, in perfect safety, while Nanny escorted Clare. The chalets were comfortable enough. I made more little summer friends at Butlin's than ever I did on the Côte d'Azur. Holiday camps were a great national institution, rubbished only by snobs who never experienced them. At twelve, my highest ambition was to become a Butlin's redcoat. Those trips represented almost the only periods of my childhood during which I never got into trouble. The sole hitch occurred when I returned to prep school after one such idyll. It was discovered that I had acquired head lice, and infected a hundred or so other boys. As we were combed and disinfected, Mother received a stiff letter from the headmaster, suggesting that in future I might be dispatched to holiday in more salubrious locations.

My prep school was generally underwhelmed by me. Horris Hill was a 'feeder' for famously clever Winchester, to which my parents wanted me to progress. When I was twelve, one of my Horris Hill headmasters, a bald-pated and sinister figure named Richard Andrews, a taller version of *Eagle*'s the Mekon, was about to administer a routine whacking (headmasters snapped their fingers in irritation at their own forgetfulness if a month or so passed, and they noticed that they had forgotten to beat Hastings). As Mr Andrews exercised his refined judgement upon selecting a cane, he said: 'Winchester have just asked us whether, in our opinion, you are the sort of boy they should wish to have. We have been obliged to tell them that you are not.' He gave me the sort of look which Captain Bligh inflicted on one of his less lovable mutineers, then addressed my bottom. When Mr Andrews died suddenly a year or two later, I found myself hoping that the stokers of hell were in especially vigorous form that day. Rejected by

Winchester, I went to Charterhouse instead, where I proved as considerable a disappointment as I had been at Horris Hill ('His performance both in and out of school falls below the standard we would expect from a scholar . . . His contemporaries do not like him, and they are not bad judges of character').

By that stage, however, my parents were relieved to have identified any institution willing to admit me. In a brief flash of optimism when I had been at Charterhouse for a few weeks, Mac wrote to my housemaster: 'There is no doubt that he is idyllically happy at the school.' Even Father the heroic fantasist, however, was unable to sustain this delusion for long. When he and Anne found nothing else to talk to each other about, there was plentiful scope for debate about what should be done to preserve their son from descent into a semi-criminal abyss. A considerable factor in Anne's mounting exasperation with Mac was her belief that he should play a larger role in taming me. His eccentricities, which so delighted television audiences, seemed less sympathetic in a domestic context. His lack of interest in all practical matters, the assumption that somebody else would change plugs, mow lawns, fill cars with petrol or read bedtime stories, did little to promote harmony.

I would be surprised if Mac indulged in much sexual misbehaviour during his married life. His persistent infidelities were committed, instead, with firearms. He was fascinated by the cold, black metal of the barrels, the sublime beauty of crisply crafted actions and walnut stocks. His eyes glittered at the sight of a Purdy or Churchill shotgun, a fine Colt revolver or Mauser rifle. He fondled guns with the passion which many men reserve for women. Besides his battery of Churchill 12-bores, the house was strewn with eighteenth-century duelling pistols (off one of which I sheared the hammer, to my chagrin and Father's not unreasonable fury), nineteenth-century revolvers, percussion and flintlock sporting pieces. Even in my most reckless moments, I never dared to fire those frail old weapons. Mac, however, indulged a phase when in place of a modern shotgun he deployed his 1820s Mantons against partridges and pheasants. It was an awesome sight to behold the flash of the flint as he fired, the black powder smoke which wreathed him for half a minute thereafter. The birds were seldom much troubled by these assaults, but they provided Father with enormous pleasure.

It is not surprising that I was infected by his enthusiasm. Sometimes I bicycled a couple of miles to the spinneys and cornfields of a farmer who was grudgingly willing to let me attack his pigeons with a 20-bore. Maybe twice a year, Mac would take me with him to a pheasant day to which he was invited. I loved rifle practice on the lawn, writing from prep school at ten, 'Please, please when I come out can Daddy gets lots of lovely .22 ammunition.' But most of my dealings with his guns were illicit. From the age of ten or eleven onwards, whenever my parents absented themselves I took possession of the family armoury. Nobody in those days locked up guns, and most of Father's stood ready to hand in a rack in the hall. Nanny was oblivious, my sister an uneasy spectator. I experimented with the hand-loading of cartridges, which caused Father some astonishment when he used them, unaware of their provenance. Those which I had over-charged with powder yielded thunderous explosions, following which a few pellets sped towards the planets. Where I had underdone the propellant, a shower of lead trickled limply out of his barrels.

The whiff of cordite whetted my appetite for more ambitious pleasures. In an oak chest in Father's room he preserved his war souvenirs: a Polish Radom, a broomhandle Mauser and two Luger automatics, and – most thrilling of all – a Schmeisser machine-pistol, together with a plentiful stock of 9mm ammunition. At first I confined myself merely to stripping and reassembling the guns, at which I became probably the most proficient eleven-year-old in the world. Soon, inevitably, I dared to fire them. This proved exhilarating. When the coast was clear and parents safely absent, I invited a few friends round for tea, cucumber sandwiches and pistol practice. They giggled nervously amid the cannonade and later, I fear, told their parents, as I discovered a growing reluctance among playmates to accept invitations. I emptied a Luger magazine into the garden seat, which still bears the scars. I took to carrying a pistol or two on bicycle rides around the village, which provoked public resentment when reports spread that these were not

206

toys. A local view gained currency that the Hastings family, always known to be mad, were also bad and dangerous to know.

Late one dark night when Mother was at home and we were all in bed, I was awakened by stirrings outside the front door, obviously an intruder. Thrilled that here was my opportunity to repel an assault on the household, I seized a pistol, flicked a round into the breech and crouched beside the open window, drawing a bead on a shadowy figure below. A knock on the door prompted my mother to peer out of her window. A voice said: 'Good evening, madam. Constable Jones. As I was passing, I noticed a bicycle outside and thought that somebody might be up to no good here.' No, said my mother wearily, it was merely her son's machine, carelessly abandoned at the garden gate. The constable saluted and disappeared into the night. Fortunate man, he never knew how close he came to a sticky end in the line of duty. I suffered a stab of vague awareness that I was in danger of carrying a good thing too far.

Nanny was oblivious of my games with guns, but my mother was dismayed by rumours which reached her. A report swept the family that on Father's return from his latest foreign assignment, all the World War II weapons would be removed from circulation. Appalled, I chose my favourite pistol, the Radom, and secreted it in the luggage, together with a generous supply of ammunition, when we returned to London from the cottage. An evening or so later I was sitting in my room in the flat watching an instalment of an American TV drama – *Perry Mason*, as it happened. Most of my attention was on the screen, but as I viewed I caressed, stripped and reassembled the Radom, pushed in an ammunition clip, and snapped the gun at the screen. Mother, more than forty years later on *Desert Island Discs*, did me a notable injustice by suggesting that I became over-excited while watching a Western. It was not a Western. What happened was the fruit of momentary carelessness, such as could befall – well, any male member of the Hastings family.

I remember as if it were yesterday the spectacle of the TV disappearing in a sudden eruption of smoke and a cascade of glass, with much tinkling and clatter. I was so surprised by the effect, as was inevitable on hearing a gunshot at close quarters in Cromwell Road, that I slumped back in the chair, pistol dangling limply in my hand. This caused Mumsy, rushing in seconds later, to assume the worst. I reassured her that all was well with everything except the unfortunate television. Should you be contemplating firing a pistol in a Victorian mansion block, and wonder whether the noise would trouble the neighbours, I can offer comfort. Nobody else in our flats, which housed such exalted residents as the novelists C.P. Snow and Pamela Hansford Johnson, along with H.G. Wells's old lover Baroness Budberg, complained about a thing.

Even by the standards of our family, however, the ensuing row was a corker. I remained in disgrace for weeks. Father, on his return from foreign parts, first demanded my assistance to sieve the wreckage of the TV and retrieve the bullet, lest its discovery by some third party led to trouble. All those wonderful war souvenirs vanished forever from the house, to a destination unknown. Father announced that a shooting expedition on which the two of us were scheduled to embark a fortnight later would henceforward become a fishing holiday. Even he, I think, was shocked by the intensity of my mother's fury, which was evenly distributed between the two of us.

My enthusiasm for shooting was undiminished by the death of the television. But once childhood passed, I ceased to be as keen on guns as artefacts as was Mac. I was in my mid-twenties before I enjoyed more than occasional opportunities for pursuing pigeons and pheasants. At Rose Cottage in my teens, I was obliged to return to such humdrum pastimes as making plastic and balsa-wood model aeroplanes. Looking back, I cannot honestly say that I regret the era of pistol practice. Like all young malefactors, I was simply sorry that I had been caught. It was such fun until that silly moment when I overplayed my hand. I knew exactly how my grandfather felt when he blew up the toy fort in Trinity Square, Borough – I was already familiar with Basil's account of that episode.

Mac, meanwhile, turned his attention to more serious matters. He was tuning up for the most dramatic, indeed preposterous, episode of his journalistic career, which also proved the final landmark before the break-up of our family.

TWELVE

Castaway

Three Hastingses – Mac, Anne and myself – have at different times featured as guests on the BBC's *Desert Island Discs*. Mac possessed unique credentials for his appearance: he had himself experienced life as a castaway, albeit a voluntary one. It was the apogee of his unflagging and often ill-judged pursuit of adventure. In the summer of 1960 he was pressed for money, desperate to make a coup to rescue him from the insistent clamourings of the Inland Revenue. His relations with Anne had become sulphurous. He was seized by a yearning for escape, a breathing space. Most people in such circumstances go walking in the Lake District or catch a boat to Le Touquet. Mac chose to have himself marooned on an uninhabited island in the Indian Ocean, equipped only with a gun and a hunting knife.

That bald statement improves only marginally upon reality. He loved wild places, was unafraid of loneliness, and had a deep and ill-founded faith in his ability to fend for himself. He was heedless of the fact that, at fifty, he was absurdly old to undertake such an adventure. Journalists frequently decide that they want to fulfil a fantasy, then look about for someone to pay them to do it. Mac had always been more successful than most in achieving this, through his assignments for *Picture Post*, *Eagle* and BBC TV. Now he sold the idea of emulating Robinson Crusoe to the highest bidder, which proved to be *The People* Sunday newspaper. Its editor agreed to pay him £5,000, which seemed good money in those days, to spend five weeks marooned in conditions of suitable privation. With his usual enthusiasm, Mac began searching for somewhere sufficiently awful to fill the bill. His friend the novelist C.S.

Forester suggested an outpost of the Grenadines in the Caribbean. A club acquaintance who had just retired as director of the Ordnance Survey favoured a pimple off the east coast of Malaya.

Finally, however, Mac settled for an atoll in the Amirantes chain, just beyond the Seychelles. His mother, Billie Hastings, scribbled in her diary on 11 July: 'Mac rang to tell me that he is flying immediately to an island in the Indian Ocean until the end of September. Very worrying!' Anne was beyond argument, and perhaps also concern, about any folly which Mac chose to commit. While the castaway stunt was still in the melting pot, she set off on her own long-planned and pleasantly glamorous assignment in Kenya for the *Daily Mail*. All her bills were of course being paid by Lord Rothermere. Her trip was profitably completed inside three weeks, a very different proposition from the challenge Mac now set himself.

My own farewells to him were nonchalant, however, because his departures had become so familiar. My faith in his powers was unbounded. I responded to news that he was departing for a desert island much as Superman's son, had he possessed one, would have received news that Dad was off for another bout with Lex Luthor. The outcome never seemed in doubt. The insurance broker who covered Mac's life for £10,000 had a similarly exaggerated confidence in his client. He charged a premium of less than £30.

The haste of Mac's going was prompted by the fact that in those days the Seychelles were reachable only by rare steamship sailings from East Africa. There was no airstrip. Mac, however, discovered that the Royal Navy's frigate *Loch Insh* was due to sail in a week from Mombasa for a goodwill visit to Mahe, the Seychelles' capital. His celebrity enabled him to hitch a lift for the three-day passage, with Admiralty blessing. He packed his beloved African bush jacket, the aforesaid gun and hunting knife, together with a blank journal and some borrowed Leica cameras with state-of-the-art self-timers, and caught a plane to Nairobi. Anne was astonished to be confronted at the New Stanley Hotel by her husband, who displayed no interest in her bush odyssey, and merely plunged into describing his own plans for self-immolation. They parted without much display of emotion on either side, he for Mombasa and she for the Masai Mara. Anne was especially annoyed that Mac had without consultation breached a longstanding pact, whereby during school holidays they should never both simultaneously absent themselves abroad.

A week later, he took up residence at Government House in the Seychelles, to organise his outing in the sun. In those days when not much happened in the islands between Christmases, the arrival of a well-known journalist on a mission of such startling battiness provided a welcome variation of the diplomatic round. The British community rallied round enthusiastically, to ensure that Mac's ordeal was a success.

He found a tough old skipper, an Irishman named Harvey Brain, known locally as 'Cyclone' because he talked so much about storms. 'Cyclone' agreed to carry him to the Amirantes as soon as his schooner, the *Marsouin*, had offloaded its cargo of salted shark. Bemused locals instructed Mac in the arts of splitting coconuts with a panga, weaving rope out of palm stems and constructing a fish trap. He lay awake nights reading a borrowed copy of the classic *Fishes of South Africa*, a catalogue of the Indian Ocean's monsters of the deep which alarmed him somewhat. To provide company, the local Botanical Department presented him with a giant turtle, which he christened Fifi. A British civil servant about to return home bequeathed to him Richard, a tough young terrier of exotically mongrel origins. Mac added the dog to his entourage, happily without its discovering the responsibilities which it must fulfil to earn its new name – Friday. His luggage expanded to include an axe and mattock, panga, cooking pot, fishing lines, coil of rope, paraffin lamp, antiseptic and bottle of brandy for emergencies. A cheerful local doctor warned him that if he could not find greenstuff, symptoms of scurvy should show after a month: aching muscles, foul breath, bleeding gums. Mac surrendered his wristwatch for safekeeping, knowing that he would have no appointments to keep. Then Harvey Brain took the *Marsouin* to sea, where the schooner promptly sailed into one of the worst storms the region had known for years.

Fifi the turtle was flung hither and thither across the hold, among the remnants of the sharks. Friday crawled into the fo'c'sle to die. Movement aboard was impossible save on hands and knees, as the vessel plunged and soared through towering seas. The mainsail boom swung wildly to and fro, threatening the unwary with being smashed overboard. On the first night, the Creole cook somehow prepared a mess of food over an open fire on deck, which Harvey, Mac and the three crewmen ate jammed into the little wheelhouse. It proved their last meal for thirty-six hours. The seas rose to a frenzy. Mac staggered forward and retrieved the terrified, pulsating Friday from his refuge, then wedged himself with his head against the ship's sternpost, legs dangling over the companionway, with the dog in his arms through the long hours that followed. Mac's narrative will sound familiar to any modern aficionado of Patrick O'Brian's sagas of sailing ships amid the elements at their most fearsome:

Below the waterline the crash of the sea on the bows, the whining of the rigging, made a noise as if all the people in the Seychelles were whispering behind their hands about me. The stink of shark made me retch. The crash of the sea slapping against the planking, the tumult of loose stores, scared the wits out of me. Friday was piled in a tangle of luggage. The bunk was tipped upright, the companion way behind me was horizontal, and the door into the hold had burst outwards. For a moment the bow of the *Marsouin* was pointing straight into the air. It wasn't until she was sinking into the trough of the swell again that I got my bearings. This happened three times. I was exhausted with the mere effort of staying put and keeping some sort of control of the stuff clattering about, like dice in a box, in the sweating acrid heat of the black hole I was incarcerated in. In the glimmering light, I imagined that grimacing faces were drawing towards me and drawing away again like images in a nightmare. Gargoyles, not people, seemed to be saying ugly things close to my ear. It was a form of delirium, I suppose, induced by the claustrophobic horror of the reeling cabin, the fever-heat of the atmosphere, and lack of food. Friday clung to me.

Brilliant red cockroaches crawled from their holes in the planking and scuttled about the cabin. With a crash, the skylight shattered, littering Mac with fragments of glass. Under heavy rain and with seas relentlessly breaking inboard, he and Friday were soon awash. Harvey Brain shouted down the hatch that he was heaving to until daybreak. In those shallow, reef-ridden waters, he no longer dared steer a course until he could fix a position. The sails flapped in the shrieking wind. The *Marsouin* rolled through an ever more unnatural arc, each sidelong descent threatening to be its last. It seemed an eternity before the motion began to ease. After thirty-six hours at the wheel, Brain dropped onto the netted frame that passed for a bunk, and fell into a sleep which eluded his passenger.

Next morning, once more under sail on a less turbulent ocean, they made their landfall. The seas were still too heavy for the schooner to deliver Mac directly to his chosen atoll, which bore the name of Ressource. Instead, Brain steered to the nearby island of Darros, where three hundred labourers gathered copra under a British manager, Marshall Dyer. It was months since they had received a visitor. A pirogue, a long, narrow craft rowed in perfect rhythm by a team of sweating Seychellois, put out from shore. When it came alongside, Mac explained his purpose. With astonishing lack of astonishment, Dyer agreed to drop him at his destination, a few miles distant. Mac, dog, turtle and baggage were loaded into the pirogue, and the castaway bade farewell to Harvey Brain, who said he would return in five weeks to retrieve the bits. The skipper offered him a parting gift of three onions, saying that he would need them to ease the pain of scorpion bites. Then the oarsmen bent to their labour. The craft raced over the reef, collecting six inches of green water in its bottom as it shot the surf. Finally, it grounded on the flat stretch of sand and palms which was to be Mac's residence for the next thirty-five days.

Friday bounded joyously ashore. Mac threw away his last cigarette. Putting a hand into his bush jacket pocket, he found himself clutching a final warning from the Post Office about failure to renew his TV licence. Marshall Dyer said that if Mac wanted to bottle out – though he described such a contingency more delicately – he should hoist his shirt aloft a pole on the sandy point at the tip of the island. Somebody would spot it sooner or later. Then the pirogue's crew pushed off, leaving Mac sitting atop his modest heap of possessions,

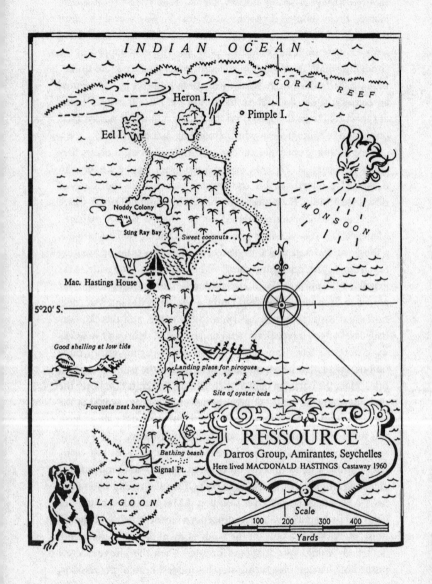

INDIAN OCEAN

CORAL REEF

Heron I.

Pimple I.

Eel I.

MONSOON

Noddy Colony

Sting Ray Bay

Sweet coconuts

Mac. Hastings House

5°20' S.

N

Good shelling at low tide

Landing place for pirogues

Site of oyster beds

Fouquets nest here

Bathing beach

Signal Pt.

RESSOURCE

Darros Group, Amirantes, Seychelles

Here lived MACDONALD HASTINGS Castaway 1960

LAGOON

Scale

100   200   300   400

Yards

cursing mildly to himself for not having thought of trimming his nails while he still had access to scissors.

The adventurer felt no great emotion as the craft vanished beyond the reef. He had determined to make himself a castaway, and now here he was. With Friday leaping eagerly ahead of him across the virgin sand under the sun, he set out to explore: 'Ressource was so cosy, so much the very model of the desert island of romance, that it had the unreality of a film-set,' he wrote. The island was three-quarters of a mile long, and at its narrowest point no more than fifty yards across. The beaches were fringed with wild laurels, the entire atoll clad in coconut palms, some rising forty feet. 'Every wrinkle in the shoreline,' he wrote later in his sojourn, 'every irregularity in the floor of the lagoon, almost every tree on the island is now so familiar that I find it difficult to recapture the mood in which I first explored it.'

On the first day, the habit of going clothed remained ingrained. He wore underpants as he paced his new domain. Thereafter he donned shorts only when he was photographing himself. 'One part of me,' he wrote in the journal which he began to keep, 'is still listening for the sound of people and traffic, looking for electric lights to switch on, half-expecting someone to call. When I was gathering wood for the fire this afternoon, there was a moment when I imagined that I could hear a telephone ringing.' He was pleasantly surprised by the absence of unfriendly creatures: 'In Africa, the ground seethes and the air hums in daytime with warring insects. There's a savage stillness in the night, an atmosphere of watchful menace, of eyes pricking the dark. Here, under the broad dial of the moon making a fretwork pattern of the palms, it's hard to believe that there's any hostile element at all.' He was enchanted by the absence of fear in the birds, the terns which brushed his head and dive-bombed Friday. Hump-shouldered herons strutted up to examine their visitor. Yellow-legged bitterns peered from the scrub on the shoreline. Vast shoals of tiny fish flung themselves exuberantly into the air amid their cruising grounds in the shallows.

Mac was never a heavy eater, and in the first days he took little trouble about foraging. Friday turned up a clutch of wild chicken eggs in the scrub above the shore, which his master boiled and shared with the dog. He slept poorly. The night was rendered hideous by the wailings of fouquets, a species of shearwater, in their burrows around his bivouac. When Friday woke, which was often, he licked Mac's face with unwelcome enthusiasm. Dog and man alike were pestered by land crabs, some of them huge red brutes with claws big enough to crack a coconut. Every half-hour or so, with the regularity of a temple gong, a coconut fell from one of the palms and thumped 'ker-boomp' on the sand.

When the blazing red tropical dawn came, Mac rose, and used a finger to clean his teeth in salt water. He ran a dissatisfied hand over the stubble on his chin which he now had no means to remove. He and Friday then set off on the scrounge, looking for wild pigs, which they had been told they might expect to encounter. Nothing so useful appeared. Instead, they saw a ginger cat, which the dog chased up a tree. A deserter from a ship's company? They never knew, and only once again glimpsed the animal during the weeks that followed. Friday caught a scrawny wild chicken, which they boiled for the pot, recklessly sacrificing one of Harvey Brain's onions for a relish. It proved delicious. Mac used the bird's innards as bait to catch a fish of indeterminate identity, weighing around two pounds. On the beach they found the lid of an oil drum, which made a serviceable frying pan. Mac realised that, in the fierce heat, there was no possibility of husbanding food overnight. He and the dog must live from meal to meal, day to day. He was conscious that he had failed to identify edible greenstuff.

His big mistake, entirely in character, was a failure to do any botanical homework before surrendering himself to the hazards of Ressource. Had he but known it, for instance, palm 'salad' – the greenery at the growing heart of the tree – offered an important source of vitamins. All manner of nutrients could be extracted from available fish and vegetation. But Mac had fallen in love with a fantasy of himself as castaway, shooting and fishing for survival with the insouciance of an English gentleman, the dash of a Hollywood white hunter thrust amid savages. The notion that some boring biological knowledge might be useful, indeed indispensable, to his welfare was alien to him. Most of the Hastingses have been ignorant of science. An unkind critic might have said that Mac's decision to land on Ressource, then make up the story as he went along, represented no lesser hubris than a similarly casual commitment to turn up at the Royal Opera House and attempt to dance *Swan Lake*. Mac cherished a romantic delusion that any man who could pull down a pheasant, skin a buck and cast a good line on the Spey was equipped for survival on an atoll in the Indian Ocean. This view was now confounded.

It was fortunate that whimsy had not prompted him to compose his essay in survival on the Polar icecap, for instance, where such careless braggadocio would have killed him. The Indian Ocean was more forgiving: not much so, but sufficiently to enable him to live to tell the tale. He set about constructing a shelter, some ten feet by twenty. At the end of the first day, he perceived that his clumsiness with axe and mattock was making heavy labour of a task that would have taken a Seychellois a quarter of the time. In the soft sand, it proved hard to sink parallel headposts and keep them upright. With infinite sluggishness, a framework of poles rose amid the trees, roughly knotted with palm strands, then thatched with palm fronds.

He had done nothing, before embarking, to make himself fit. Indeed, until the moment he stepped ashore he sustained his life-long regime of fifty cigarettes and the best part of a bottle of gin a day. For years he had taken no more physical exercise than was required to walk to a pub, a riverbank or a shooting peg. In the unremitting heat of Ressource, he discovered that each day he could manage only two hours of manual labour, after which he sank down exhausted. Far from missing books or amusements, he found himself falling asleep as he scribbled his journal each night.

By the end of the first week, hunger had begun to gnaw at him. The island's modest supply of wild chicken eggs soon expired. Mac thrashed Friday when he caught the dog wolfing eggs wholesale. This was not only unjust, but futile. It was too late to preserve any stock. Thereafter, the diet of dog and man alike consisted of fish, oysters, and a prodigious quantity of coconuts. Fortunately many trees had been bent almost horizontal by the wind, and thus required no exertion to harvest. Salt was not a problem, for it was easily dried from seawater. Mac lit fires by focusing a camera lens on driftwood under the sun. He found a pleasant-smelling herb to flavour each night's stew. But bulk and vitamins were lacking. He was garnering only sufficient food to provide coconuts for breakfast, together with a cooked meal at night. Remarkably soon, even a man as careless of his own health as was Mac began to notice the pleadings of his stomach. Ben Gunn in *Treasure Island* became obsessed with thoughts of toasted cheese. Mac hankered for sardines – and soon, indeed, for any substantial fare at all.

On the seventh day, he was momentarily careless as he slashed at a palm frond with his panga. The blade buried itself in his right thumb. It was three days before he discovered that, by mistake, the pirogue crew had landed among his luggage a box of medical supplies intended for Darros. He was then able to bind his finger with plaster, but it ached fiercely. To compound his troubles, as he contemplated his almost completed house, the structure groaned, tottered, then crashed in ruin. For the first time he experienced real anguish, even despair. There was nothing to be done, save start the whole construction over again. A rainstorm pelted down on his waterlogged encampment, causing his hair to hang in rats' tails, Friday's body to steam.

He found that, more even than nails, he lamented a lack of containers capable of holding liquids and food. He scoured the flotsam on the shoreline for cans and boxes. It was a red-letter day when he found a glass buoy with a stopper, such as Japanese deep-sea fishermen used on their nets. He found three bottles, and amused himself by casting them back into the sea with appropriate messages, though none was ever returned to him. Having only a knife with which to eat, he was troubled by lack of a spoon. He tried in vain to carve a suitable wooden substitute, and resorted instead to shells. To his surprise, he discovered that the gun, which he had supposed would be indispensable to a castaway, was redundant. Edible birds were easily caught. He killed stingrays in the shallows with a spear.

Mac the hunter unexpectedly found himself feeling that it would anyway be sacrilegious to break the spell of the island's silence with the detonation of firearms. His beloved 12-bore lingered in its case, unfired from the first day on the island to the last.

When Friday ate his leather belt, Mac fashioned a replacement from a stingray tail. He found seaweed an acceptable substitute for toilet paper, but his own filthiness increasingly irked him. However often he washed himself and his shorts in the ocean, his body itched, even in the absence of biting insects. A man who had always disliked facial hair on others, he became increasingly bothered by his beard, and picked at it irritably. Confronted by necessity, he hardened his heart to cruelty. Meat could not be preserved dead for even a few hours, so he kept it alive. He caught wild chickens at dusk as they fluttered up to roost, then kept them trussed by his fireside until next day. He began to yearn for a woman – not, I think, for sexual purposes, but simply to feed him. Mac was no twenty-first-century domesticated man, indeed he was barely a twentieth-century one.

Friday, oddly enough, flourished on the island routine. The dog, to which Mac became devoted, bounded hither and thither with irrepressible energy, plentifully fed on local birdlife. Fifi the tortoise, by contrast, was a social disappointment. From the day they arrived on the island until that on which they left, she scarcely moved. A tap on the shell caused her cautiously to project her head; a second tap induced her to withdraw it again. From an early stage, Fifi displayed absolute lack of interest in Mac's great experiment in wilderness survival. Disgusted by her inertia, he observed crossly that it was not surprising giant tortoises live for two hundred years, given how little they exert themselves. Afterwards, he decided that he should have eaten Fifi.

Mac himself, at a disturbingly early stage, began to fall prey to a lassitude attributable to lack of nourishment. 'It's probably the usual reaction when you go to the sea for a summer holiday,' he wrote in his journal on the tenth day. 'At first, you're bubbling with enthusiasm; swimming twice a day, going for long walks, planning picnics and motor-coach rides, and walking along the promenade to see the illuminations. But, after a week, you're quite content to hire a deckchair on the pier and listen to the band. I'm in the deckchair mood.'

There was a middle period in his sojourn on the island, around the third week, when for a time he experienced remarkable contentment. He felt that the absence of gin and cigarettes was doing him good. A near-alcoholic at home, he was pleased to notice that, for the first time in years, his hands had ceased to shake. His emergency brandy bottle remained untouched. He yearned for a handkerchief; a shave; soap; boiled silverside of beef with carrots, dumplings, jacket potato; and, so he claimed, a woman's voice.

Mac's own narrative of the desert island experience is sorely incomplete, because it records much about what he did, little about what he thought. He must have spent many hours contemplating his arid relationship with Anne and his own unhappiness. Even in after years, however, he admitted to no such reflections. Proper Englishmen in that inhibited, pre-Diana era supposed it indecent to give vent to emotion, even in the privacy of a journal. Both Mac and Anne lacked self-knowledge, but there must have been moments on that ridiculous island when the castaway asked himself whether such an expedition represented a proportionate or even sane response to an unhappy marriage.

During his happy days in the third week, he completed construction of a table, which he could now use to write his journal, seated on an old crate. His new house was much more successful than the first one. Finding a plank on the shoreline with three nails embedded, he wrote on it in neat charcoal 'MR. MACDONALD HASTINGS' and fixed the sign proudly to a tree outside the hut. He began to weave a bed to enable him to sleep off the ground, completing this on the twenty-first day. He found himself untroubled by the absence of either books or company. But the tyranny of food, the need to provide it and the misery of being without it, became a mounting obsession: 'Every day that passes my heart goes out to the ordinary housewife. How women can go on feeding men every day for a lifetime is beyond me. I work on my house with patience, because I can see a result, the end of the task. But within a few minutes of providing a meal there's nothing to show for it, nothing to look forward to except repeating the performance over again.'

On the evening of his twenty-second day, as he prepared to eat boiled white fish, he experienced a wave of nausea. The doctor on Mahe had warned him to expect this. It was a first sign that his stomach was commencing a revolt prompted by deprivation and lack of vitamins. He found two tins of corned beef among the medical kit. Hacking one open with his knife, he found the contents dissolved into a stinking goo. When he tried to eat a little, he threw up. Friday finished the beef, of course. Mac went to bed hungry. Later, he was told by doctors that if he, like the dog, had eaten fish raw rather than cooked, his health might have deteriorated much less swiftly.

Afterwards, he claimed to have been ashamed of how little useful work he did during his later weeks on the island. Once the hut was complete, he spent hours collecting cowry shells exquisitely polished by the elements. He pottered in the shallow water, peering fascinated upon the riches of the reef: 'Turning over the coral, iridescent in paintbox colours, is like turning over the contents of a colossal junkshop in which, every now and again, your eyes light upon a little masterpiece. The lagoon is a patchwork of glittering greens, the shades determined by the character of the marine landscape below – a landscape peopled with fantastic creatures: tiny squids, hermit-crabs, silver sea-snakes, green and red anemones, myriads of small fish, winkles, crabs and limpets – often in water so thin that it doesn't cover their backs – rays, sharks, and shoals of big mullet.'

His mind was wandering. He found that, like many prisoners, whole days passed without a thought of his former life, or contemplation of his future. Only Ressource was real. Sometimes he forgot even to carve a daily notch in the tree beside his hut to mark the progress of his sojourn. The soles of his feet had grown sufficiently hardened for him to abandon shoes on the coral. He slept for longer and longer periods. His chief activity was to photograph himself at the daily routine – cooking, writing, manufacturing furniture. Mac was always a gifted cameraman, and he brought back some remarkable images from Ressource.

The thirtieth day, night of the full moon and highest tide, precipitated a bad fright. The sea lapped up to his camp, extinguishing the fire with an abrupt hiss. Mac bent furiously to work with a mattock, pushing up a frail rampart of sand which just sufficed to hold back the water until the ebb. Next day, he suffered another attack of nausea. His journal, in which each of the early entries ran to hundreds of words, now filled only a few lines, amid 'the lassitude that keeps on overcoming me now'. By the thirty-fourth day he had become too weak to gather food, too ill to eat it. Afterwards, he decided that part of the problem was that he knew he needed only to survive for a fixed period. Had he been a genuine castaway, anticipating a possible eternity on the island, he would have forced himself to work much harder at finding sustenance. As it was, he sought merely to keep himself alive until the vital day when salvation would come. In this, he almost failed.

With ebbing strength and wit, he carved a sign which he hung outside his hut: 'TO LET'. On the afternoon of the thirty-sixth day, he pursued a tottering path to the southern tip of the island. With difficulty, he hoisted his filthy shirt on a pole – the signal for rescue. He photographed himself in the pose, then found his head spinning. He slumped down in the shade of a palm. A sudden gust of wind blew down the pole. He was too weak to hold it up, and experienced a surge of fear that, in the absence of the agreed signal, his deliverers would stay away.

Somehow he stumbled to his camp, found a fishing line and wooden pegs, and returned to the point to tie up his pole. Then he staggered back to bed, and collapsed into unconsciousness. When he heard voices, he assumed that delirium had overtaken him. Opening his eyes, however, he beheld Marshall Dyer and a group of grinning ebony faces peering down at him, teeth gleaming in the dusk. 'Delighted to see you,' said Mac, with what he hoped was appropriate dignity. 'How do I look?' Dyer eyed him in silence for a moment, then responded: 'My wife has sent a thermos of tea and some jam sandwiches. You look as if you need them.'

Mac could stumble ashore on Darros only by clinging to Dyer's shoulder. He sobbed when Dyer's wife helped him into a bath and gently bathed his body. He had landed on Ressource weighing 160 pounds. Scales at the manager's house showed that he had lost thirty-two pounds. His legs were covered in jungle ulcers, and he was displaying early symptoms of scurvy. In five weeks, he had reduced himself to something approaching the condition of a wartime prisoner of the Japanese.

Yet this ghastly predicament – for his condition in the last weeks became indeed ghastly – was entirely self-inflicted. In the Middle Ages, religious zealots employed acolytes to inflict upon them the sort of sufferings which he had contrived all on his own. Only Mac at his maddest could have devised, planned and executed a journalistic stunt which destroyed his health. This was flagellation advanced to an art form. Here was he, a respected fifty-year-old writer and broadcaster, earning a decent living in Britain, who had wantonly embarked upon an expedition which rendered him, quite literally, a stretcher case. He returned to our flat in Cromwell Road prostrate between two ambulance men.

I was a bemused spectator of the terse exchange of incivilities when Mac and Anne's paths crossed in the hall as he returned from Ressource, and she left for a long-planned holiday in the South of France. It required the passage of a decade or two before I acknowledged that Anne's behaviour deserved sympathy. Mac retired to a hotel, where he could receive the nursing which he needed. Granny wrote in her diary: '2 October: news of Mac at last. Seems to have been an awful ordeal. Will that boy never learn? 7 October: Beryl rang Anne to get news of Mac as I was so worried and he answered the phone, and had been home (we think) nearly a week. Very hurt he did not get someone to write or phone me. 5 November: Mac came to dinner and told us all about his travels. He seems to have been in a coma when they found him and it was obviously a very near thing. He is still very ill.'

Mac duly received his £5,000 cheque from *The People*, but the articles he wrote did nothing like justice to his experience. The paper was an unrewarding platform for thoughtful writing. Mac felt inhibited from telling anything like the truth about why he had sought the assignment, or how he felt while he fulfilled it. He was no more self-revealing in the book he later wrote, *After You, Robinson Crusoe*, which proved a surprising commercial failure, given the sensational battiness of the story. Worse, it was months before he was fit to work again. He threw away the only positive effects of the island sojourn by reverting immediately to a diet of cigarettes and gin.

At vast expense, including six months in quarantine kennels, Mac brought home his beloved Friday, a dog which proved to possess great strength of body and character, of the wrong kind. Friday adored humans, but hated animals. Other dogs, not to mention sheep, were as dust beneath his chariot wheels. Mac sought to turn Friday's murderous career to advantage, by making a little film for *Tonight* in which he showed a cure being wrought by the old shepherd's remedy of tying the dog to a ram for ten minutes. On camera, Friday indeed looked suitably chastened by the experience, as should Mac have been by the flood of viewers' letters denouncing his cruelty. But within days the incorrigible canine offender returned to his bloody ways. After eighteen months of carnage and compensation payments, a tearful Mac recognised the inevitable and had Friday put down.

Sceptics might suppose that Mac exaggerated his tale of terror at sea, during the storm which his schooner experienced on the way to Ressource. A few months after returning home, however, he learned that the vessel which recovered him from the island had foundered with all hands in a similar blow.

It is curious to look back and reflect that, at the age of fifteen, I perceived Mac's desert island adventure merely as one more chapter in the picaresque saga of his life, one more giant obstacle on the assault course which I myself must some day undertake in order to live up to his awesome achievements. It was years before I recognised that the ideal journalistic stunt should involve the appearance of hardship and danger, but a minimum of their realities. His experience represented the antithesis of *I'm a Celebrity, Get Me Out of Here!*. He exchanged appalling suffering for relatively modest reward. His health never entirely recovered. 'I'm sorry I did not do better,' he wrote ruefully. His experiment did not disprove the notion that a castaway could survive on an atoll in the Indian Ocean. It merely showed that one as ill-prepared and impractical as himself was unlikely to prosper.

Forty-five years later, a senior executive of the *Daily Mail* telephoned me bright and early one summer morning to announce in tones of high excitement: 'We've just had a marvellous idea! You must go and relive your father's desert island adventure.'

'Not a chance,' I said.

'We'd pay you lots of money.'

'There is not enough in Lord Rothermere's piggy bank to induce me to do anything of the sort. I'm fifty-nine years old, for God's sake! Father was fifty, and that was twenty years too old.'

My crestfallen caller put down the phone, no doubt to transmit word to higher authority that they were no longer making Hastingses like they used to do. I mopped my brow, reflecting gratefully upon the lessons in life which I had learned since 1960. I revered Father's memory not a whit less in 2005 than I had cherished his prowess in my teens. But I recognised that a jury composed of his mother, sister, wife and colleagues could not all be wrong. Diminished responsibility represented the most charitable verdict.

THIRTEEN

Late Editions

In the last years during which my parents professed to occupy the same home, Mummy and I often shared a giggle over her breakfast tray about Daddy's excesses, of which drinking was the most conspicuous. Mac was never a violent drunk, but he became an increasingly morose and habitual one. Sober, he could still be an enchanting companion. At work, he usually controlled himself sufficiently to do the business. But at home, his passages of conviviality and indeed dignity narrowed. Nanny's lips pursed deeply as she was obliged to see 'Mr Hastings tiddly' with ever greater regularity. My mother withdrew into a cloud of contempt. A few months after his return from the Seychelles, Anne gave Mac his marching orders. Prominent among the reasons why I threw in my lot with Father was the anguished memory of past mocking of his misery, verbal betrayals which I felt that my mother had incited me to share in. It all seemed her fault. For years afterwards, even when he was remarried, Father would assert defensively: 'The divorce represented your mother's wish, not mine.' Anne's decision to evict him was founded upon a simple belief that enough was enough. In a final chivalrous gesture, he provided the then customary but unfailingly sordid contemporary grounds for divorce, by passing a night in a Brighton hotel with a professional co-respondent.

Like all children in such circumstances, I was stunned by my parents' parting. Despite the long disharmony, and their final period of open alienation, divorce seemed very dreadful. I felt a chill and shame, reading in newspapers at school the brief paragraphs announcing the rift in the Hastings household. I saw little of Mother during the time that followed. Indeed, over the next thirty years there were long periods when we scarcely spoke.

Frustrated and miserable at home, I enlisted Father's help to get me a holiday job. His name was still affectionately remembered at Lyons, and as soon as I was fifteen and legally able to work, I was admitted to the company's Olympia sales team, hawking choc ices and lollies at Bertram Mills's circus and assorted exhibitions such as the Ideal Home. I threw myself into the role, sometimes earning as much as six pounds a week in commission. I was good at selling ice cream, and passed several successive holidays peddling trayloads of frosty delicacies in the aisles at Olympia amid clowns and elephants or show houses. Those were the happiest interludes in an unhappy time.

My last years at school were landmarked by earnest conferences between Father and my teachers. Charterhouse took the view that it would be wisest for me to leave immediately after taking A-levels. If I stayed on, it seemed likely that I would commit some excess which made it necessary to sack me. I was thought a disruptive and even dangerous influence, unfit for any position of responsibility. When my contemporaries became monitors, I was passed over. There was an episode in which I discovered a mortar bomb on Hankley Common while training with the cadet corps. I brought this souvenir back to my house, and was interrupted by a monitor while dismantling it. He confiscated the bomb, and continued my technical studies on his own account. The resultant explosion caused him to spend a disagreeable few nights in Guildford General Hospital. Since he was thus unavailable to be chastised, I was invited to stand in, and received the usual six from my housemaster. I left Charterhouse amid expressions of relief on both sides. I would have been a misfit in any school, but was especially so at that one. It was a sordid place, dominated by seedy men with anachronistic values. I have always applauded the sentiments of the Emperor Septimus Severus, who had a man scourged for drawing attention to the fact that they had been at school together.

When there was no work for me with Lyons, I spent holidays in Father's rented cottage near Winchester. There I watched with dismay and pity as he struggled to make some sort of new life for himself, and to sustain his career, while growing ever more dependent upon gin. One legacy of that period is that I have never since been able to see a Gordon's bottle, far less to sample one, without a shudder of revulsion. Even Mac's old Thursday Club friends were appalled by his consumption. One day we lunched with the actor James Robertson Justice, then famous for his portrayal of Sir Lancelot Spratt in the 'Doctor' films, at his Hampshire millhouse. James turned to me afterwards and enquired, in his inimitably fruity tones: 'Can you drive?' No, I could not. James, himself scarcely teetotal, was moved to observe that we had better hope God was our co-pilot on the journey home, because our safe arrival with Father at the wheel would require divine intercession. Somehow we made it, and many other such trips. But we did not deserve to.

More than thirty years passed, and I suffered a broken marriage of my own, before I learned to adopt a more temperate view of my parents' relationship. The attribution of blame was as absurd as it is in most such cases. Mac and Anne were simply two people who lacked anything in common beyond the shared parentage of children. At the time, however, my commitment to Mac's cause was strengthened by the fact that he seemed helpless on his own. I learned a lot about cooking during the year or two in which we were much together, because he was scarcely capable of boiling an egg. We forged a closer relationship than ever before, founded upon his sudden need to confide. I was just old enough to contribute something towards filling his emotional void, though his soul-baring would probably have been better done in company other than that of a teenage son. My animosity towards my mother was intensified by some brutally frank conversations about the family which I held in those days with Mac's sister Beryl. Aunt Beryl, herself childless and now widowed, spoilt me delightfully, and won my devotion in proportion. Never one to mince words, she made some intimate observations and surmises about my mother's shortcomings which caused my naïve sixteen-year-old hair to stand on end.

In maudlin moments, Father offered me two pieces of counsel which I remember, one enlightened, the other not. First, he urged me to learn to respond to 'the challenge of a blank sheet of paper'. At the time, the phrase meant nothing. Later, when I became a professional writer, it came to seem everything. Father's invocation echoes in my memory to this day, when I sit down at my desk, switch on the computer and feel a surge of excitement as I stare into an empty screen which it is my happy responsibility to fill. Second, Father advised me gravely to marry a girl with fat legs, 'because they are better in bed'. Even at an age when I had no opportunity to explore the sexual merits of girls with either fat or thin legs, this seemed a questionable proposition. Poor Father. Thereafter, though he sometimes bestirred himself and sparkled in company, a melancholy possessed him which became ever more oppressive with the passage of the years.

My mother, by contrast, flourished without him. Always highly competent, she enjoyed a more successful professional life, and soon a livelier personal one, than she had ever known. She wrote a scintillating column for the *Daily Mail*, for which she was handsomely rewarded. She went on holiday to the Mediterranean sunspots and great cities she had always loved. She was spared the wretchedness of Mac's drinking, and of her alienation from him. She was lonely for a time, and clung as closely to Clare as Mac did to me, which served to deepen a divide between brother and sister. Mac, never much interested in girl children, made matters worse by taking scant heed of his daughter for the last twenty years of his life.

Anne wrote a 1963 column for the *Daily Mail* in which she reflected at the age of fifty about regrets in the first half of her life. She described herself as having just passed an important watershed: the previous Thursday, she had stayed in bed all morning reading *La Chartreuse de Parme* without a sense of guilt. She lamented the oppressive discipline of her upbringing which, she said, had induced in her 'no real virtue, but a tedious, blighting conscientiousness. I have always been nervous of pleasure. In my twenties, and even in my thirties, I was obsessed with work before play, reluctant to read a novel in the morning or go to the movies in the afternoon.' She regretted, she said, her first forty years in which she never touched a drink. She claimed at last to have cast off the old Puritan legacy, to have forsworn competitiveness. She asserted that her greatest happiness now lay in her children, and said that she felt much pride that I had lately gained my parachutist's wings: 'I think that unless a woman has a vocation, like teaching or music, which absorbs her emotionally, she is only half a woman if she is childless.' Almost half a century ago, I read that bit with a curling lip.

Anne went on to say that she regretted setting her own professional sights too low: 'I do not find journalism a fully satisfying career, but I am afraid that after years of writing captions, paragraphs and short articles, I may have lost the powers of concentration needed to write something longer and deeper. I ought to have written bad poetry at 17 and bad novels at 25 to get my hand in.' She never wrote a big book, but now undertook some ambitious foreign reporting assignments for the *Mail* – for instance contributing a series from America after the assassination of President Kennedy. Somewhat to my surprise and disbelief, now as in 1963, she described herself in print as 'naturally amorous'. Although her liking for men was not in doubt, she frightened the life out of most. I have always believed that she enjoyed the experience of receiving admiration more than the reality of intimacy. In any event, for a time she threw herself into work because her personal life was sterile.

Mac was rescued from disaster by a woman. In June 1963, after eighteen torrid, alcoholic months in the wilderness, he married Anthea, widow of his publisher, Michael Joseph. She was thirty-eight, which then seemed to me impossibly old, while Father was fifty-four. A woman of energy, intelligence, wit and almost saintly disposition, she required all these qualities to deal with Mac, and indeed with me. She already had two children of her own, aged ten and twelve, and soon gave birth to another with Father – my half-sister Harriet, born in 1964. In a perverse moment Mac invited cousin Stephen, whom he had always detested, to become one of Harriet's godfathers. I suspect that Anthea's wishes influenced the choice – Stephen was one of our few apparently reputable family connections. The reconciliation was short-lived, and Father soon returned to bad-mouthing his cousin.

Mac – and I at erratic intervals – moved into Brown's Farm, Anthea's house in the village of Old Basing, near Basingstoke. There was no alternative, for he was effectively penniless. Anthea embarked upon the Herculean task of house-training him. Gin had played too large a part in Father's life for too long now to be abandoned. His consumption could only be controlled. He loved his new wife, and was deeply grateful for what she did for him. But he was no more convincing a stepfather to her children than I was a stepbrother. He could not undo the self-destructive habits of a lifetime. The happiness of their marriage was a tribute to her fortitude. She controlled her temper even when, for instance, Mac parked the car outside the local pub with its handbrake off, whereupon it rolled into a wall. She humoured his whims, even though she was obliged to limit his expenditure. He became dependent upon her counsel, management – and income. She remained a director of Michael Joseph, by then owned by the Thomson Organisation, and eventually became the firm's chairman. Anthea's money paid almost all the bills at Brown's Farm. At the outset, I think she supposed that she was marrying a successful writer and 'television personality'. She soon discovered, without any evident display of resentment, that Mac's career had entered a decline which could not be reversed.

Her energy and versatility were astonishing. She was born into a generation of working women who tried to do it all, almost single-handed. She embraced the domestic round far more convincingly than Anne. Many evenings, I saw her sweep into the kitchen at Brown's Farm, back from a day's work in London, toss aside her briefcase and address cooking the dinner without breaking step. She arranged the flowers in church, read the children bedtime stories, took a manuscript to bed, watered the gin, picked broad beans, pursued a vigorous social life. She was astonishingly restrained in her complaints about my excesses – emptying cigarette boxes, injuring cars, eating extravagant quantities of food and bringing home conspicuously unsuitable girlfriends. Once, after we had been discussing a woman in the village whom everyone found tiresome, Anthea muttered to herself, quite unself-consciously, 'I must learn to like her more.' I knew she meant it. Thenceforward she would do her utmost to be nicer to this dreary creature. Even though I was incapable of such generosity myself, I deeply admired it in Anthea. I have always thought that the strain of bearing so many burdens, in her career as well as her domestic life, contributed decisively to her early death.

Living with Anthea, Mac acquired a new circle of acquaintances, in some cases friends, among 'her' authors at Michael Joseph. They saw a lot of Dick Francis, the champion jockey turned champion thriller-writer, and his wife Mary who contributed so much to his books. Alan Wykes, a fellow Savage Club author, dedicated one of his books to Mac, who was characteristically untroubled – unlike Anthea, who was mortified – when it proved to be about venereal disease. There was John Masters, whose novels of British India are terrific, and sadly neglected today; Richard Gordon, author of the 'Doctor' books; Alf Wight – 'James Herriot', best-selling Yorkshire vet; the veteran Winifred Clemence Dane; country writer Dora Saint – 'Miss Read'; and more unexpectedly, James Baldwin. Jimmy once left a niece as a guest at Brown's Farm for some days while he went off on an expedition of his own. The village was amazed and vastly entertained by the spectacle of Mac walking the lanes hand-in-hand with a small black child. Only Anthea could have reconciled him to such a responsibility.

From the mid-1960s onwards, however, while Mac found much happiness in marriage, his career flagged. Intensely stubborn, he adopted courses which he thought appropriate for himself, heedless of the view of others, including employers. Then, as always, any successful television performer needed to take close heed of the tortured, Byzantine politics of the BBC. Without the support of some reigning patrons in the corridors of power at Television Centre, talent alone has never sufficed to maintain access to the airwaves. Father's indifference to the shifting sands at *Tonight*, his refusal to notice the rise of new powers and the eclipse of old ones at Lime Grove Studios, cost him dear.

His advice to me about forswearing sunglasses on camera reflected an almost pathological distaste for this affectation. He himself never wore them, even amid Arabian sands. At *Tonight* in those days there was a talented director, with an intake of alcohol notable even by

Mac's standards, named Derek Amoore. Among other peccadilloes, Amoore wore shades indoors and out, by day and night. Mac grew to dislike this habit, and its noisily trendy perpetrator, so passionately that he could scarcely bring himself to speak to the man, never mind work with him. In 1966, when he wrote the last of his 'Mr Cork' thrillers, *Cork on the Telly*, he introduced a thinly disguised Amoore figure as the plot's chief villain. In all this, Mac was ill-advised. Though Amoore was indeed awful, he was a rising power, who returned Mac's contempt. The young producers at Lime Grove did not achieve the celebrity of the performers, and worked for pittances. But many were highly gifted. Several, such as Jack Gold, Ken Russell and Kevin Billington, went on to careers as feature film directors. Others rose to become senior BBC executives. They represented the future, and it was they who made the key decisions about appointments of presenters and reporters. The support of Grace Wyndham-Goldie, Donald Baverstock and Alasdair Milne counted for a lot, but Mac paid heavily for his disdain towards the young turks coming up behind, soon occupying big desks and decreeing who was 'in' and who was 'out' within BBC TV's Talks Department.

As the 1960s advanced, Mac found himself marginalised. His defiant adherence to the standards of old Britain, his contempt for the 'swinging' decade in which he now found himself, seemed ever more fogeyish. He commanded affection among colleagues, but some were exasperated by his refusal to accept advice, sometimes even direction. Gin affected his fitness for work. Producers joked that if Mac had to shoot a piece to camera after lunch, it was prudent to locate a doorpost for him to lean against while delivering it. There came a day in 1965 when some remote administrative figure wrote a bland letter saying that with regret 'the Corp' would not be renewing his annual contract. He continued to make occasional appearances, persuading the BBC to let him present a dramatised documentary series about Robert Churchill the gunmaker's appearances as a witness in famous murder cases early in the century – *Call the Gun Expert*. He wrote and presented *The Hated Society* about the Jesuits, in whose bosom he had been reared. But for four programmes he was paid a mere £500 for a notional two weeks' writing and three weeks' filming – pin money even in those days. For some time he presented a little weekly magazine show for Tyne-Tees Television, *Man Bites Dog*. His glory days as a broadcaster were done. He was not yet sixty, but he had blown it.

I understood why. Anthea understood why. He never did. He continued to write books, contribute occasional pieces to magazines, cherish the public recognition he retained. But his income declined steeply. He owned no property, and had made no pension provision. I was shocked to discover after his death that by the late 1960s he was bringing in less money than me – just £1,500 in 1969, compared with £6,500 three years earlier, his last serious earnings. His books made little. He got £100 for *English Sporting Guns*, the same for *After You, Robinson Crusoe*. He continued to do the work he wanted to, heedless of its marketability. But this was only possible because my stepmother bankrolled the family.

The most significant contribution Mac could make to their finances when these were strained was progressively to sell personal treasures: a few pictures including a cherished Rowlandson watercolour, some guns. Save for his wonderful good fortune in marrying Anthea, Mac would have been stony broke in the last fifteen years of his life. We know that all careers end in failure, but I was deeply moved by the waste. Mac threw away his talents, forfeited the fruits of the real love his TV fans felt for him, long before his time should have been up. His financial difficulties, together with the awareness that as a family the Hastingses have been shockingly improvident, made a profound impression on me. After emerging from my spendthrift youth, throughout my later working life I have been almost obsessed with the importance of avoiding being old and poor.

Anne began a time of great happiness when she formed a new relationship with Osbert Lancaster, the artist best known for his pocket cartoons on the front page of the *Daily Express*. Not long after Mac's expulsion, or maybe even before – Anne was exceedingly coy about such matters – they encountered each other at a cocktail party given by former *Express* editor Arthur Christiansen. She had known Osbert for years as a Fleet Street acquaintance, but without enthusiasm. She found him supercilious. He, in his turn, professed to have been terrified of her: 'She was always so elegant, so aloof and so much taller than me.' Now, however, at the Christiansen party where neither he nor she encountered any other congenial company, they went off to dine together at the Ritz. They discovered much in common, and the relationship blossomed – Osbert was already living apart from his wife Karen.

Physically, it was an implausible pairing. Anne towered above the world, dwarfing her new man, who was notably short. An intensely mannered figure, born in 1908, he modelled himself on the Edwardian writer and caricaturist Max Beerbohm, who like him and indeed me was educated at Charterhouse and thoroughly disliked the place. A dandy, meticulous about his appearance even unto the daily carnation, perhaps in response to a lack of physical advantages which he cheerfully acknowledged, Osbert had become celebrated not only for his newspaper work – including the creation of his famous characters Lord and Lady Littlehampton – but also for his deeply informed and wonderfully witty studies of architecture, in words and pictures.

I always wondered whether Osbert fell in love with Anne because of her resemblance in style if not pedigree to Maudie Littlehampton. Often, noting Maudie's succinct and scornful judgements upon the follies of mankind on the front page of the *Express*, I heard my mother's voice. She shared almost all Osbert's enthusiasms, save his taste for clambering into white tie and tails to attend City livery dinners – formal occasions bored her. At first the relationship was discreet. But following the death of Karen Lancaster in 1964, they began to be seen together openly. After a lifetime of worrying about money, it was a relief for Anne to share the life of a rich man. Osbert, whose grandfather was among the founders of Prudential Assurance, had inherited a fortune sufficient to enable him to indulge his own lifestyle, independent of his income as an artist.

In 1967, when a reporter telephoned him to enquire whether it was true that he was to marry Anne, he acknowledged the impending wedding, adding in character: 'Living in sin would have been much cheaper, but you can say that we are still good friends.' So they remained through the years that followed. Osbert's establishment in Eaton Square was notably more elegant than Anne's rambling old mansion flat in Cromwell Road. She loved first nights with him at Covent Garden and Glyndebourne – Osbert designed many ballet and opera productions – together with the accompanying social life. He was inexhaustibly gregarious.

His father had been killed on the Somme in 1916, and he spent much of his childhood in the homes of rich grandparents. During four years at Oxford he forged a reputation as an aesthete, one of the few to be resolutely heterosexual. He became celebrated among his contemporaries, and left with an impenitent Fourth in English. His family wanted him to become a lawyer, but after his studies were interrupted by a brush with tuberculosis, he went instead to the Slade. Thereafter his social persona, as one of the landmarks of upmarket London, evolved in step with a burgeoning artistic career. Hugh Casson wrote of a wartime encounter in a restaurant, where Osbert's ringing tones as usual commanded the room: 'The sonorous voice, the elaborate phraseology, the bristling moustache and staring eyes, the physical presentation – half Balkan bandit, half retired Brigadier – was at first terrifying, and then almost immediately endearing. Osbert, it quickly became clear, is a performance, meticulously practised and hilariously inflated and at times disturbing.' Among Osbert's peccadilloes was a distaste for Winston Churchill, matched by a loyalty to the prime minister's son Randolph, whom he had first met at Oxford. Osbert claimed to be the only man on earth who liked Randolph.

Vermeer was his favourite painter. Unsurprisingly, given his passion for gossip, he retained a lifelong addiction to Boswell's *Life of Johnson*. Alan Pryce-Jones, who first met him at university, wrote in the 1960s that Osbert seemed quite unchanged by the intervening forty years: 'He might, then as now, have been an Edwardian dandy, moustached and pinstriped, perhaps a trifle trimmer at twenty than today, but already with the communicative air – since he remained passionately interested in the doings and foibles of countless friends – of a bigger and rounder Max Beerbohm.'

It would be quite inadequate to describe Osbert's political views as conservative. He was a shameless enemy of 'progress' in all its manifestations, mocking change and supposed improvement in the condition of society with relentless scorn. He was never apologetic about his taste for the high life, observing that he made jokes about the smart world because it was the only one he knew. 'It would be silly to try to make working-class jokes. One can make jokes about bus conductors, because one meets them. But not jokes about agricultural labourers, because I don't know any.' Interviewed on *Desert Island Discs*, he chose as his castaway's luxury a live sturgeon, to provide a secure source of caviar.

'Tell me, Canon, are you as bored with Premarital Intercourse as I am?'

In those days the *Daily Express* used the great Giles's cartoons to portray the working class; The Gambols strip to tease suburban Britain; and Osbert's pocket cartoons to divert its upmarket readers. It is doubtful how many Giles fans understood Maudie Littlehampton when she said, for instance, in 1964 after Prime Minister Harold Wilson refused to make a statement in the House of Commons: 'But darling Aunt Ethel, I do assure you that it was *quite* a different Mr Wilson who was so terribly keen on open covenants openly arrived at!' Likewise *Express* readers may have felt unsympathetic to a drinking companion at the bar of White's Club who remarked to Lord Littlehampton: 'You know, Willy, I've been thinking and I've come to the conclusion that the trouble with us is that we were never educated for leisure.' The *Express* prized the Littlehamptons' creator, however, because he provided important people with an excuse to buy a paper they might otherwise have spurned. 'My dear, have you seen Osbert Lancaster today?' was for thirty-five years as familiar a line at fashionable parties as is the same enquiry today about Matt's cartoons in the *Telegraph*.

'Mountbatten's right! One wouldn't so much mind the thought of Denis Healey's finger on the button if only one could be reasonably certain that the Pentagon's thumb weren't on Denis Healey.'

I never achieved a comfortable relationship with Osbert. My first physical impression of him was that he resembled one of the villains of Ian Fleming's thrillers – Sir Hugo Drax, perhaps, or Goldfinger – misshapen and hirsute. He had no sporting enthusiasms, and I then supposed that every right-thinking Englishman shot pheasants or pursued foxes. He had spent the war in the Foreign Office rather than on battlefields, albeit with a memorable eighteen-month stint as press attaché at the British Embassy in Athens during the 1944–45 Greek Civil War. He had never, so far as I could discover, attempted to kill even a small German.

I was bemused by the manner in which he allowed my mother to belabour him for his impracticality. He took pride in the indifference to domestic matters that wealth makes possible. He went to his grave without, so far as is known, having washed up so much as a cup and saucer. Not long after he and Anne began their relationship, John Betjeman – Osbert's oldest and closest friend – took me to lunch at the Great Western Hotel at Paddington, one of those railway establishments which he loved. He said: 'Dear boy, it would give everybody such pleasure if you could be just a little bit nicer to Osbert.' I said: 'John, I don't see how he can bear to sit in the corner and let himself be bullied by my mother.' Betjeman answered: 'But don't you understand? Osbert *adores* it!'

'Is that the one we swopped for Burgess?'

My own attitude to Mother's new domestic arrangements was coloured by a muddled sense that, while I had not the slightest desire myself to share a roof with Osbert, it was unjust that she and my sister Clare should be luxuriously ensconced in Eaton Square, while I was then eking out an existence in Belsize Park. My wildly exaggerated sense of entitlement was similarly affronted when I encountered them in Athens, staying at the Grand Bretagne Hotel, at a moment when my own resources encompassed a bunk in the city's youth hostel. I record these unworthy sentiments not in quest of sympathy, but as symptoms of crass immaturity. Beyond my own lack of appreciation for Osbert's gifts, on his side he was understandably reluctant to welcome the excesses of a large, noisy, bellicose adolescent as part of the baggage which came with Anne. His present to me, the first Christmas that he and Mother spent together, was a 1953 American edition of one of his own books. Keenly materialistic, I interpreted this gesture as a declaration of war. Our relationship remained distant. I regret this, and accept most of the blame. To my sister Clare, incomparably more sweet-natured and accommodating, he displayed affection and generosity to the day of his death.

Many times since, people have said: 'It must have been fascinating to have somebody as clever and funny as Osbert as a stepfather.' It should have been. But few children are as indulgent towards their parents' love lives as mature judgement recommends. We may reluctantly accept the notion that they slept with each other often enough to conceive us, but we recoil from the vision of them making love to third parties. In disgust at Mother's perceived betrayal of my father, on visits to Rose Cottage I treated Osbert as an unwelcome interloper.

I was not alone, however, in finding his manner a trifle ponderous. Graham Greene, who admired Osbert's drawing but was impatient of his prose, described him as 'a charming creature with a heavy moustache, looking like a miniature Guardsman . . . He has a curious pompous style which is excellent when he is being funny, but is heavy when he's serious.' James Lees-Milne observed of Osbert in a passage of his famously bitchy diaries: 'He is more facetious than funny. And the text of his latest book which he brought for us, *The Littlehampton Bequest*, bears this out. The incomparable illustrations (and they are marvellous) are far more amusing than the text.' Lees-Milne thought better of Anne: 'extremely tall, with a splendidly lissom figure, very pretty face, dresses admirably and is elegant. Is the exact opposite to Osbert in looks, demeanour and behaviour, although O is always neatly dressed, too neatly for the country. She told me that Osbert is not in the least interested in individuals, only in people in the mass. He knows nothing whatever, she asseverated, about the heart, a piece of anatomy which bores him stiff.' This chimed with my own perception – that for all his geniality, Osbert was a cold fish.

Mother concluded that it was in all our best interests to get on with a new life, with a minimum of violent intrusions from me. I wrote to her, during one of our many rows: 'I understand you much better than you like to think, because in character we are very much alike. I've always admired you immensely, but you can frighten me very much…When you tell me how boring my girlfriends are, I'm often well aware that you're right, but it doesn't help me much.' Father wrote to me in those days, dissenting from something Anne had written in her *Mail* column, and observing: 'I am afraid that she has a lot of the ruthlessness of character which you have yourself, and which I hope you will grow out of.'

For long periods of the 1960s and 1970s, Mother and I saw little or nothing of each other, largely by my choice. To a remarkable degree, from the age of sixteen onwards I lived my own life, and indeed at seventeen I moved into a rented flat in Holland Park. I saw my parents as a visitor, rather than as an established resident at either of their homes. In the years thereafter my peripatetic, chronically restless existence would have commanded the respect of the Flying Dutchman. Relations with Mother did not improve when she told me, soon after I was twenty-one, that she had just made a new will, leaving everything to my sister. She believed, she said, that I would always be capable of taking care of myself, while Clare would need her support. This painful little revelation coloured my attitude to her for the ensuing forty-odd years. Her judgement was entirely rational, especially as I had chosen to throw in my lot so decisively with Father. Father, indeed, excluded Clare from his own will. But I have always regretted that she thought it necessary to tell me what she had done.

Likewise, she later came to see me, urging that I should withdraw my name as a candidate for the Beefsteak Club, which then seemed to me to represent the summit of glamour and august company: 'It's a typical nonsense of your father's, to organise this. Osbert's a member, and it will be too embarrassing for him to have to meet you there!' I joined the Beefsteak anyway, with the aid of John Betjeman and Alec Waugh, and the roof did not fall in. A few years later she wrote to her old friend Charles Wintour, then my boss at the *Evening Standard*, urging him to make me an executive rather than allow me to continue a career as a war correspondent which she thought likely to get me killed. She said: 'He is not good with people – nobody knows it better than I – but most of the good executives I know in Fleet Street have been bastards: think of H. Keeble and Chris[tiansen].' I knew nothing of those remarks for thirty years after they were written. Reading them in middle age, when I became editor of the *Evening Standard* and found myself in possession of my predecessors' correspondence, I felt unsure whether to be touched by her anxiety for my survival, or mortified by her brutal assessment of my character.

Belatedly, I acknowledged that with Osbert, Mother achieved a happiness and security which she had earned after so many years of toil and trouble. My own behaviour, my fiercely aggressive support for Father, provoked her beyond endurance. She was correct – though I wish she had not said it in writing – to assert to Charles Wintour that I lacked any gift for getting along with people. My late teens and early twenties were a lonely period, full of more anger and frustration than even most adolescents inflict upon themselves. In the eyes of the world I was a prime specimen of what Victorian novelists called a hobbledehoy – awkward, selfish and charmlessly assertive. I blamed my parents for the fact that I possessed no social circle, rarely got invited to parties, and was utterly at a loss when I did attend one. I maintained the habit of making trouble in any house in which I found myself, long after the age at which most young men grow out of it.

I was rescued from delinquency by work. At an early age I found happiness and an early flicker of success in a life which I embraced with passion. In 1963, Father's influence at Lime Grove narrowly sufficed to assist me to a gap-year job in the gift of Alasdair Milne, as a researcher on a huge project which BBC TV was then launching, *The Great War* series. This proved a wonderful initiation to the world of adults, and of the media. I thrilled to the glamour of the business, and exulted in the perquisites of admission to the BBC circle – for instance, joining the Saturday-night studio audience of *That Was The Week That Was* with a young BBC librarian named Penny Levinson, whom I dated for a while. She found me at seventeen too alarming to deserve a lasting place in her life, and a few years later she married Michael Grade. I had to wait another thirty years for her to marry me.

It is hard to exaggerate the thrill of working for the BBC, even in the humblest capacity, during the early 1960s. Brimming over with talent and novelty, it seemed the place where the most exciting things in Britain were happening. There came a moment when I chanced to meet Mac amid the throng at the bar of the BBC Club. After we had exchanged greetings, he murmured to me: 'My boy, I think the moment has come at which you should stop calling me "Daddy" and address me as "Father".' It was a significant rite of passage. In the offices of *The Great War* I was charmed to discover that, for a change, my grown-up colleagues were in trouble more often than I was, usually as a consequence of complex sexual intrigues. I began to discover that happiness could be something more positive than freedom from imminent indictment. I took two days off from work to sit the Oxford entrance exam, and was surprised and not altogether pleased to be rewarded with an exhibition to University College, which some months later removed me from the BBC.

I found Oxford no more congenial than had my mother thirty years earlier. Nobody seemed to appreciate me, and I gave them no reason to do so. Having started to earn a living wage, I hated becoming a broke student again. I began to moonlight as a fixer for foreign TV companies filming in Britain, and spent vacations working on the *Evening Standard*'s Londoner's Diary – an introduction I owed to my mother, who did her best to help my career when I would allow her to. She heavily rewrote the drafts of the first two newspaper articles which appeared under my byline in the *Standard* in 1964. One was entitled: 'IN ATHENS, THE HUNGRY HITCH-HIKER SELLS HIS BLOOD', which is what I had done. The other piece was a lament for my inability to find a girlfriend at Oxford.

At the end of my first Oxford year, the *Standard*'s editor Charles Wintour offered me a staff job. 'I am impressed by your potential,' he wrote to me at Univ., 'and am prepared to make quite an investment in you, if you stick around for a reasonable period.' Here was an unprecedented assertion of confidence in the possibility that I might have a future outside a reformatory, for which I will remain grateful to Charles for the rest of my life. Rumour within the paper, deeply resentful of my precocious admission to the payroll, suggested that the editor was my mother's lover, or, even more exotically, that I was his illegitimate offspring. In reality, I think, mere commonplace nepotism was at work. Charles also at the time employed the sons of Eric Linklater and Alan Moorehead on the Londoner's Diary. He liked to suppose that journalistic talent could be inherited.

Ignoring protests from family and tutors I quit my college, thus following my great-great grandfather, grandfather and mother in a family tradition of entering universities, then failing to graduate from them. Eighteen months later, in 1967 when I was twenty-one, I won a fellowship from an American foundation to spend a year in the US, during which I was also able to report for the *Evening Standard*. Indeed, at the paper's behest I returned to America for several months to contribute to its reporting of the 1968 presidential election.

This protracted absence proved a blessing, perhaps above all to my parents. I recently reread their letters to me during that period, written in response to many homesick and self-pitying communications from me. Both wrote sympathetically but hard-headedly. Anne said, for instance, that I made far too much fuss about the difficulties of living up to the family reputation.

> Your father and I are not – repeat not – famous people. I am a successful journalist and your father had a good reputation [I noted the past tense] as a TV personality on a certain type of programme, but that doesn't make us a difficult family to live up to. The way you talk, we might be the Churchills. I foresee a much better career for you than either of us had.
>
> You are bad at providing interests from within yourself. I

remember when you were 15 or 16 you used to sit in the flat and complain that you had nothing to do, and nothing I suggested seemed to interest you. It is hopeless if you are always going to be dependent on parties and constant action. Your father's tragedy has been a longing for recognition and fame which made no sense at all, and an opinion (or so he pretended) that he was a great celebrity. Followed, of course and alas, by a corresponding sense of failure if things went wrong. I always thought you were more balanced and saw things more clearly. I'll go dotty if you, too, are going to be tortured by a false ambition.

Immediately following my return from America in the autumn of 1968, Father wrote me a long letter, full of advice about both my behaviour and recent published examples of my journalism.

I must give you a little paternal advice on prose style. In some of your reports from the US, you have employed too many clichés. Get emphasis out of the construction of the sentence – not by messing about with capital letters and exclamation marks. You use that hackneyed phrase 'right now' several times. Think on it, and you will appreciate that it means precisely nothing. It is an Americanism which has dribbled into the Queen's English because it's a convenient way of starting a new paragraph when the writer can't think of a more meaningful way of doing so.

You are such a born writer that you must watch out for these vulgarisms. I am more anxious to underline them because I appreciate the pressures on your style while you have been living in an American idiom. My impression is that, at the moment, in print you are pressing your prose too hard. You are better in many of your letters to me, when you are talking with your hair down. Nothing will stop you from being a successful popular journalist. What I want is for you to be recognised as a fine writer.

Be very careful not to command conversation about your experiences, remarkable as they have been. People can get very bored. Before you know where you are, they will write you off as

an arrogant young fool. The art, my dear son, is to lie low like
Brer Rabbit. The great reporters (excluding Bernard Levin,
perhaps) are great listeners. I know that I myself am a compulsive
talker. I have always regretted it. At your age, it is far more important than it is at mine to play *sotto voce*. I beg you not to show
off. Concentrate on letting the other fellow think how much you
admire him. That's the way to get on. If you try to impose your
own personality – and this is your especial vice – you will find
that you are out in the cold. The game, in getting to the top, is to
persuade people that you think they are cleverer than you.

Rereading the other side of that correspondence, there seems no merit
in quoting my own twenty-two-year-old words, because these were
so conceited, foolish and self-absorbed. I find myself marvelling at
the good fortune which enabled me eventually to extricate myself
from the mindset into which I had sunk, consumed with impatient
and extravagant ambition. The American experience provided the
material for my first book, *America 1968: The Fire This Time*, a portrait
of the US amid race riots, assassinations and one of its most bitterly
contested elections in modern memory. This was published early in
1969, when I was twenty-three. Thereafter my work for the *Evening
Standard*, and later the BBC, provided a foundation which compensated, in some degree, for my social shortcomings. I was preserved
from self-immolation by the discipline and opportunities offered by
Fleet Street and television.

Almost all the counsel offered by both my parents was wise. Yet
for years I paid inadequate heed to it. I could never resist picking
a fight and airing my opinions. Once, after some rustic lunch
guests at Brown's Farm had gone home, Father said to me: 'I
suppose you think those people are full of admiration for what a
clever chap Max Hastings is. They are not. They are saying to each
other, "What a cocky young idiot!" You chose to argue with them
because you thought they were saying silly things, and so they
were. But the great principle in life is to pick enemies your own
size. Don't waste your fire on little people. Fight big people, if you

must, but always be civil as butter to little ones, even if you think they are bloody fools.'

Sometimes, however, differences with big people could also cause trouble. Anthea's father was a law lord, a grave, humourless, digni-fied septuagenarian named Charles Hodson. He was a lifelong friend of the notorious hanging judge, Lord Goddard. When Goddard died, Bernard Levin wrote a lacerating column denouncing the old monster and all his works. At the following Sunday lunch, Lord Hodson deliv-ered an enraged broadside against Levin, in which I fancy the words 'rotten little Jew' featured. I took issue. Hodson said: 'Either you leave this table, or I do.' Family opinion was decisively against me.

There is no purpose in rehearsing such yarns any further. Readers will have got the picture. It was a tribute to Anthea's forbearance that she continued to endure my visits to Brown's Farm with good grace until I was belatedly tamed. I tested almost to destruction Bacon's observation that 'Youth and discretion are ill-wed compan-ions.' I learned eventually to love and respect Anthea as a close friend, rather than as a stepmother. By the time I delivered the address at her memorial service in 1981, I knew what a debt of gratitude I, as well as my father, owed to her intelligence, warmth, wit and generosity.

Anne's life in the years after she began to live with Osbert glittered both socially and professionally. As a famous wit, Osbert was asked everywhere, and now she went with him. At Rose Cottage and in Eaton Square she entertained as she never had done before – artists such as John Piper and Elisabeth Frink, both close friends, the inevitable John B and Elizabeth Cavendish, Roy and Jennifer Jenkins, Anthony Powell, the historian Michael Howard and Mark James, Alan and Lucy Moorehead and many others. The garden at Rose Cottage, sadly neglected in the last years of Anne's marriage to Mac, was dramatically revived under the stimulus of her new happiness and enthusiasm. In London, the Lancasters were regulars at the Euro-pean embassies, a milieu for which Osbert had retained a taste since his wartime Foreign Office days.

Mac, in a rare moment of bitchiness, observed of Osbert that in the days when he drew for *The Strand*, 'As he came up the stairs, you could see him working out the joke he would make when he got to the top.' It was true that, to Osbert, every social appearance was a theatrical performance, crafted for effect: the lift of the great bushy eyebrows, the flick of the moustache, the devastating line delivered in a fruity, emphatic, booming voice that could be heard across the bar of his beloved Garrick Club: 'There they all were in 1945; gongs for Matthew, gongs for Mark, gongs for Luke, *but no gong for Colonel Peter* [Fleming].' There was a host of stories, enlivened with vivid mimicry, of Isaiah and Maurice – Berlin and Bowra – and of Churchill and Macmillan. He possessed an encyclopaedic familiarity with Debrett, and a marked taste for titles, especially if their holders were semi-literate. For Osbert with his talent to amuse, all manner of grand doors were thrown open.

Anne delighted in her new-found intimacy with John Betjeman. She described him as the only man in England from whom she was happy to accept such invitations as this one: 'I'm giving a lunch party next Tuesday on Southend Pier. Do come – such a lovely ride, just an hour each way by train from Fenchurch Street. Southend is at its best in January, all that icy wind and huge grey waves.' On the train, Betjeman delivered a running commentary, of a kind perfectly familiar to any viewer of his television masterpieces: 'Keep your eyes open for a really splendid cemetery on the left – it must be the largest in Britain, all overgrown like a jungle. Now move over to the right for Upminster windmill – oh, what a pity, it's cloaked in fog. Now back to the left for Basildon New Town; you mustn't miss it at any price, it's the most hideous thing in Britain, an education in itself. Now there's ten miles of absolutely unspoilt country – oh dear, they do seem to have run up a few things, in fact I see it's continuous building all the way. Never mind, we'll soon be at Westcliff, that's the *better* end of Southend. There are some fine 1890 boarding houses you'll see as we pull out.'

Anne described how they bought cockles and prawns, which John B recommended as a speciality of Southend ('Oh, I see they're Norwegian'), then looked at an art gallery and a church which she and Osbert found devoid of any architectural interest whatsoever, before taking the train home. 'It had been a glorious day,' she wrote, without irony. 'Indeed, in my experience, all days were glorious with John B.' She was fascinated by watching Betjeman and Osbert together:

> Their humour, their love of architecture, their deep knowledge of all the arts except music, their phenomenal visual memories, their capacity for enjoyment at every level, their shared religion (high C of E), their beautiful voices, their charm, their selfishness, made them two characters who had been cast in the same mould, but hand-finished differently. They both looked extraordinary, John with his rabbity teeth, Osbert with his huge head on a short body and bulging, all-seeing blue eyes. They were both scintillatingly but effortlessly witty, surpassing each other in each other's company. There was no niche nor buttress of a cathedral that they were willing to pass by, no thumbnail sketch in a major exhibition of paintings that they would not pore over. A single parish church would occupy them for two hours, and I confess that I often grew tired, and would rest on a tombstone wondering prosaically where and when we would lunch.

However frosty my relations with Osbert, I too adored Betjeman. In my turbulent youth he was as kind to me as to a host of others. He once took me to lunch in St John's Wood (always pronounced '*Sinjun's*' by John B) to meet Dame Veronica Wedgwood, a friend of his who was among my heroines as a historian. Before I departed for America in 1967, he invited me to lunch at his little house in Cloth Fair, and presented me with a briefcase from Swaine Adeney, which embarrassed me. I knew it must have cost a lot, and in those days John was never flush. Then he took me on a whirlwind tour of the City of London, of exactly the kind which my mother experienced in Southend, and offering far more beauty. 'Dear boy,' he said, 'I want you to see all the wonderful views that will have vanished behind concrete by the time you return to these shores.' We galloped from church to church for an hour or two before John halted in a street and said: 'Shut your eyes. Walk five steps. Turn right. Now, open your eyes, and you will see the view of St Paul's from the east exactly as Wren conceived it – for the last time before they put a new office building in the middle of it.' Even in those years when my aesthetic sense was woefully underdeveloped, I was moved. I was more grateful than I could say to John B for offering me the most precious gifts he could offer – not the briefcase, though I still use it, but his time and wisdom.

While Anne's delight in intellectual society was uninhibited, her attitude to grander company was more equivocal. She had always been conscious that her own background was modest. Once, in my childhood, I fatuously enquired of her whether the Hastingses were upper-class. Absolutely not, she said sharply, 'upper middle-class at best'. She interviewed Nancy Mitford at the time of the great rumpus surrounding *Noblesse Oblige*, the book Mitford edited and part-wrote on class, U and non-U. 'Am I U?' Anne demanded with characteristic directness. The great social arbiter looked her up and down and conceded evasively: 'You have U legs.' One night the Lancasters dined at the Garrick with Miss Mitford. For Anne, this was not a comfortable experience. Osbert and Nancy had known each other for almost forty years, and spent the evening shrieking with laughter about long-dead grandees and newly remembered feuds and teases. The third party felt distinctly *de trop*.

Yet, plunged into the clever U world – for Osbert had no more patience than herself with philistines, coroneted or otherwise – Anne adapted to it with growing pleasure. Her manner, always commanding, assumed something of the *grande dame*, of Lady Littlehampton perhaps – for when Osbert received a knighthood, she became Lady Lancaster. The historian Michael Howard said simply of Osbert: 'He was a life-enhancer.' Their friends found Anne a perfect companion for him, though she remained exasperated by his dogged indifference to practical matters: 'He behaved during our marriage as though we had a full Edwardian staff, from butler to boots.'

Osbert himself wrote: 'For sheer pleasure few methods of progression can compare with the perambulator. The motion is agreeable, the range of vision extensive and one has always before one's eyes the rewarding spectacle of a grown-up maintaining prolonged physical exertion . . . The gondola alone, I think, can compare with the pram for pleasure.' Anne added sardonically to that passage: 'Or sitting in the passenger seat admiring the scenery while one's wife drives a hired car up a precipitous mountain road at dusk.'

Nonetheless, she adored her travels with Osbert, especially in the Mediterranean – not infrequently on Lord Camrose's splendid yacht – and above all in his beloved Greece and Turkey. Though she always professed herself to be a socially humble, politically liberal professional woman, disavowing any taste for high life, she acquired a growing appetite for stately-home weekends. Her cultural hunger, unassuaged during the years with Mac, at last found fulfilment. She admired Osbert's tireless crusading and lobbying, often in cahoots with Betjeman, for the cause of architecture and the preservation of fine buildings. She respected his dedication to his craft: he wrote a thousand words a day in addition to drawing for the *Express* and for his own books. 'The emotional security was a revelation,' she wrote. 'Osbert was born with a self-confidence rare in my generation. I personally attribute this to his innate talent – there was so much that he did well – but he put it down to the fact that, being five years older than I, he was born into a securer world. He remembered carriages, butlers, bootboys, visiting cards and coming down to tea in a blue silk suit with a Brussels lace collar.'

As her new life became settled, Anne reviewed her career. She was weary of Fleet Street life, and the pressures of writing a regular column. In 1968, soon after her remarriage, she resigned from the *Daily Mail*. Thereafter, she did little newspaper journalism, but became a panellist on the BBC's hugely popular radio quiz show, *My Word*, alongside Dilys Powell, Frank Muir and Denis Norden. Through thirteen years that followed, once a week they disported their wit and knowledge of language, much to their own amusement as well as that of the audience. Anne adored her broadcast companions, once remarking that Frank Muir was the only brilliantly talented man she ever met who might be described as socially normal.

Most of her time and energy, however, were devoted to a new writing career. In her childhood she had acquired a considerable familiarity with wildflowers. She learned something about plants, and much about practical gardening, during thirty years at Rose Cottage. Moreover, she had the gift of all good journalists for extracting information from experts and presenting it to the public with a sparkle and lucidity of which they themselves were often incapable. Hugh Johnson, then the young editor of *Queen* magazine, invited her to contribute a monthly gardening column. The feature flourished, and led to a series of books which gave her a new reputation.

The first, *Down to Earth*, was published in 1971. She described it as 'not so much a textbook as a treasury of ideas, by a devoted but amateur gardener'. Illustrated by Osbert, the book reflected her practical approach. She argued, justly, that the limitations of her knowledge also represented a virtue, because they enabled her to see the challenges as most gardeners do: 'always pushed for time and cash, the reality never quite catching up with their dreams'. She wrote about the new gardening world in which skilled help was hard to obtain at any price, and thus labour-saving was vital. The new-age garden must be founded upon shrubs, more hardy and less tender plants, less staking, more paving and permanent planting. Though Anne had seen many great gardens, she knew that 86 per cent of those in Britain occupy less than a quarter of an acre. She refused to lament the changing pattern of design, observing that 'Some of Miss Jekyll's surviving gardens seem quaint and fussy to modern eyes.'

She argued that the greatest of all contemporary styles was the 'New Cottage', idealised at Sissinghurst. Here was the principal theme of the sort of garden she addressed in her book: three-dimensional, with important trees and climbing plants; full of slow-growing plants; dominated by shrubs, roses and ground cover; so profusely planted that most of the year no bare soil is to be seen. Colours are muted, giant blooms spurned. There is an emphasis on preserving beauty through the winter, which Miss Jekyll cared little about. 'Any snobbery is of the inverted kind,' Anne wrote. 'We use our houses hard, and want pleasure from the garden all the year round . . . The most important law in the designer's code is that a garden must harmonise with the landscape.' If some of this sounds familiar, indeed old hat, almost forty years later, when Anne first took up garden writing it was fresh. A host of readers responded to her cheerful, straightforward approach. Just as Mac's shooting manuals articulated technique with a clarity which better shots than himself could not match, so Anne's elegant prose more than compensated for any weakness in her knowledge of plants.

Down to Earth, which reached the best-seller lists and was serialised in the *Evening Standard*, was followed by *Sissinghurst: The Making of a Garden*. This was, in effect, an authorised portrait of the great creation of Harold Nicolson and Vita Sackville-West, for which Anne spent some weeks, in fits and starts, living at the castle. She was the third writer to attempt the project, and the first to succeed. 'To me,' Anne wrote, 'Vita had a physical presence in that house, in the tower, in every corner of the garden…She was undeniably an egotist, but, working for many hours in the garden and among the letters and books, I came to like her very much. In the rose garden, I was infected by her romantic love of profusion, her desire to "cram, cram, cram every chink and cranny". The atmosphere was so intense that sometimes I felt that I was staying in a religious precinct. My days at Sissinghurst, though in some ways alarming, gave me deep pleasure and intensified my love of plants, and because Sissinghurst is an intimate garden, not majestic or grand, I found there was much I could learn there to help me with my own amateurish plot.' Anne spent many hours talking to Vita's son Nigel, to the head gardener – who had worked for Vita for three years before her death – and to local people who had known the couple. She spent a year on the project, because she wanted to see the garden at every season.

The book sold well, and was followed by *The Pleasure Garden* and *The Cottage Garden*, the former illustrated by Osbert, both warmly received. Anne became increasingly involved in the Royal Horticultural Society, judged at its shows and sat for some years on its Council. She was thrilled by her new status as a gardening queen, adoring the excuse and opportunity to travel the land, visiting great gardens and their owners, adding to her store of expertise. Every journalist with an ounce of self-knowledge knows how transient is newspaper writing, and deservedly so. Books and their repute last a little longer, plough a marginally deeper furrow. Anne made a real contribution to promoting the explosion of gardening enthusiasm and knowledge that overtook Britain in the last quarter of the twentieth century. She was almost humbled by an invitation to compose a slim volume on flowers for the British Museum. Her books were published in America and widely translated. She never claimed to be 'a gardening expert', but instead used her gifts as a writer to translate a great mass of the accumulated wisdom of others onto the printed page, which is what most good journalism is about. This role gave her immense pleasure for twenty years.

Mac continued to produce books – he claimed a final total of twenty-seven – until the last year of his life. Their themes became ever more whimsical and their sales were very modest, but his pleasure in writing them never diminished. His political judgement did not improve. In 1967 he wrote to me predicting that Rhodesia's rebel prime minister Ian Smith would go down as one of history's great men, and that a confederation of Rhodesia, Mozambique and South Africa would ensure that southern Africa remained white-dominated. He adored Enoch Powell. He contributed occasionally to country magazines, but his pieces described sporting experiences of his past, not present. After his marriage to Anthea, he scarcely shot or fished again. Partly, this reflected the fact that he lost the desire to kill things; partly also, the reality that there was no spare money to pay for grouse and pheasant shooting, or salmon fishing.

Nonetheless, I was able to share with him one last, wonderfully happy sporting experience. In 1970 I was twenty-four, and a reporter for BBC TV's *24 Hours* programme. I harboured passionate yearnings to fish and shoot, above all in the Highlands of Scotland, but seemed likely to die of old age before receiving invitations to do this for free. From Saigon, where I was working at the time, I wrote to the agents Strutt & Parker, asking whether they had any Scottish lodges available for rent. If my own children at the age of twenty-four had begun renting Scottish shooting lodges, I should have rushed them into counselling, but such a course seemed to me in 1970 perfectly reasonable. I was starting to tiptoe down Father's path towards fulfilling fantasies at the cost of financial ruin. Strutts sent back particulars of several places, of which I fixed upon one named the House of Tongue, on the north coast of Sutherland, possessed of 35,000 acres of hill and heather. I arranged to take it for a fortnight in September, and persuaded some friends to come with me and share the cost. I also invited Father.

When September came, chance dictated that I was in Amman, reporting the onset of a Jordanian civil war. With the utmost difficulty and some exercise of subterfuge, I wangled my way back to London on one of the last planes to leave the country for weeks. After reaching Heathrow, I just had time to collect clothes and gear from my flat before meeting the rest of the Tongue party at Euston, to catch the night train north.

Then began one of the romantic idylls of my life. As we sat in the restaurant car, in those days when sleepers possessed such splendid relics of fading grandeur, Father held us entranced with tales of the Highlands, some perhaps founded in reality. He was physically fifteen years more frail than he should have been at the age of sixty-one, but all his old enthusiasm was restored, together with his genius for imbuing a new experience with a sense of adventure.

At Inverness next morning I had arranged to rent two Land Rovers, in which we drove north towards the farther remotenesses of Britain. I was apprehensive, for I had no idea at all of what we were going to. As we topped the hill overlooking the estuary of Tongue, and looked down upon one of the finest and wildest views this island offers, my hopes soared. They were dashed on descending to the shore. The only large house we could see was an undistinguished brick construction. Had I brought a dozen friends here, to share a dump? I knocked on the door. The man who responded explained that this was the youth hostel. The House of Tongue? He pointed around the turn of the estuary.

A few hundred yards along the coast, set on the shoreline encircled by trees, was a great rambling seventeenth-century stone mansion. I ran inside, through room after room carpeted in tartans, beautifully furnished in the period manner. Each window commanded a perfect view. The borders behind blazed with the sort of colour that had faded in England two months earlier. We discovered, quickly enough, that Tongue possessed one of the finest gardens in Scotland. 'You're very lucky, my boy,' said Father wryly. I was laird for a fortnight of the sort of paradise both of us had dreamed of all our lives.

Each day that followed was more blissful than the last. We climbed the great heather hills, shot pigeons, fished mackerel, took a little boat at mortal risk to the offshore islands, struggled to catch salmon in the nearby river, on which we had a beat. The Borgie was wonderfully pretty, but very low. Day after day the fish defied our best efforts with a fly, and even with worms. Then, one morning on a pretty pool named the Shepherd's, Father tempted a salmon to his fly, played and landed it. Glowing with pleasure, clad in his usual impeccable plus-fours and brogues, he held it aloft for a photograph. It was the last fish he ever caught. I bottled that enchanted moment with him, laid it lovingly in the cellar of memories, and have cherished it ever since. Through several years that followed, I continued to rent the House of Tongue, though the bills nearly ruined me. I regretted not a farthing. Tongue remained, above all, the place where I saw Father as I always imagined him, in sporting fellowship with me. Those days in the northern Highlands laid many ghosts, and opened the promise of all manner of hopes for the future.

Mac's and Anne's lives thereafter lapsed into relatively humdrum domesticity, as is the destiny of most of us. The exotic phases of both their careers were ended. My parents, in their respective remarriages, found more contentment than they had ever known. The baton passed to the next generation.

FOURTEEN

Headstones

My great-uncle Lewis Hastings died in 1966, at the age of eighty-five, after suffering a stroke while on holiday in Spain with the sorely tried, unlovable Marigold. For all the old boy's extraordinary appetite for life, he would not have wanted to go on. There was no future for one who anticipated with such distaste the Britain of the forthcoming millennium, prophesying: 'Soon the pheasant woods will be cleared for corn, mechanised farming will uproot the hedges, the cathedrals will be turned into industrial flats, and in Africa what remains of the antelope will be penned in well-ordered Whipsnades. Virtue will be compulsory, we will buy all our meat from the butcher, and there will be no more cakes and ale. Hunting, in particular, will be put down with a strong hand by the Security Police.'

I know. Don't say it. Those sentiments seemed hoary even two generations ago. Later, in the 1970s, when I quarrelled with my cousin Stephen, by then a Tory MP and member of the notorious Monday Club, about his impassioned support for the illegal white minority regime in Rhodesia, he said: 'You always claim to have loved my father so much, but he would turn in his grave to hear all your liberal claptrap.' This was probably true, but did not diminish my regard for Lewis. He was neither a good nor an enlightened man. But he walked by himself in a manner that seized my imagination, as it had that of my father, and retains it to this day.

Mac was sore that Lewis's longstanding promise to bequeath his hunting rifles to his favourite nephew went unfulfilled. He often spoke to me of this as a theft from my own ultimate heritage, an instance of cousin Stephen's dastardly meddling. In truth, it is more likely that Lewis forgot. In any event, even forty years ago I found it hard to imagine what either Father or I could usefully have done with a couple of elephant guns. As a reporter in Rhodesia during its civil war, I was once offered a chance to shoot a tusker. A game warden suggested that I should join a national-park cull then taking place, to address elephant overpopulation. For a moment I was tempted to accept, as an act of obeisance to the shade of old Lewis. In the end, however, I declined. I am not at all squeamish about other people killing large animals, if it becomes environmentally necessary to do so. But I felt no urge to press the trigger myself. Stephen lived until 2005. I sustained a desultory relationship with him, but the memory of Lewis's and Father's disdain lingered in my consciousness, together with a distaste for his rabidly conservative view of society, and in my eyes exaggerated idea of his own rightful place in it.

Nanny died in 1968, at the genteel Kensington hotel to which she retired when my mother could no longer house her. The problem that arises when old retainers work for decades in a modern middle-class family is that such employers have no ready supply of estate cottages in which to accommodate redundant treasures in old age. 'The pay-off to the system of the old-fashioned nanny,' Anne wrote crossly and ungratefully, 'is that they do in time dominate the house to an absurd degree.' In practical terms, it is hard to imagine what else could have happened to Nanny once Clare was into her teens. But I have always harboured a lingering guilt that we accepted so much from Jessie Strafford for so long, then ruthlessly discarded her.

Money was not an issue, for Nanny's carefully nurtured savings enabled her to live in comfort. But it was a terrible blow to the poor old thing, after more than sixty years living in the bosom of families – indeed, offering her own ample bosom to the comfort of those families – to find herself alone and friendless in her mid-seventies, left with her football pools and her memories. By a final feudal gesture, she left Clare and me £500 apiece in her will. Clare also inherited her little sapphire engagement ring, relic of an attachment of which none of us ever knew the nature. Yet another among so many tragedies of the First War, perhaps? My legacy almost paid off my first overdraft, a purpose of which Nanny would have disapproved deeply, never having owed a shilling in her life. The bulk of her estate, some £14,000, she left to the Imperial Cancer Fund, with a legacy to her Sheffield neighbour Mrs Green. Our daily, Mrs Elmer, remarked with bemusement rather than resentment: 'The funny thing is, Mrs Green told me that she never liked Nanny.' But who else did the poor, lovely woman have in her lonely life?

Mac died in October 1982, suffering a cerebral haemorrhage a few days before his seventy-third birthday. I was saddened – indeed, deeply angered – that, though his old *Tonight* boss Alasdair Milne was then director-general, the BBC ignored his passing, and sent no representative to his funeral. The Corporation possesses no collective heart or memory. It was left to old colleagues to say nice things. David Attenborough paid a wonderfully generous tribute to Mac as one of the first to bring nature and the countryside to the small screen. A producer who often worked with him, Peter Bale, wrote to me about 'the debt many of us TV mortals must owe to Macdonald Hastings Esq.: for enlightening us about "English as she is spoke"; for the delight he passed to colleagues through his skill with words, first written, then spoken before the camera, on cue – and usually first take'. Alan Whicker spoke of Mac's 'distinctive brand of dauntless enthusiasm'. His old editor at *Picture Post*, Tom Hopkinson, described him as 'a most lovable man, all the more so for his irascibility, often dissolved into laughter, and his carefully-cherished prejudices'. Antony Jay, who went on to create *Yes, Minister!*, remembered him in his heyday as 'a master craftsman'. Many television viewers and readers of his books sent me letters telling me how much pleasure they had gained from his work.

I grieved for myself at Father's death, because I forfeited the joy of his company and the comfort of his pleasure in my successes; but not for him. Years before, he wrote exuberantly: 'I reckon that if it was appointed that I appear at The Last Judgement seat to account for my sins on earth, with Hilaire Belloc as my first witness, I might be forgiven; my crime was that I seized all the splendid things life had to offer.' Those days were gone. Anthea, his rock, had died the previous year of cancer, tragically young at fifty-six. After her passing, Father was tired, lonely, ill and bored. He had done everything he wanted, ruined his health with gin, cigarettes and finally the desert island fiasco. In old age he became ever more quirky and fractious, as most of us do. One night after we had dined together, he said impulsively: 'Take my Churchills when you go home. I want you to have them, and now is as good a time as any.' Exulting because Father's shotguns had totemic status in my eyes, I carried the guncase home with me. Next morning, like Joseph after discovering the loss of his cup, Father rang me in a rage: 'You've stolen my guns!' he cried in outrage. 'Bring them back immediately.' I returned the case without resentment, knowing that this flash of petulance was merely a malady of lonely and alcoholic old age.

I always thought of Father as he had been in his prime, glowing with enthusiasms often mistaken, sometimes absurd, but which his passionate personality never failed to infuse with charm. He was a fine reporter, though at the last a disappointed man. He was nagged by the injustice that, though his own father Basil, together with Lewis and Stephen Hastings, Rolfe and Anne Scott-James, Osbert Lancaster, Anthea Joseph and indeed myself had all been listed in *Who's Who*, his own name was never deemed worthy of inclusion. On such trifles are our sorrows founded.

I never doubted that he was eccentric, and I came to understand how unsuited he was to marriage, but I loved even his nonsenses. He bequeathed to me a passionate admiration for Britain's past and its rural heritage, a belief that to be born English, into the nation that spawned Drake and Marlborough, Cobbett and Kipling, is to draw the finest card in the pack of life. If such an admission invites derision in the twenty-first century, it is real nonetheless. From my teens onward, I became acutely conscious of Father's failings and follies – as what son does not? He was a careless parent to me in childhood, and always so to Clare and Harriet. But from my late teens onward he became an unfailing believer in my star, and at his best an enchanting companion. I adored him. Today, he lies beside his third wife in Old Basing churchyard, beneath a common gravestone, sculpted to his own design as an open book. The left-hand page reads 'MACDONALD HASTINGS – AUTHOR – 1909–82'; the right-hand says 'ANTHEA HASTINGS – PUBLISHER – 1925–81'.

Osbert died at seventy-seven in 1986, having been cruelly disabled by a stroke in 1975. John Betjeman went before him, in 1984. During Osbert's last years, he often rent Anne's heart by saying, 'Oh dear, I do miss John B.' For my part, whenever now at Covent Garden I see a revival of the enchanting production of the ballet *La Fille Mal Gardée* designed by Osbert, I am reminded of his remarkable gifts. An exhibition of his life and work in 2008 proved the most popular in the Wallace Collection's history. I regret that I was not more appreciative of him during his lifetime.

For Anne, the loss of Osbert was an almost unbearable blow. Having waited so long to find domestic happiness, it was snatched from her. She wrote: 'I have been just half a person since.' The last twenty-three years of her life were shadowed by loneliness. In the immediate aftermath of Osbert's death, although not in the least morbid by disposition, she spent many hours gazing at his photograph, and indeed talking to it. She wrote him a long series of letters, which she found a great consolation: 'I poured out all my feelings and unhappiness, but also gave him the day's gossip about our friends. I reported the news of the day, including political incidents. I felt that Osbert would now, as always, want to be in the swim.' A year after his death, she stopped writing the letters, because she had come to terms with her loss. Anne's last decades were redeemed chiefly by her pleasure in the successes of my sister Clare and her clever daughter Calypso. She made no secret of her boredom, often remarking, 'I've lived too long. I want to go.' Dismissing talk of a birthday present as one late anniversary dawned, she observed caustically: 'Getting to ninety-five is scarcely a cause for rejoicing.'

I was moved by Mother's courage in the final phase of her life, and grew to understand that this had always been among her virtues. As infirmity increasingly dogged her, she never complained of it. Alone, her mind razor-sharp to the end, she returned to reading Virgil in Latin, Flaubert in French, to pass the long, dreary days in her Chelsea flat and finally in a Hampshire retirement home. Her judgements on politics, newspapers, the arts, and her children's conduct of our own lives, remained trenchant on her good days, acidic on her bad ones. At the age of ninety-three, after she reread Kingsley Amis's *Take a Girl Like You*, a novel I have always enjoyed, she deflated my enthusiasm with a critique of the book's repetitive jokes and excessive length. She rediscovered Trollope with a pleasure that surprised me, because his novels are characterised by their generosity of spirit, a quality absent from her own nature.

Her capacity to make Clare and me quail remained undiminished to the last. One day when Mother was in her late eighties, I told her that I entirely respected her decision, declared to me thirty years earlier, that she would leave her entire estate to my sister, and now also to Calypso. But I added that I would love to have one of her good pictures. She said nothing, and I went home knowing it would be foolish to cherish expectations. A year or two later, however, she telephoned: 'You know how much you've always liked the Picasso?' Yes, indeed – this was a coloured drawing of a woman bequeathed to her by a close friend which always seemed to me, and to others, rather wonderful. 'Would you like to buy it?' I choked. She went on: 'I've decided to sell the picture. I thought you should have first refusal.' I said to my wife Penny, 'If I murder her, I shall plead extreme provocation and no jury will convict.'

Anne's judgements on human frailties, including those of the family, were rarely mistaken, but often drove the knife deep into old wounds. For more than sixty years I failed in my quest to gain her approval – which was, of course, what many of the difficulties in our relationship were about. In 2002, when I told her I was getting a knighthood, she at once suspected – perhaps correctly, for all I know – the hand of my close friend Roy Jenkins. 'I suppose Roy fixed it for you!' she observed laconically. I went away amazed that I still cared so much that she was pleased so little. I lacked Clare's gift for bending with the storms and evading confrontation. Maybe also Penny is right in her surmise, that in Mother's later years she came to believe I had received more than was my due in life, while she herself had garnered less.

While she may have lacked charity and self-knowledge, my admiration for her gifts, and gratitude for whatever share of them she passed to me, were very great. Michael Howard once said, in response to some stricture I expressed about her, 'I think your mother is the most intelligent woman I have ever met.' This was no mean tribute from a former Regius Professor. All that was lacking between her and me was love. We had too much in common ever to feel comfortable with each other. The success of human relationships is determined by who makes who feel good. In this, Mother and I failed. Had I taxed her about her behaviour towards me, she would have answered: 'What can you expect, after years in which you scarcely spoke to me, and I barely met your children?' Touché. Each of us inflicted savage emotional wounds upon the other. I tease my own offspring by asking them how they would define the perfect parents. The proper answer, of course, is that there are no such animals. Our perceptions of the virtues of other people's daddies and mummies by comparison with our own are almost invariably founded upon incomplete knowledge. But only in late adulthood do most of us acknowledge this.

I look back without much embarrassment on my childhood, because children may expect absolution for crimes committed in short trousers. I feel shame, however, about the discourtesies, follies and cruelties I committed in my late teens and twenties towards family and friends. I am tempted to write a circular letter of apology to all those who had to live, work, worst of all sleep with me in those years. Nothing in my parents' or step-parents' faults of omission or commission could have justified the selfishness of my behaviour. I was raised in comfort and well educated, inherited some talents, went out into the world fit and qualified to earn a living. How could I have supposed myself hard done by, and for so long borne such a baggage of anger and aggression? 'Your family has a lot of issues,' my daughter once observed in some bewilderment after an evening among them.

I am profoundly grateful for the heritage I received from my parents. Each of their enthusiasms has brought pleasure into my own life: reporting, adventure, shooting, fishing and gardening, a commitment to books and newspapers. I feel not only the blood, but also the tastes and passions, of past Hastingses and Scott-Jameses coursing through my own veins. I occasionally smoke Por Laranaga cigars, for no better reason than that they were the favoured brand of grandfather Basil, who died almost twenty years before I was born. Whenever I ride a horse among the great wild animals of Africa, as I have ridden so often and so happily in recent years, I think of Lewis. On the day I became editor of the *Daily Telegraph* and looked down from the window of my office upon Fleet Street, I reflected with deep emotion on the line of earlier Hastingses and Scott-Jameses who laboured and scribbled in its environs. I cannot today shoot a grouse or catch a salmon without recalling Father, and the pleasure it would have given him to see me living in reality a sporting life such as he was obliged to enjoy mostly in fantasy.

Some years ago, I made a modest donation to the Royal Literary Fund, which assists impoverished writers. The secretary, writing back to acknowledge this, told me that his records showed Basil Macdonald Hastings as a beneficiary of the Fund's aid in 1927. I was moved to find myself, in a trifling and entirely accidental fashion, completing a circle. It delights me to have added twenty-odd titles to a collective family output of eighty-seven books in three generations, an achievement that may compensate in quantity for what it lacks in quality. None of us attained great wealth, nor forged a reputation that has survived, or is likely to, beyond a lifetime. Our nineteenth-century experience was dominated by disappointment, represented indeed a struggle to cling to a modest place in the professional middle class. In the twentieth century, however, all of us enjoyed our spells in the sun, and what pleasure these gave!

On 13 May 2009, just before Mother was anaesthetised for an operation after a fall, she held what proved the last conversation of her life with my sister Clare, who recorded her entirely characteristic remarks as she sat in a bed at Hampshire County Hospital looking out on a vista of roofing, scaffolding and workmen:

'Don't take the notebook, it has addresses I need in the back – tear it out. I love it here. I've had the most intelligent chat I've had in weeks with the doctor about the hereafter. The nurses are so kind. They do their work and just chat around the bed, perfectly normally, not like the home, where they never smile, you know. I'm really looking forward to breakfast. Yesterday I had a nice soft roll – really fresh, not like those bits of toast you get in the home. I'd just like to move in here, but the view's not lovely, is it? And it won't get any better when they take that lot down. You remind me of that Chekhov line, dear – *The Cherry Orchard*, or was it *The Three Sisters*? – 'You are all in black, are you in mourning for your life?' The papers? Oh well, I just had to have them. I got the last from the trolley. Those dreadful MPs. I was asked once to sign a resident's parking permit for a friend who lived out of town and came to London a couple of times a month and wanted one. I refused. Other friends said they would have done it, but I just couldn't lie on a form. Would you have done it, dear? She never liked me much afterwards. I'm not a bit worried. I feel like it is all happening to somebody else. Any news? Well, you had better go now, dear. No point in coming for the next couple of days. They tell me I shall be in some pain, but they will be monitoring it, so I shan't be worth seeing. Do keep in touch . . .

Her energy, spikiness, curiosity, persisted to the last. A few hours later, a month past her ninety-sixth birthday, she was dead.

The Hastingses' little saga over the past couple of centuries has been as unsatisfactory as that of many families, marked by more divisions and feuds than beset most. Each of us has striven as best we could, much mindful of generations of the Tribe who went before. It is left to those who come afterwards to say whether we fared better or worse than we deserved. The adage that truth is the daughter of time is quite mistaken. Years do, however, assuage pain and teach us to thank our stars and our genes.

Appendix

Books Published by Members of the Hastings and Scott-James Families Since 1908

By R.A. Scott-James:
Modernism and Romance (1908)
An Englishman in Ireland (1910)
The Influence of the Press (1913)
Personality in Literature (1913)
The Making of Literature (1928)
Education in Britain (edited) (1944)
The Day Before Yesterday (1947)
Fifty Years of English Literature (1951)
Thomas Hardy (1951)
Lytton Strachey (1955)

By Basil Macdonald Hastings:
Faithful Philanderers (1923)
My Permitted Say (1924)
Memoirs of a Child (1926)
Essays of Today and Yesterday (1926)
Ladies Half-Way and Other Essays (1927)
Published plays:
The New Sin (1913)
Love – and What Then? (1913)
The Tide (1914)
The Advertisement (1915)

The Angel in the House (with Eden Phillpotts) (1915)
Q (with Stephen Leacock) (1915)
Victory (from Joseph Conrad's novel) (1919)
Hanky-Panky John (1921)
If Winter Comes (with A.S.M. Hutchinson) (1923)
Bedrock (with Eden Phillpotts) (1924)

By Lewis Hastings:
The Painted Snipe (1937)
Dragons are Extra (1947)

By Stephen Hastings:
The Murder of TSR2 (1964)
The Drums of Memory (1994)

By Macdonald Hastings:
Passed as Censored (1941)
Cork on the Water (1951)
Cork in Bottle (1953)
Cork and the Serpent (1955)
Cork in the Doghouse (1957)
Cork on the Telly (1966)
Eagle Special Investigator (1953)
Adventure Calling (1955)
The Search for the Little Yellow Men (1955)
Churchill on Gameshooting (with Robert Churchill) (1955)
Men of Glory (1958)
More Men of Glory (1959)
A Glimpse of Arcadia (1960)
Macdonald Hastings's Country Book (1961)
The Other Mr Churchill (1963)
London Observed (with John Gay) (1964)
How to Shoot Straight (1967)
English Sporting Guns (1969)
Sydney the Sparrow (1971)

Jesuit Child (1971)
Diane: A Victorian (1972)
Mary Celeste (1972)
Wheeler's Fish Cookery Book (with Carole Walsh) (1974)
After You, Robinson Crusoe (1975)
Why We Miss (1976)
Gamebook (1979)
The Shotgun (1981)

By Anne Scott-James:
In the Mink (1951)
Down to Earth (1971)
Sissinghurst: The Making of a Garden (1975)
The Pleasure Garden (1977)
The Cottage Garden (1981)
The Language of the Garden (edited) (1984)
The Best Plants for Your Garden (1988)
The British Museum Book of Flowers (with Ray Desmond and
    Frances Wood) (1989)
Gardening Letters to my Daughter (with some replies by Clare
    Hastings) (1990)
Sketches from a Life (1993)

By Max Hastings:
America 1968: The Fire This Time (1969)
Ulster 1969: The Struggle for Civil Rights in Northern Ireland (1970)
Montrose: The King's Champion (1977)
Yoni: Hero of Entebbe (1978)
Bomber Command (1979)
The Battle of Britain (with Len Deighton) (1980)
Das Reich (1981)
The Battle for the Falklands (with Simon Jenkins) (1982)
The Oxford Book of Military Anecdotes (edited) (1983)
Overlord: D-Day and the Battle for Normandy (1984)
Victory in Europe (with pictures by George Stevens) (1985)

The Korean War (1987)
Outside Days (1993)
Scattered Shots (1998)
Going to the Wars (2000)
Editor (2002)
Armageddon: The Battle for Germany 1944–45 (2004)
Country Fair (2005)
Warriors (2005)
Nemesis: The Battle for Japan 1944–45 (2007)
Finest Years: Churchill as Warlord 1940–45 (2009)
Did You Really Shoot the Television? (2010)

*

WILL: 'Bah! Your plays are just prostitution.'
JIM: 'I'm not proud of them, but I'm proud of the fact that I can
    sell them.'
        From *The New Sin* by Basil Macdonald Hastings, Criterion
        Theatre, February 1912

Index